SOURCES OF BAILIFF LAW

JOHN KRUSE

PP

Disclaimer

This work is not a substitute for legal advice in relation to any particular case. Although the authors have attempted to produce a work which is designed to assist the practitioner, neither they or the publishers undertake any duty of care to any person or entity whatsoever, without limitation, in relation to any of the statements in, or omissions from this work, and accepts no legal liability or responsibility in respect of any statements in or omissions from this work.

Published by

PP Publishing
Suite 74, 17 Holywell Hill
St Albans AL1 1DT, UK

www.peerpractice.com

ISBN 978 1 85811 717 1

Printed and typeset in the UK

CONTENTS

Acknowledgements

I wish to thank the following for their assistance with cases and other materials over the years: all the patient librarians who have assisted over the years; Peter Madge, Citizens Advice Specialist Support Unit; Steve Everson, CIVEA; Chapeltown CAB; Birmingham CAB; the late Steve Beinoras of Nottingham Law Centre; Mrs Susan Oddy, Sheila Harding and an adviser from Nottingham CAB who inspired this book!

Table of Cases

Table of Statutes, Rules and Regulations

Glossary

Abandonment	failing to retain possession of impounded goods;
Action	a civil court claim;
Avowry	in replevin, the defendant's plea justifying their distraint;
Bar	a plea which challenges the basis of a plaintiff's case;
Amercement	a penalty imposed by a court;
Complainant	person commencing a prosecution;
Conusance	in replevin, a creditor's ratification of the bailiff's actions;
Conversion	wrongful dealing with or use of another's goods;
Counsel	a party's barrister;
Curtilage	the garden or yard surrounding a property;
Damages	compensation for a tort. *General damages* are the compensation to which a person is entitled as of right because they have been the victim of a trespass; *special damages* are compensation for a loss which must be proved and quantified;
Demurrer	a plea by a party to the effect that the other party had no valid or sufficient legal claim against them;
Disseisin	an illegal dispossession of land;
Fieri facias (fi fa)	a writ issued to a High Court enforcement officer; it is a means of enforcing a High Court judgment by seizing goods;
Fine	a criminal penalty; also a sum paid in settlement of a claim;
Interpleader	in the county or High Court, a procedure for determining adverse claims to goods seized in execution;
Judge's titles	judicial titles are generally abbreviated to letters after the surname in the reports, as follows:

B	Baron, a judge in the Court of Exchequer;
CB	Chief Baron, senior judge in Exchequer;
HHJ	His Honour Judge X in the county court;
J	Justice X in the High Court;
LJ	Lord Justice, judge of the Court of Appeal;
CJ	Chief Justice, senior judges of the courts of King's/ Queen's Bench or of the Common Bench;
MR	Master of the Rolls, judge of the Court of Appeal;

Nonsuit	a judgment that a plaintiff has failed to establish a legal case or abandoned a case at a late stage because of a procedural error;
Obiter dictum	a judge's passing remarks not directly relevant to a judgment;
Plaintiff	the person initiating an action or claim in the civil courts;
Plea	a defendant's response to a claim;
Ratio decidendi	the basis of a court decision;
Replevin/ to replevy	a county court procedure for release of goods illegally distrained;
Respondent	person responding to an appeal;
Rule	an order made by a superior court upon application; generally used here in the sense of an appeal against the judgment of a lower court;
Serjeant	the older equivalent of a barrister;
Tort	a civil wrong giving rise to damages- for example, trespass or assault;
Trespass ab initio	an act which has been rendered wrongful and a trespass from its outset;
Trover	now included within 'wrongful interference with goods'; a claim for 'conversion' of goods;
Ultra vires	an act by a public body which is outside its legal powers.

Introduction

There are several reasons for preparing this book:

- The physical inaccessibility of the law - many of the reports are only to be found in the medieval Year Books, in the 'English Reports' dating to before the 1860s and in unreported cases;
- The linguistic inaccessibility of some of the reports which can be in French or in older English;
- The obscurity and complexity of older English court procedures; and,
- The obscurity and complexity of English enforcement law.

The nature of the law

The last of the above bullet points is what I wish to discuss now. Until (if ever) the Tribunals, Courts and Enforcement Act 2007 is implemented, bailiffs' law will remain multifarious- dozens of statutes and regulations and thousands of cases. Were that not enough, the law is further complicated by its division into execution, common law distress and statutory distraint. This tripartite classification has practical consequences:

- There are differences in the personnel involved: civil court bailiffs, landowners and public bodies;
- Differences in specific powers; and,
- Differences in remedies for creditors and debtors.

As important as the differences listed are, and as much as they must be borne in mind, they can work as much to conceal similarities of procedure as to alert us to unique features. The Tribunals, Courts and Enforcement Act acknowledges that core of commonality - that regardless of the debt being recovered or the label given to the enforcement agent - ultimately enforcement of debts by seizure of goods is a single process with features shared across the technical boundaries. In other words, what a High Court enforcement officer enforcing a writ and a bailiff enforcing a distress warrant for a fine do are substantially the same.

This Source Book will substantially be concerned with the law that is shared across the sector. Leading cases and statutes will be selected that illustrate these points. It is particularly in the first chapter that the most debt-specific material will be found. I have provided texts of the various Distress for Rent Acts from 1689 to 1908. In their detail, these are unique to levies of distress for rent arrears; however, they are worth quoting at length because of their broader importance for other forms of enforcement. For example:

- Section 10 of the Distress for Rent Act 1737 first permitted impounding on a debtor's premises. This evolved into walking possession which is now in universal use. Equally, an understanding of the provision and its background throws light on the arguments about the legality of clamping and other forms of impounding on premises; or,
- The Law of Distress Amendment Acts 1888 and 1895 introduced the process of certification for private bailiffs.

To properly understand the complexity of bailiffs' law readers need to appreciate how distress for rent has often formed a model for other forms of enforcement, how aspects of rent law have been shared across the field but how, still, most features of rent distress remain unique to rent distress.

Format of the book

This book is organised into a chapter of statutes and then chapters dealing successively with the key stages of the enforcement process. Each source (statute or case report) is supplemented with a commentary discussing its significance and linking it with other sources quoted here or to other applications of the principles brought out.

The book is intended as a complement to my other books- *Bailiffs' law, Law of seizure of goods* and *Powers of distress* - and as a convenient guide to the cases for debtors, creditors, bailiffs, voluntary sector advisers and lawyers.

A note on sources

Most of the cases quoted here predate the twentieth century. Court procedures were different and, in some cases, even the language used was different. Some of the earliest reports have been translated from Law French (these are mainly to be found in the 'black letter' folio volumes of the so-called Year Book reports of medieval law courts).

Year Books

The Year Books provide the foundations of English common law, but are very hard to find and, for the uninitiated, very hard to read and understand as they are written in French with some Latin. The Year Books were not written as reports of judgments: they were records of the arguments used in court intended as a tactical guide for other lawyers. The result can be that the facts and the outcome are treated as minor details, making it difficult to uncover the actual law about which the barristers and the bench were debating.

English Reports

These are unofficial law reports complied between the late sixteenth and mid nineteenth centuries. The various reports are collected together as the multi-volume *English Reports* or they can be consulted individually. The reporters sometimes recorded cases for their own purposes, sometimes (increasingly) for publication and profit. The authors were mostly practicing lawyers, many were (or became) judges. The reports are predominantly in English, but French (and Latin) continued to be used until the late seventeenth century (even though the use of French in courts had officially been prohibited in 1362). I have edited some of the case reports in order to focus on the key elements of the judgments useful to readers. In older reports previous stages of the case and counsel's arguments might be cited at length. These are often missed out. I have left in the technical terms of pleading (the different stages of the lawyers' arguments) but provided a glossary of these terms at the end. For statutes, naturally, I only include those sections which are directly relevant to our focus on civil enforcement.

Law Reports

Since 1865 there has been an official series of Law Reports for each of the higher courts (Chancery Division, Queen's Bench etc). These are supplemented by various commercial publications which are treated as providing accurate records of decisions. Increasingly now, of course, judgments are published on the Ministry of Justice website.

Unreported cases

Several of the judgments printed in this book have not been officially reported, mainly because they are county court or magistrates' court decisions and therefore are not binding on other courts. Nonetheless, they are often the only recent interpretations we have on many aspects of bailiff law and I felt that it was important for readers to see them and to understand how the courts and lawyers currently approach these subjects. The cases must however be cited with due caution bearing in mind their status and authority.

Themes of the book

A number of essential elements of the distraint process are brought out through the cases selected:

- *the significance of the licence* in being permitted or refused entry;
- *the complexities of impounding* and the ambiguities of walking possession; and,
- *the strictness* with which fee scales should be interpreted.

Underlying these specific themes are some more general concepts:

- the surprisingly conditional and temporary nature of many of bailiffs' rights;
- the fact that the bailiff is increasingly obligated to interact with the debtor to achieve his purpose; and,
- the truth (several times referred to by judges) that many practices which have been widely adopted and which are in daily use are not justifiable in law.

Statutes

Chapter 1

STATUTE LAW

Introduction

The history of common law distress and execution is a story of progressive encroachment by statute - to the extent that now the largest use of the remedy of seizure of goods is by way of statutory distraint for taxes and other duties, whilst common law distress for rent faces abolition under the Tribunals, Courts and Enforcement Act 2007. At the same time existing statutes are replaced by newer Acts of Parliament on a periodic basis. It should not be supposed, though, that this implies innovation or modernisation of the law. The Statute of Marlborough, discussed later, simply confirmed and codified existing common law rules. Many modern provisions are just the latest versions of much older clauses. For example, the Insolvency Act 1986 (see later) consolidated and repeated sections from older Companies and Bankruptcy Acts whilst the rules regulating county court bailiffs and High Court enforcement officers are derived from earlier Acts. This necessarily imports into modern law a considerable amount of much older case law which continues to be relevant.

By and large, the interference of Parliament has been for the protection of the debtor, but it has at the same time added a further layer of complexity on top of an already involved body of common law rules. This chapter provides the text of statutes of general interest and application.[1]

---

[1] For further information see *A lawful trespass* c.8 & *Persons of no value?* Cc.6 & 9.

Part One - Rent Statutes

Distress for Rent Act 1689

"s.1 Right to sell distresses Whereas the most ordinary and ready way for Recovery of Arrears of Rent is by Distress, yet such Distresses not being to be sold but only detained as Pledges for enforcing the payment of such Rent the persons distraining have little benefit thereby. For the remedying whereof be it enacted that: Where any Goods or Chattels shall be distrained for any Rent reserved and due upon any demise, lease or contract whatsoever and the Tenant or Owner of the Goods so distrained shall not within Five Days next after such Distress taken and notice thereof (with the cause of such taking) left at the chief mansion house or other most notorious place on the Premises charged with the Rent distrained for replevy the same with sufficient Security to be given to the High Sheriff according to Law then in such Case after such Distress and Notice as aforesaid and expiration of the said five days the person distraining shall and may with the Sheriff or Under Sheriff of the County or with the Constable of the Hundred Parish or place where such Distress shall be taken (who are hereby required to be aiding and assisting therein) cause the Goods and Chattels so distrained to be appraised by two sworn Appraisers (whom such High Sheriff, Under Sheriff or Constable are hereby empowered to swear) to appraise the same truly according to the best of their Understandings and after such appraisement shall and may lawfully sell the Goods and Chattels so distrained for the best price can be gotten for the same towards satisfaction of the Rent for which the said Goods and Chattels shall be distrained and of the Charges of such Distress Appraisement and Sale leaving the overplus (if any) in the Hands of the said High Sheriff, Under Sheriff or Constable for the Owner's use.

s.2 Sheaves or Cocks of Corn & Hay And whereas no Sheaves or Cocks of Corn loose or in the Straw or Hay in any Barn or Granary or on any Hovel Stack or Rick can by the Law be distrained or otherwise secured for Rent whereby Landlords are oftentimes cousened and deceived by their Tenants who sell their Corn Grain and Hay to Strangers and remove the same from the Premises chargeable with such Rent and thereby avoid the payment of the same for remedying the said practice and deceit, be it enacted that: It shall and may be lawful to and for any person or persons having Rent Arrear and Due upon any such Demise Lease or Contracting as aforesaid to seize and secure any Sheaves or Cocks of Corn or Corn loose or in the Straw or Hay lying or being in any Barn or Granary or upon any Hovel, Stack or Rick or otherwise upon any part of the Land or Ground charged with such Rent and to lock up or detain the same in the place where the same shall be found for or in the nature of a Distress until the same shall be replevied upon such Security to be given as aforesaid and in default of replevying the same as aforesaid within the time aforesaid to sell the same after such appraisement thereof to be made so as nevertheless such Corn Grain or Hay so distrained as aforesaid be not removed by the person or persons distraining to the damage of the Owner thereof out of the place where the same shall be found and seized but be kept there (as impounded) until the same shall be replevied or sold in default of replevying the same within the time aforesaid

s.3 Pound-breach or rescue Upon any poundbreach or rescue of goods or chattels distrained for rent the person or persons grieved thereby shall in a special Action upon the Case for the Wrong thereby sustained recover his and their treble Damages . . . against the Offender or Offenders in any such rescue or Pound-Breach, any or either of them or against the Owners of the Goods distrained, in case the same be afterwards found to have come to his use or possession."

s.4 created a penalty where a landlord distrains when no rent is due. The landlord will forfeit double damages based upon the value of the goods levied.

Commentary

Until this Act came into force distresses had been taken as pledges only. They could not be disposed of by the landlord in order to raise money to settle the debt; rather, depriving the tenant of the use of chattels would hopefully provoke payment. It is because deprivation of goods was the effective element in the process that impounding off the premises (which will be discussed later) was particularly significant (see chapter 3).

Introducing a power of sale for the landlord was a fundamental change to the remedy and it was accordingly hedged about with restrictions in order to protect tenants. For example, the landlord had to value the goods and the exact procedure laid down for appraisal had to be strictly observed in order to entitle the landlord lawfully to sell.[2] These rules have since been relaxed, although the requirement in section 1 to supply a notice of distress is still

---

[2] See for example *Lamb v Cloves* (1847) 10 LT 231. See too *Westwood v Cowne* (1816) 1 Stark 172 - the distrainor may not appraise and *Burroughs v Smith* (1869) 4 LJ 22 - damages for failing to leave surplus with sheriff- though not being able to find the tenant is a good excuse for failure! (*Stubbs v May* (1822) 1 LJCP 12).

central to the process, as it informs the tenant of the cause of the distress and the goods distrained so that the person may pay or replevy.[3]

The Distress for Rent Act 1689 also allowed, for the first time, the seizure of harvested crops and the impounding of these on the premises. Finally, a civil penalty for poundbreach was created to give extra protection to landlords now that tenants faced forced sale of their goods (including previously exempt grain and hay).[4]

Distress for Rent Act 1737

"s.10 Distresses may be secured & sold on the premises And whereas great difficulties and inconveniences frequently arise to landlords and lessors and other persons taking distresses for rent, in removing the goods and chattels or stock distrained off the premises, in cases where by law they may not be impounded and secured thereupon, and also to the tenants themselves many times, by the damage unavoidably done to such goods and chattels or stock in the removal thereof, be it enacted that: from and after June 24th 1738, it shall and may be lawful to and for any person or persons lawfully taking any distress for any kind of rent, to impound or otherwise secure the distress so made, of what nature or kind so ever it may be, in such place or on such part of the premises chargeable with the rent as shall be most fit and convenient for the impounding and securing such distress, and to appraise, sell, and dispose of the same upon the premises in like manner and under the like directions and restraints to all intents and purposes as any person taking a distress for rent may now do off the premises by virtue of the Distress for Rent Act 1689 or of the Landlord and Tenant Act 1730 and that it shall and may be lawful to and for any person or persons whatsoever to come and go to and from such place or part of the said premises where any distress for rent shall be impounded and secured as aforesaid, in order to view, appraise, and buy, and also in order to carry off or remove the same on account of the purchaser thereof, and that if any pound-breach or rescous shall be made of any goods and chattels, or stock distrained for rent and impounded or otherwise secured by virtue of this Act, the person or persons aggrieved thereby shall have the like remedy as in cases of pound-breach or rescous is given and provided by the said Statute.

s.19 Irregular levies And whereas it hath sometimes happened that upon a distress made for rent justly due, the directions of the Distress for Rent Act 1689 have not been strictly pursued, but through the mistake or inadvertency

---

[3] See *Davies* later in Chapter 4 and *Green v Brown* (1852) 13 Ir LR 329 QB regarding a defective notice of distress.

[4] See further discussion of this in *Abingdon RDC v O'Gorman* - see chapter 7.

of the landlord or other person entitled to such rent, and distraining for the same, or of the bailiff or agent of such landlord or other person, some irregularity or tortious act hath been afterwards done in the disposition of the distress so seized or taken as aforesaid, for which irregularity or tortious act the party distraining hath been deemed a trespasser *ab initio*, and in an action brought against him as such, the plaintiff hath been entitled to recover, and has actually recovered, the full value of the rent for which such distress was taken: And whereas it is a very great hardship upon landlords and other persons entitled to rents, that a distress duly made should be thus in effect avoided for any subsequent irregularity, be it enacted that: from and after June 24th 1738, where any distress shall be made for any kind of rent justly due, and any irregularity or unlawful act shall be afterwards done by the party or parties distraining, or by his, her, or their agents, the distress itself shall not be therefore deemed to be unlawful, nor the party or parties making it be deemed a trespasser or trespassers *ab initio*; but the party or parties aggrieved by such unlawful act or irregularity shall or may recover full satisfaction for the special damage he, she or they shall have sustained thereby, and no more, in an action of trespass or on the case, at the election of the plaintiff or plaintiffs: Provided always, that where the plaintiff or plaintiffs shall recover in such action, he, she, or they shall be paid his, her, or their full costs of suit, and have all the like remedies for the same as in other cases of costs."

Commentary

Not all of this Act is reproduced here. The opening sections deal with the tenant's offence of 'fraudulent removal' of goods in order to evade distress. This is of very little practical relevance today, although it is discussed in *Law of seizure of goods.*[5]

Section 10, however, continues to be of considerable importance. This section enabled landlords for the first time to impound all manner of goods and chattels on the debtor's premises where they were distrained. It seems that this power went through three broad phases of development:

1. the locking up of goods in some or building on the debtor's premises. This was quite lawful so long as the tenant was not ejected entirely from possession.[6]
2. Leaving the goods *in situ* under the supervision of a possession man employed by the bailiff; and,

---

[5] See section 3.5.2.
[6] *Purcell v Nolan* (1839) LR Ir 1 CL 258; *Josephs v London & County Stores & Evans* (1911) 77 EG 170.

3. leaving the goods *in situ* under the care of the debtor or another occupier subject to a 'walking possession' agreement.

Section 10 refers to situations where "by law" goods may not be impounded on the premises. What is meant here is the common law rule against impounding at the place of seizure, which is discussed in chapter 3 and later. There were clearly exceptions to this rule: section 2 of the Distress for Rent Act 1689 allowed produce to be impounded on the premises and in *Abingdon RDC v O'Gorman* Russell LJ suggests that tenants may have already consented to such impounding for their convenience.[7] Be that as it may, this alteration to the law had profound consequences for the remedy of seizure of goods as a whole, leading to the development of walking possession in the late nineteenth century and its almost universal adoption since.[8]

Secondly, section 19 of the 1737 Act created an exception to the common law rule that any error made by the distrainor made that person a trespasser *ab initio.* This concept of irregular, as opposed to illegal, distress, is returned to frequently in several of the cases that follow.

Law of Distress Amendment Act 1888

"*s.4 Exempt goods* The following goods and chattels shall be exempt from distress for rent; namely, any goods or chattels of the tenant or his family which would be protected from seizure in execution under section ninety-six of the County Courts Act 1846, or any enactment amending or substituted for the same.

Provided that this enactment shall not extend to any case where the lease, term, or interest of the tenant has expired, and where possession of the premises in respect of which the rent is claimed has been demanded and where the distress is made not earlier than seven days after such demand.

s.5 Appraisement So much of the Distress for Rent Act 1689, as requires appraisement before sale of goods distrained is hereby repealed, except in cases where the tenant or owner of the goods and chattels by writing requires such appraisement to be made, and the landlord or other person levying a distress may, except as aforesaid, sell the goods and chattels distrained without causing them to be previously appraised; and for the purposes of sale the goods and chattels distrained shall, at the request in writing of the

[7] See chapter 7.
[8] See chapter 3.

tenant or owner of such goods and chattels, be removed to a public auction room or to some other fit and proper place specified in such request, and be there sold. The costs and expenses of appraisement when required by the tenant or owner shall be borne and paid by him; and the cost and expenses attending any such removal, and any damage to the goods and chattels arising therefrom, shall be borne and paid by the person requesting the removal.

s.6 Extension of time to replevy at request of tenant The period of five days provided in the Distress for Rent Act 1689, within which the tenant or owner of goods and chattels distrained may replevy the same, shall be extended to a period of not more than fifteen days if the tenant or such owner make a request in writing in that behalf to the landlord or other person levying the distress, and also give security for any additional cost that may be occasioned by such extension of time: Provided that the landlord or person levying the distress may, at the written request, or with the written consent, of the tenant or such owner as aforesaid, sell the goods and chattels distrained, or part of them, at any time before the expiration of such extended period as aforesaid.

s.7 Distress to be levied by certificated bailiffs No person shall act as a bailiff to levy any distress for rent unless he shall be authorised to act as a bailiff by a certificate in writing under the hand of a judge assigned to a county court district, or acting as a judge so assigned; and such certificate may be general ... and may be granted at any time after the passing of this Act in such manner as may be prescribed by rules under this Act.

A county court registrar may exercise the power of granting certificates hereby conferred upon a county court judge in cases in which he may be authorised to do so by rules made under this Act.

If any person not holding a certificate under this section shall levy a distress contrary to the provisions of this Act, the person so levying, and any person who has authorised him so to levy, shall be deemed to have committed a trespass.

s.8 Power to make rules The Lord Chancellor may from time to time make, alter and revoke rules-[9]
(1) for regulating the security (if any) to be required from bailiffs;
(2) for regulating the fees, charges, and expenses in and incidental to distresses; and,
(3) for carrying into effect the objects of this Act."

---

[9] These are now the Distress for Rent Rules 1988 as amended.

Commentary

The most significant provisions of this Act were the improved protection for tools and household goods under section 1 and the increased control over bailiffs achieved through the process of certification created by section 7. These were further enhanced by the Law of Distress Amendment Act 1895 - section 4 of which created a penalty for the sale of exempt goods and tools or allowed magistrates' courts to order their return; in addition improvements were made to the certification regime by limiting their duration, by allowing judges to cancel them and by imposing a fine for acting without a certificate.

Certification continues to be the sole form of regulation of individual bailiffs and much more recently has been extended to distraint for local taxes and to road traffic executions too.[10] The rules referred to in section 8 are currently the Distress for Rent Rules 1988, although various previous versions will be met with in the case reports. The Rules set out the process whereby certificates are granted, coupled with a complaints procedure that permits revocation if the bailiff proves to be unfit. The charging of fees is controlled by a fee scale and specific regulations. There is also an ultimate sanction of revocation through a link between the assessment of fees and review of a certificate in cases of gross abuse of the scale by a bailiff.

From the early experience of certification in county courts a number of clear these emerge which are still relevant today:

- *the use of uncertificated staff*- the degree to which work can lawfully be delegated to unlicenced individuals was (and remains) doubtful. The general feeling of county court judges seems to have been that uncertificated assistants could not work except under the direct and personal supervision of certificated individuals- although one certificated bailiff could pass work to another. A levy conducted without a certificated bailiff present could be trespass;[11]
- *the charging of excessive or illegal fees* which could lead to revocation of a certificate;[12] or,

---

[10] See *Persons of no value?* chapters 8 & 9.

[11] *Hawes v Watson* (1892) 94 LT 191; (1890) 29 LJ 556; contrast *Varden v Shread* (1890) 36 EG 449 or 25 LJ 363, *Harker v Browne* (1890) 36 EG 59, (1892) 40 EG 402, *Thomas v Millington* (1894) 2 PMR 472, *Bray v Naldred* (1894) 2 PMR 227 & *Rodgers v Webb* (1912) 20 PMR 186.

[12] *Duncombe v Hicks* (1898) 42 Sol Jo 393- certificate cancelled because illegal possession fee charged; *In Re: Longstaffe ex. p. Robinson* (1897) 49 EG 60- bailiff charged double the permitted percentage for an auctioneer & (1896) 47 EG 49 & 171.

- *unfit behaviour* - whether on the part of the bailiff or an assistant. Illegal levying, abuse of the position or improper conduct could all lead to revocation.[13] This could even include wrongful acts when undertaking uncertificated work.[14]

Generally, the courts have used certification as a way of raising standards in the sector, by reminding certificated bailiffs of their duties. It has been accepted that the law is "obscure and difficult" and that bailiffs cannot be expected "to express a very definite opinion on it". Nevertheless they have a duty to the community and to the state to protect the poor from abuse and they should normally err on the side of caution and generous treatment of debtors. These comments by certificating judges echo remarks made by Baron Gurney in a case in 1843, when he stated that brokers [bailiffs] have a duty to protect the interests of both the creditor landlord *and* the indebted tenant.[15]

In addition, the obligation to appraise distrained goods was abolished by the 1888 Act, whilst tenants benefited from the extended period possible for seeking replevin, often a necessity given the fact that no prescribed county court forms exist for the application and the procedures are both obscure and potentially costly. Accordingly time may well be essential for a person to get legal advice and either to raise the necessary funds or to apply for legal aid funding.[16]

---

[13] *Woodward v Day* (1894) 2 PMR 753 & *Re: Gurden* (1894) 2 PMR 872- drunk or assaulted debtor; *Mutton v Sheppard* (1905) 66 EG 806 - deceiving a tenant; *Villenueva v Clark* (1890) 33 EG 458 - drunk; *London Central Meat Co v Rae* (1905) 13 PMR 825 - illegal distress; (1912) 20 PMR 972 & *The Times* December 3rd 1894 4c.

[14] *James v Proctor* (13 PMR 442.

[15] (1898) 104 LT 345; *Taylor v Ashworth* (1910) 129 LT 578; *Harrison v Mearing* (1843) *The Times* May 10th 8b, Exch.

[16] See *Law of seizure of goods* 9.2.

Part Two - General Statutes

Statute of Marlborough 1267

"*c.4. Distresses shall not be driven out of the county & shall be reasonable* None from henceforth shall cause any distress that he has taken to be driven out of the county where it was taken. If one neighbour do so to another by his own authority, and without judgment, he shall make fine ... as for a thing done against the peace; nevertheless, if a landlord presume so to do against his tenant, he shall be grievously punished by amercement.

Moreover, distresses shall be reasonable, and not too great; and he that takes great and unreasonable distresses, shall be grievously amerced for the excess of such distresses.

c.15. Where distress cannot be levied It shall be not lawful for any man from henceforth, for any manner of cause, to take distresses out of his fee, nor in the king's highway, nor in the common street, but only to the king or his officers, having special authority to do the same."

Commentary

The Statute of Marlborough is the oldest Act of Parliament still (partially, at least) in force in England and Wales. It is of interest for this reason alone. In addition, the three provisions which still operate place significant restrictions on the exercise of powers of distress. Mostly they relate to rent distresses, but the second part of chapter 4 is of general application, as a result of which this statute is dealt with in the 'General' section of this chapter.

- *Chapter 15* - this chapter has been held only to apply to landlords levying for distress for rent and not to other levies.[17] For a levy off the demised premises, the remedies are either trespass or a claim based on the Statute. For a levy on the highway, the remedy is a claim founded on the Statute. The justification behind the clause, as Bullen stated, is "the convenience of passengers and the encouragement of commerce." Be that as it may, it is now accepted that executions and statutory distraints may be levied on the highway.[18]

[17] Coke, 2 Inst p.130.

[18] Bullen, *A practical treatise on the laws of distress,* London, 1842, p.125; see *Quinlan v LB Hammersmith & Fulham* later in chapter 7.

- *Chapter 4, first section* - this part of c.4 limits the location where goods taken in distress for rent (or distress damage feasant) may be impounded. A landlord who impounds distrained goods outside the county in which they were seized will face 'grievous amercement.' What this penalty involves is discussed in the next paragraph.[19]
- *Chapter 4, second section* - this clause prohibits excessive or unreasonable levies. A disproportionate levy was unlawful already at common law and the Statute of Marlborough merely confirmed and formalised this. The remedy will be a general claim for damages or a claim based on the Statute. There is no need for the claimant to prove malice on the part of the bailiff.[20]
- It is widely accepted that an excessive levy is one in which more than is reasonably needed is seized. However, the courts have entertained some broad applications of the term 'excessive distress.' In *Earl of Shaftesbury v Russell* (1823) the Earl was allowed a plea to the effect that a levy on goods held in trust for the debtor was both trover and excessive distraint.[21] The label has also been attached to levies for more than was lawfully due and to cases where a tender of the debt was refused and possession retained.[22] It is arguable that it may be understood in yet another manner.
- The second clause of chapter 4 may be better translated from the original Latin as "Distraints are ... to be reasonable and not too severe [23] and, if anyone makes unreasonable or undue [24] distraints, he is to be heavily amerced on account of the excessive nature of those distraints." As will be seen, an unreasonable distraint is one that is "severe (or harsh)" and is "undue (or improper)." These terms, it seems, may be as applicable to a levy which is excessive in the sense that it could not be justified by the value of the goods taken as to one in which too much was taken. In other words, seizing a few goods of minimal worth which do not even cover the costs of the process- rather than abandoning the levy- may be as wrongful as seizing too much. Some support for this wider interpretation comes from the judgment in the case of *Nargett v Nias* (1859). This decision is primarily concerned with the circumstances in

[19] It used to be said that claims under statute or for common law violations of distress should not be combined in one action (*Anon,* Case XLVI, Jenkins 24).

[20] *Field v Mitchell* (1807) 6 Esp 71. Note too, that if both excessive distress and interference with goods are claimed together in one action, damages cannot be awarded for both and the claimant must choose one for judgment: *Clarke v Roe* (1854) 4 Ir Ch R 1.

[21] (1823) 3 D&R 84. NB: if an officer levying execution seizes and sells more than is required to satisfy the writ, it is not a trespass - *Hughes v Brown* (1845) 7 Ir LR 492 Ex.

[22] Respectively *Wilkinson v Terry* 1 M&R 377 & *McGuckin v Dobbin* (1863) 15 Ir Jur 311; *Holland v Bird* 2 LJCP 201.

[23] "*non nimis graves*"

[24] "*indebitas*"

which tools of the trade can be seized in distress for rent.[25] However, during the argument before the court, the application of the Statute of Marlborough was raised and it was accepted by all parties and by the bench that one remedy for seizing tools would be by way of proceedings under chapter 4 of the Statute because such a levy would be "unreasonable." Counsel for the defendant cited the case of *Piggott v Birtles* (1836) which in turn relied on the writings of Lord Justice Coke in the seventeenth century.[26] There is a duty in the common law for all those distraining to act reasonably and justly, breach of which gives rise to a claim for damages. This right to recover compensation where the bailiff has levied in an unreasonable, undue or excessive manner "agreeth with the reason of the common law" according to Coke. What he meant by this is revealed elsewhere in his writings: courts would intervene because "all excessiveness is abhorred by law."[27] In *Nargett v Nias* in particular the words of the Statute are read in a broader sense than has become the norm. 'Unreasonable' levies therefore may be not just those in which far more is seized than is required to cover the debt due; they may include those where privileged goods are levied or those where worthless goods are levied.

- To violate this provision of the Statute there will have to be disproportion and oppression in the bailiffs' actions. It may be useful to have some guidance as to what the courts have considered excessive. For example, in *Fitzgerald v Longfield* (1855) a claim for excess levying was rejected as the sum produced on sale was only 3.6% higher than the rent arrears due. The court could not accept that such a slight excess was unreasonable.[28]
- By way of contrast, in *Sullivan v Bishop* (1826) the court accepted that distraining an item worth nearly three times the amount of the rent arrears was an excessive levy.[29] Counsel for the defendant argued that "A landlord is not bound to look around with a microscopic eye to select the nearest article in value to the sum claimed." The Court did not agree and awarded damages and the return of the item seized. Later in the book in commentaries on cases reported it will be argued that a number of the judgments indicate that the proper conduct of levies should involve careful and thorough inspections of premises. The judgment in *Sullivan v Bishop* does not discourage this view of a bailiff's duties. In *Josephs v London & County Stores & Evans* (1911) rent arrears of £1 were enforced by distraint on furniture in a shop said to be worth £35

[25] (1859) 1 E& E 439.
[26] (1836) 1 M&W 441; 2 Inst 107.
[27] 1 Inst lib.1, cap.9, section 74.
[28] (1855) 7 Ir Jur 21.
[29] (1826) 2 C&P 359.

which sold for £5. The jury found the levy to have been excessive and awarded £10 damages.[30] See too the outcome in *Lowry v Read* (1889): the landlord distrained for £11 rent arrears on goods he valued at £6. Lowry valued the possessions at £100 and sued. The county court awarded damages of £50 for the excess; an appeal to the High Court was settled on payment of £30 by the landlord, which is still triple the debt. The circumstances of a levy will nonetheless be important: in *Skene v Midland Railway* (1911) the High Court accepted that as the tenant was facing imminent business failure, an extensive levy and a quick sale were justified.[31]

- The exact nature of the penalty that is to be imposed for an excessive levy is difficult to define. Amercements were penalties imposed by medieval courts and do not now exist. However, it seems that the sum payable, presumably as damages, is not based solely on the degree of the excess, but will reflect the court's disapproval of the wrongful act.

Insolvency Act 1986

The main impact of the Insolvency Act on debt recovery procedures is to prevent further enforcement against the insolvent individual or company. Whatever the form of insolvency involved, the same kind of provision will be encountered: further levying of distress or execution will be prohibited, although there will be a provision allowing a court or a person acting in the insolvency to give permission for recovery to continue if it is felt appropriate. This is the case for company voluntary arrangements, administration orders, windings up, debt relief orders, individual voluntary arrangements and, also, county court administration orders.[32]

Several other features of the Insolvency Act 1986 are worth noting. Both in company and personal insolvencies provision is made to deal with ongoing enforcement against the insolvent's property. A distinction is made between distress for rent, other forms of distraint and executions, county court bailiffs and High Court enforcement officers are subjected to a far more onerous set of responsibilities than private bailiffs. It is important, though,

---

[30] (1911) 78 EG 170; see too *Leyland v Benson & Hartley* (1894) 2 PMR 130 & *Redmond v Ward* (1910) *The Times* May 4th 3c - levies on the entire contents of houses were excessive; also, *Merry v Lovell* (1888) - a levy on goods worth 175% of the arrears would be treated a excessive (*The Times* November 16th 3g, QBD) - or *Webb v Pennell* (1907) *The Times* December 5th 10a- furniture worth £602 sold for £73, damages of £350 awarded.

[31] *Lowry v Read* (1889) *The Times,* March 9th 5b & 33 EG 159; (1911) *The Times* February 28th 3b.

[32] See respectively Insolvency Act section 1A & Sch.A1 para.12(1)(h), s.8 & Sch.B1 para.43(6); ss.128 & 130(2); s.251G; ss.252 & 254 and County Courts Act 1984 s.114.

that *all* enforcement agents should make enquiries about possible insolvencies, but it is especially important that officers levying execution should do so.[33]

There is also a practical distinction between the treatment of bankrupts facing statutory distraint and most other insolvents. Insolvent companies are substantially protected from recovery action (except in limited circumstances under s.130(2) for windings up). The same is true for individuals subject to individual voluntary arrangements, debt relief orders and (also) for county court administration orders. However, in bankruptcy, distraint for taxes and the like can continue despite the bankruptcy order (see s.347(8)), a curious and largely unjustifiable anomaly:

"s.347 Distress...

(8) Subject to ss.252(2)(b) and 254(1) above, nothing in this Group of Parts affects any right to distrain otherwise than for rent; and any such right is at any time exercisable without restriction against property comprised in a bankrupt's estate, even if that right is expressed by any enactment to be exercisable in like manner as a right to distrain for rent.

(9) Any right to distrain against property comprised in a bankrupt's estate is exercisable notwithstanding that the property has vested in the trustee."

For extended discussion of these issues and the considerable case authority, see *Law of seizure of goods* c.4 or *Powers of distress* c.1 Part II.

Conclusions

The legislature has increasingly modified (or created) powers of distress by statute. This may in due course result in the extreme of a wholly statutory code of powers for most bailiffs and most debts (though not all- see my *Powers of distress*). Even should this occur, enforcement law will inevitably continue to be an interaction between many spheres of law and, given the daily difficulties of its actual implementation, the guidance of the courts will still be essential.

[33] *Balme v Hutton* (1833) 9 Bing 471; see also *Cooper v Chitty* (1753) 1 Kenyon 395, *Dillon v Langley* (1831) 2 B&A 131, *Garland v Carlisle* (1837) 4 Bing VC 7 HL.

Cases

Chapter 2

ENTRY RIGHTS

Introduction

This chapter is concerned with the initial stages of the levy of distress – the access to a debtor's premises. Vital as this is to the ability of the enforcement agent to continue at all, or to avoid prejudicing subsequent actions, it is surprising how many misconceptions – or complete blanks in knowledge- there are about the process. The principles of English law on rights of entry date back at least to the early thirteenth century, so that ignorance of this unbroken heritage may seem more shameful still. Three themes underlie the cases discussed- the right to use force to enter, the concept of the licence to enter and the situations in which resistance might legitimately be offered (and when it would be an offence).[1]

Adherence to the law here is crucial. Any default or omission on the bailiff's part may render him a trespasser *ab initio* and liable to penalties in tort (see chapter 7). The entry may also be a breach of article 8 of the European Convention on Human Rights if it is not made "in accordance with law."[2]

Part One: Entry - general principles

P.18 Ed.IV fo.4 pl.19

Facts "Catesby came to the bar and explained how a writ of *fieri facias* had been directed to the sheriff of Middlesex to make execution on a judgment obtained by J against B. The said B placed all his goods in a locked and enclosed chest. The sheriff broke open the door and entered the house and took the goods away with him. Had the sheriff committed any wrong?

---

[1] For more discussion see *Law of seizure of goods* 7.4, Powers of distress 2.7 or A lawful trespass cc.4 & 7.

[2] See for example *Jokinen & Jokinen v Finland* (2009) 37233/07.

Judgment Chief Justice of the Common Pleas Littleton, and all the other judges, held that the plaintiff was entitled to a writ of trespass against the sheriff for forcing entry to the house notwithstanding the fact that he acted on a writ of execution, because that could not excuse breaking the door open, only taking the goods away."

Commentary

This is a quite typical *Year Book* report in which the state of the common law has to be inferred, by reading between the limes as it were. It is very clear that force could not be used in order to gain entry to the house. It is implicit in the decision, though not discussed directly, that breaking open an internal door (or, in this case, a chest) was *not* wrongful and that the sheriff could only be criticised by the Court for the means by which he got access to the hidden goods so as to be able to remove them. These principles are seen applied in *Semayne v Grisham* and all subsequent cases.

Semayne v Gresham (1604) Yelverton 29

Facts Gresham and Beresford were joint tenants of a house in London, in which Beresford kept his goods. Beresford was indebted to Semayne and judgment was entered against him for the sum due. He soon afterwards died but Gresham continued to occupy the house. Semayne then issued execution on his judgment against the goods of Beresford. The sheriff of London came to the house to serve the execution but Gresham shut the door before the sheriff entered and would not allow him access to view and appraise the goods. As a result Semayne sued Gresham for disturbing his execution.

Judgment (by Fenner and Yelverton) "The action does not lie; for Gresham has done nothing but what he may lawfully justify, that is- shut his own doors. Although the execution had been for the debt of Gresham, yet before the sheriff's entry into the house it had been lawful for him to shut the door; for, unless it is upon the Queen's suit, for the contempt of the party, it is not lawful for the sheriff to enter the house unless it is open; as in 18 Ed. IV (see previous case). This was agreed by all the justices, contrary to the *Year Book* case of 18 Ed. II 'Execution.'[3] Also in this case (according to Fenner J) if the sheriff himself might have entered, yet it is not lawful to bring a jury into the house to praise the goods; for it was very inconvenient to have so large a company in a house, and might be

[3] This case is correctly 8 Ed. II - the bailiff put his hand through a hole in a wall in order to pull back the bar on a door. This was ruled to be a trespass. See *Ryan v Shilcock* later.

prejudicial to the party, by the loss of the goods, but Popham J and others disagreed, because by this means justice is hindered; for execution is the effect of the whole suit; and if execution cannot be made, but is prevented by this means, then it will be in vain to sue; and therefore he conceived the decision in the Year Book case in 18 Ed.II *Execution*, is better law than 18 Ed.IV and he was of opinion that upon an execution between party and party, the sheriff might enter and break the door; to which Fenner Justice answered, that if the sheriff might by law in such case break the house, then also clearly the action does not lie; for then, although Gresham shut the door of the house, it was the sheriff's fault that he did not break it: Judgment was given against the plaintiff by the whole court."

Seyman v Gresham (1604) Croke, Elizabeth 908

Facts "Action upon the case; supposing, that one G. Berisford was indebted unto him for £200 and that he sued execution, and the sheriffs of London, by force of that writ, impanelled a jury, to enquire what goods there were and that there were divers goods of the said G. Berisford in such a house in London; and that the sheriff came with the said jury, to have a view of them, and to appraise and seize them for this debt; and that the defendant, *præmissorum non ignarus*, shut the door, and disturbed him to make execution. The defendant entitles himself to the possession of the house, by reason of a joint lease made to him and one Berisford, and that he had it by survivorship; and that he shut the door for the salvation of his possession. The plaintiff replies, that the said Berisford mentioned in the bar, and he who was obliged in the statute (i.e. the judgment debtor), were all one person. And it was thereupon demurred.

Judgment The principal question was, whether this shutting of the door was a disturbance of the execution and, whether the plaintiff might thereupon maintain this action?

Whether he might upon a *fieri facias* enter the house of any to take execution of the goods, and to break the party's house to make execution, they doubted. See the *Year Book* cases18 Ed.II Execution 252, 13 Ed.IV pl.9 and 18 Ed.IV pl. 4. But if the door be open, there is no doubt but that the sheriff might enter to do execution; for the law gives him authority thereto. And for this cause Gawdy and Popham held, that the action here well lay; because by the shutting of the door the party was disturbed to have his execution.

But Fenner and Yelverton disagreed; for the goods being in the defendant's house, who is a stranger to the execution, he is not bound to take conusance of the sheriff's intent, in coming to make execution; and his shutting the door was lawful. And although there were loss to the plaintiff, yet it is *damnum sine injuriâ*.[4] And it appears not by what means that the goods of the conusors, which are in the defendant's house, came thither; and if they were taken by the defendant as a trespasser, the party whose goods they are, or the sheriff upon execution, may come within the house, if the door be open, to seize them, because the defendant had them by unlawful means. But if the defendant had them by lawful means, whether by bailment or otherwise, neither the party himself nor the sheriff can come within the house to seize them; and therefore the shutting of the door is no cause of action for the plaintiff. Therefore the action lieth not. Adjourned.

Note, that at a later date this cause was argued again and that Williams agreed with the opinion of Yelverton and Fenner that the sheriff might not break any man's house to take execution, unless in the Queen's case, or for a contempt. Wherefore, according to their opinions, it was adjudged for the defendant."

Commentary

The most extensive version of this judgment is that by Sir Edward Coke, but it is not really a report of the court decision at all. Rather, the case is used by Coke as the basis for an extended analysis of the law on sheriff's rights of entry as it had developed by 1604.[5] Here I quote selectively from Coke and instead provide the reports by Yelverton and Croke which more closely reflect what was said in court by the judges.

The importance of *Semayne* is that it sets out (especially in Coke's version) the essential points of English common law on bailiffs' and sheriffs' rights of entry.[6] What is striking is that these principles have not altered since, despite the lapse of four centuries. Coke extracts from the judges' remarks the following resolutions which summarised the established legal position at that date:

1. "The house of every one is his castle, and if thieves come to a man's house to rob or murder, and the owner or his servants kill any of the thieves in defence of himself and his house, it is no felony and he shall lose nothing;
2. Where any house is recovered by any possession action, the sheriff may break the house and deliver the seisin or possession;
3. In all cases where the King is party, the sheriff may break the house, either to arrest or do other execution of the King's process, if he cannot

[4] 'Damage without injury'- that is, not a legal wrong for which a person could sue.
[5] 5 Co Rep 91a.
[6] See my full discussion of the case law prior to 1604 in *A lawful trespass* c.4.

otherwise enter. But he ought first to signify the cause of his coming, and make request to open the doors;

4. Where the door is open the sheriff may enter, and do execution at the suit of a subject, and so also in such case may the lord, and distrain for his rent or service. It is not lawful for the sheriff, on request made and denial, at the suit of a common person, to break the defendant's house, to execute any process at the suit of a subject;
5. The house of any one is only a privilege for himself, and does not extend to protect any person who flies to his house, or the goods of any other which are brought there, to prevent a lawful execution and to escape the process of the law: in such cases after request and denial, the sheriff may break the house;
6. If the sheriff might break open the door to execute civil process, yet it must be after request made; and,
7. The allegation *præmisorum non ignarus* is not sufficient, where notice is material." (The Latin phrase means 'not unaware of the premises/ reasons'- in other words, Gresham could not deny that he knew why the sheriff was there. This was part of Semayne's argument as to why the exclusion was wrongful, but the Court felt that the sheriff needed to give clear notice of his purpose. Had he done so, then the defendant may have been less entitled to resist. It does not seem to be the case that this is the law any longer- see the discussion in *Vaughan v McKenzie* later.)

Two key principles of bailiffs' rights of entry are enunciated which remain law today (see *Khazanchi* later). The first is that the home is protected from forced entry in all but a couple of special cases. As Coke wrote "the house of everyone is to him as his castle and fortress, as well for his defence against injury and violence as for his repose..." If force is employed, it may be resisted (see *Vaughan v McKenzie* later). This principle is very widely known in the enforcement sector although- as we shall see- it is perhaps not fully understood. It should also be remembered that the use of force may lead to the loss of a bailiff's certificate.[7]

The second principle of entry rights is that the householder is entitled to refuse entry if she or he wishes. As Coke said "the defendant has done that which he might well do by the law, *i.e.* to shut the door of his own house." The existence of the debtor's or occupier's right to grant (or revoke) a licence to enter is far less well understood by bailiffs and needs more extensive discussion in this chapter. Bailiffs with lawful warrants have a right to enter domestic or business premises. However, this right is subject to permission being obtained and retained; for this to be done, the bailiff must of course

---

[7] See 51 Estates Gazette 739 (1898).

disclose his purpose. The occupier of premises may then grant either an *explicit licence* to enter, such as an invitation to come in, or an *implied licence:* permission may be inferred from either the circumstances (such as a door being left open) or the conduct of a person (such as standing back to allow the bailiff to walk through the open door or entry not being refused).[8] A licence to enter also must not be abused, for example by entering by improper means or methods- in other words, by force or by entry by means of unusual routes.[9]

A licence to enter may be refused by either words or conduct. Equally, although granted, a licence may be revoked: after bailiff has entered, licence may still be terminated by a person on the premises with authority. Certain conditions have been attached to this revocation by the courts:

- It must be done *before* the levy process starts;[10] *and,*
- The words used must be clear and not capable of being mistaken for mere swearing or abuse.[11]

If a licence is clearly and validly revoked, the bailiff *must* leave. If a bailiff fails to leave after permission revoked:

- s/he becomes a *trespasser*;[12]
- any levy undertaken will be *null and void*; and,
- the debtor has two *remedies*, either:
  - self help to resist the wrongful entry, using no more than *reasonable force* (see *Vaughan v McKenzie* later); or,
  - to issue a court claim for damages and an injunction if necessary.

Subsequent cases will expand on the points outlined here.

Ryan v Shilcock (1851) 7 Exch 72

Facts The plaintiff was tenant of the defendant of premises including a stable, which was a detached building. The rent for the property was in arrears, so the defendant landlord entered the stable and distrained. He made his entry in the following manner. On the stable door was a padlock attached to a staple, which was placed in the external woodwork of the door. The staple could

[8] *Faulkner v Willets* [1982] Crim LR 453.
[9] *Ancaster v Milling* (1823) 2 D&R 714; *Rogers v Spence* (1846) 13 M&W 571.
[10] *Mathews v Dwan* [1949] NZLR 1037; *Kay v Hibbert* [1977] Crim LR 226.
[11] *Bailey v Wilson* [1968] Crim LR 618; *Snook v Manion* [1982] Crim LR 601; *R (Roalfe) v Woking Magistrates' Court* [2005] EWHC 2922 (Admin).
[12] *Morris v Beardmore* [1980] 2 All ER 753; *R v Allen* [1981] Crim LR 326.

easily be pulled out and the usual way of going into the stable was by drawing out the staple, not by unlocking the padlock. The tenant sued for an illegal distress but at the trial the jury found that the staple had been pulled out without violence and that by these means the entry and distress were effected. The plaintiff appealed to the Court of Exchequer.

Judgment of Pollock CB: "In this case the question turned upon the power of a landlord to make a distress, that is, how far he was justified in making an entry into premises, for which purpose he used no more force than was necessary to open the outer door, which was shut to keep the door closed only, and not to keep people out. According to the evidence in the present case, the door had on it a padlock with a staple; but the mode by which the owner and every one else opened the door in order to obtain admittance was, by pulling out the staple, which served much in the same way as a button or nail does, which is sometimes to be found used for keeping gates "shut," an ambiguous term, and meaning either a mode of preventing a door from opening of itself, or from being opened by force or violence, or by such persons as have the key or some other means of opening the door. The jury found, upon the question being expressly put to them, that the padlock and staple were not for the purpose of keeping the door fastened, but merely closed; and as it is no part of the present question whether the verdict was against the evidence, the question is reduced to this, namely, whether a landlord, who on coming to his tenant's premises for the purpose of distraining finds the outer door closed, but capable of being opened by lifting a latch, is justified in so doing. We are of opinion that the landlord has authority by law to open the door in the ordinary way in which other persons can do it, when it is left so as to be accessible to all who have occasion to go into the premises. In the *First Institute* folio 161a, Lord Coke, in commenting upon *Littleton*, explains the meaning of the term "inclosure," to be found in the 137th section, in the following words: "Inclosure . . . . for the lord cannot break open the gates, or break down the inclosures to take a distress; and therefore the law accounts it a disseisin." Now, if these two matters be taken together, inasmuch as breaking down the inclosures would clearly be a forcible entry, we think that the breaking open the gates must be understood to be such a breaking as is also equivalent to a forcible entry; for Lord Coke proceeds to say: "But all these are intended by Littleton to be disseisins after an actual seisin had, and when the rent is behind; otherwise none of these are disseisins at all." Now, there is a passage in *Fitzherbert's Abridgment* 'Distress' pl.21, which was much relied upon by the plaintiff, "Nota, that a man came to the stable of his tenant to make a distress, and when he came, the door was shut with a bar, and he put in his hand to a hole (*il mitt eins sa main a un ptuz*) and took away the bar and opened the door, and entered and took two cows in the name of a distress; and because he opened the door in this manner, it was adjudged that the distress was tortious." On consulting the dictionary, we find that the word *ptuz* signifies a hole. It is pretty manifest that the operation alluded to in the preceding passage very much resembles that of a person who, on finding a hole in a door or pane of glass, puts his hand in through the hole to remove the fastening of the door or window, and so gains admittance into the premises, which no doubt amounts to both a burglary and trespass, as such is not the accustomed mode of obtaining admittance into the premises. The passage from Lord Coke is a direct authority in favour of the defendant; and that from Fitzherbert, when examined, turns out to be so also. We may observe that, as to the passage referred to during the argument in *Comyn's Digest*, 'Execution', that the sheriff may not open a latch, there is no reference to any authority in support of it; and it is clear that the cases cited do not support that proposition. However, that passage applies only to a sheriff entering a dwelling-house under an execution. As the rule will be discharged on this ground, it therefore becomes unnecessary to express any opinion upon the other questions in the case."

Commentary

This judgment confirms that, in distraining, a bailiff may enter by normal means, just like any other visitor to or user of premises. In other words, a distrainor may open the outer door by turning a key, by lifting a latch or by drawing back a bolt. The case concerned a landlord distraining for rent and at the very end hesitation is expressed over whether the same rules would apply in execution, but there seems no real basis for any such doubts.

Nash v Lucas (1867) 2 QB 590

Facts A bailiff went to a house to levy distress for arrears of rent due to Lucas but found the front door locked. During the day a man called Back, who was employed by the landlord, was allowed into the house by the tenant Nash in order to get access to the 'area' for the purpose of removing and repairing a grating over it which was in a dangerous state. While these repairs were still being carried out, Nash left the house, having locked both the front and area doors. As a result Mr Back, who had got into the area to refix the grating, found that he was unable to get out. The bailiff was still outside the house and suggested to Back that he try the window which opened into the area and was closed. The window was unfastened, so Back pulled the sash down, climbed into the house and then unfastened the front door from the inside. As soon as the front door was opened in this way, the bailiff entered and distrained. Nash, the tenant, claimed that the entry was trespass ands that the levy which followed was wrongful interference with his goods. Judgment for Nash was appealed to the High Court.

Judgment of Cockburn CJ: "I am of the opinion that the rule must be refused. It is quite unnecessary to decide, if the defendant and the broker had not been parties to the original trespass, whether, on the door being opened by a third person, the entry for the purpose of making the distress would have been lawful. Here the broker himself suggests to Back to open the window and get into the house, and so out by the front door, and the defendant himself was present, and the broker afterwards enters on the door being opened by Back as the broker had suggested. It must therefore be taken that both the defendant and the broker were parties to the trespass, or act, whereby access was obtained. Now the act, or trespass, was opening the window, which was closed but not fastened. Counsel for the landlord contended that it is lawful to open a window, provided you do not break anything. The old authorities do not go so far as the more modern. The later authorities say you may open a door which is only fastened by a latch: that I think was going a very long way; and I am not surprised that in America the courts have not pursued the same course as the English Court of Exchequer. In Chief Baron Gilbert's time it would appear that a landlord could not open an outer door for the purpose of distraining if it were shut.[13] The Court of Exchequer have held that he might open a door which was closed but not fastened;[14] and if a man leaves his door unfastened there may be an implied licence to any one who has business to enter the premises. But that must stand on its own ground; the principle will not apply to a closed but unfastened window. Again, it has been said that you may go in at an open window to make a distress.[15] But it is nowhere said you may open a window for the purpose. In *Sandon v. Jervis* the officer touched the execution debtor by putting his hand through a pane of glass in a window which had been broken in a scuffle to which the officer was a party, though the pane was not broken by him, and it was held a legal arrest.[16] That case also stands on its own particular ground; and the Court do not go further and say the officer would have been authorized to open the window if not fastened, but only that the window being already open, the arrest was lawful. Therefore the authorities are limited in application either to the case, where the door is shut but can be opened without violence, or where the window is open and can be entered without doing any violence. But if the window be shut, you are doing violence if you open it, when neither directly nor impliedly is the entry made by the licence of the owner of the house. The entry here was therefore unlawful, and the rule must be refused.

---

[13] *Gilbert on Distresses & Replevins*, Impey's 1823 edition p.56.
[14] See *Ryan v Shilcock* earlier.
[15] *Nixon v. Freeman* (1860) 5 H & N 647.
[16] (1859) EB & E 935; 27 LJ (QB) 279; 28 LJ (Ex) 156 - arrest through an open window or one accidentally broken is valid.

Mellor J: I am of the same opinion. The cases seem to me to have gone quite far enough. But there is no case which decides that a landlord, with a view to distrain, may open a window which is shut but not fastened. As to the point that the entry of the broker was by the door, and therefore legal: in *Sandon v Jervis* Hill, J., says: "It was also argued that the officer, by putting his hand through the broken pane, had violated the privilege of the house. But the pane was not broken by him; and I think that the officer, touching the plaintiff through the pane, had as much right to make the arrest through the pane as he would have had to go at once into the house and make the arrest if the door had been left open by the owner, or even broken by third parties and then left open." That proceeds on the assumption that the officer had had nothing to do with the breaking. Now the broker here recommends the mode of entry which led to his subsequent access to the house by the open door, and therefore the case is distinguishable; consequently as the entry must be taken to have been through the window, the distress was not lawful, and the plaintiff is entitled to keep her verdict, and the rule must be refused."

Commentary

As the judgment makes clear, entry into a house by a bailiff for the purpose of distraining by opening a window which is shut, but not fastened, is unlawful. Bailiffs are entitled to enter without using force and where they have a licence to do so. Raising a closed window may be construed a forcible *or* as an entry without permission- although the latter interpretation rests on the rather strained basis that leaving a window open is an invitation to persons on lawful business to climb in- see the remark of Pollock CB to counsel in *Nixon v Freeman* (1860).[17] Opening a closed window is certainly unlawful and cannot be justified by any means- and certainly not by some sort of implied licence.[18] Breaking a pane of glass in order to open a fastened window is even more indisputably unlawful.[19]

Long v Clarke & another [1894] 1 QB 119

Facts In levying distress for rent the bailiff for the defendant landlord climbed over a wall at the back of the rented premises and then entered through a window. The plaintiff was a bill of sale holder who already had a man in possession on the premises. He paid off the landlord to protect his existing possession of the goods and then sued to recover his money. The plaintiff argued that the curtilage of the house was protected from forced

---

[17] 5 H&N 652.

[18] *Ancaster v Milling* (1823) 2 D&R 714; *Arkins v Brunton* (1867) 4 Bar Reports 84 (Ireland, QB); *Villenueva v Clarke* (1890) 35 EG 458; *Lenty v Hunt* (1894) 2 PMR 663.

[19] *Porter v Chapman* (1855) *The Times*, January 25th, 9c, QBD.

entry in the same way as the house itself. The plaintiff's claim failed; he appealed.

Judgment of Lord Esher MR: "In this case we are dealing with a landlord's bailiff distraining for rent. What is the ordinary law applicable to such a case? It gives a right to the landlord to do that which, if any other person did it, would be a trespass, and the question is whether what has been done in the present case is within what is permitted by the law of distress. When a landlord goes into a house to distrain, whether the door be open or shut, he does that which in any other person would be a trespass, and it is just the same if he merely walks across the land to the front door. The sole question is what limitations on the right of the landlord to go on the premises and distrain the law imposes on him. He cannot go into any building or into any house if he can only do so by breaking into it. He can go in at the door, which is the most obvious way of entering; but further, he can get in by a window if it is left open. There is no trespass in doing either of these acts, because he does not break in. So it is incorrect to say, as has been suggested, that the landlord cannot go into the house if he finds a hole in the side of it, and for the same reason, that in so entering he is not breaking in. This law is applicable to any building into which the landlord wants to get for the purpose of distraining, such as a warehouse, a stable, or a barn. Thus, supposing he enters a curtilage without breaking anything, still he cannot break into any stable or building within the curtilage which is locked.

This shows that under the law of distress the curtilage is no part of the house, and it is incorrect to say that he cannot go into the house if he finds a door or a window open because he has previously got over a wall or gate into the curtilage. Another defect in the plaintiff's case is this. Supposing the curtilage to be part of the house, the bailiff did not break into the curtilage. He did not break any door or anything else; he merely got over a wall. I see no difference between getting over a wall to get into the curtilage and getting on to the wall of the house in getting in at a window in it, and it seems to me to be plain that if a landlord can get into a curtilage without breaking anything he may do so, just as he can get into a window on the same conditions.

The case of *Scott v Buckley* is cited in support of the plaintiff's case;[20] but there must be something omitted in the report, for I cannot think that Byles

---

[20] *Scott v Buckley* (1867) 16 LT 573/ The Times June 12th 11a- it seems from *The Times*' report that the fence was 5-8 feet high; as Byles J said it was "evidently a fence intended to keep people out by interposing a serious obstacle to their getting in and, that being so, the entry was illegal." This, then, seems to be the distinction made - between a fence that it is a boundary and that which is a barrier. See too *Stokes v British Mutual Banking Co Ltd* (1886) The Times July 18th 6c.

J, who decided it, would have dissented from the decision in *Eldridge v Stacey*,[21] to which he himself was a party only three years previously. I think, therefore, the action properly failed, and the appeal must be dismissed.

Lopes LJ: I am of the same opinion. A landlord may enter the demised premises to levy a distress, and may commit in so doing an act which in any one else would be a trespass, provided that he does not break open any outer door. He may walk over a garden or park to get to the building, which in any other person would be a trespass; but when he gets to the building, he cannot break open anything to gain access to it. In the word "building" I include a stable, a barn, or any other sort of building. The question raised in this case is whether the landlord or his bailiff may climb over a wall enclosing a yard, and thus get to the building, so as to be able to proceed by any unfastened door or open window to effect a levy in the house. It is clear to me that he could do so. The yard was no more part of the house than the garden or park which I have mentioned would be. The bailiff breaking nothing in getting into the yard has done nothing wrong. The case is similar to that of *Eldridge v Stacey* It is hardly possible to imagine two cases more similar to one another. It was there decided that there is no illegality in distraining for rent by climbing over a fence and so gaining access to the house by an open door. I see no distinction for this purpose between a fence and a wall. The judges who decided that case were Erle CJ and Williams, Byles, and Keating, JJ. The case of *Scott v Buckley* was relied on for the plaintiff, and certainly the head-note supports his contention. Looking, however, to the fact that it was decided by Byles, J., not long after the decision of the other case in which he took a part, I cannot think the report is correct, and I think that at least there must have been some distinction between the cases which has not been noticed in the report. However that may be, I think that the decision in *Eldridge v. Stacey* should be supported, and consequently that the present appeal should be dismissed."

Kay LJ: "If there had been a door in the wall of the yard, and the landlord had effected an entrance by breaking it, I should have thought he would have exceeded the power given him by the law and become a trespasser, and even if the house door had been open would have been a trespasser *ab initio.* It is not, however, necessary to decide that question. That is not what the bailiff did, for he got over the wall without breaking anything. In any one else the act of getting over the wall would have been a trespass, and the question is whether it is so in the case of the landlord or his bailiff. The land belongs to the landlord; but he has let it for a term, and has no right to enter, with this exception, that the law permits him to do so to distrain in the case of rent in arrear. If there

---

[21] (1863) 62 L. J. (Q.B.) 388.

were no wall, the landlord might walk over the land surrounding the house in order to reach it. The question is whether climbing over a wall to exercise his right to go on the land makes him a trespasser. If it does, he is a trespasser *ab initio*. No case has said so, and in fact if the word "wall" is substituted for "fence" in the decision in *Eldridge v Stacey*, that case would be identical with the one we are considering. We are not bound by that decision; but Erle CJ, in giving judgment, pointed out that none of the authorities cited warranted the conclusion that the distress was rendered unlawful by the broker getting over the fence, and in that view I concur.

Three years later there was a case of *Scott v Buckley*. As it reads in the report, it seems to be an authority contrary to that of *Eldridge v Stacey*. It was decided by Byles J, who was a party to the judgment in the previous case, and I am driven to conclude that there was some fact not reported which made the two cases distinguishable. The only restriction that the law imposes on the right of the landlord to enter and distrain for rent is that to do so he must not break in. He has not done that in this case, but has got over a wall, committing in doing so no further trespass than he would have committed in walking across the land if there had been no wall there. I agree, therefore, that the plaintiffs case fails, and that the appeal must be dismissed."

Commentary

This case is included not because any great importance is attached to the right of bailiffs to climb over walls, but because of the general remarks made by the judges on rights of entry. It is useful to remember that a bailiff with a lawful warrant or order has a *right* of entry which others do not possess. This may be hedged about with the provisos discussed elsewhere, but nonetheless the bailiff has legal powers bestowed upon him.

Southam v Smout [1964] 1 QB 308

Facts Two county court bailiffs called at the home of a judgment debtor to execute a warrant for her arrest for a debt of 25s. Not finding her in, they proceeded to the home of her son-in-law, bailiff B going to the front door armed with the warrant and bailiff S to the back entrance. B knocked on the closed but not latched front door several times, as a result of which it opened, and he entered. He found the judgment debtor giving her grandchildren a meal, told her that he had a warrant for her arrest, went along the passage, opened the back door by turning the knob, and let bailiff S in. The defendant householder, seeing persons whom he knew to be bailiffs in his house, told them to go out and ask to come in. They did not go, and the defendant thereupon ejected bailiff S with no more force than necessary to eject a trespasser. Meanwhile his wife borrowed the 25s. from a neighbour and paid the debt, and the bailiffs departed. On a complaint by bailiff S alleging assault by the defendant householder, the county court judge, in the exercise of his criminal jurisdiction under section 30 of the County Courts Act 1959, fined the defendant £10. Smout appealed to the Court of Appeal against the decision and the sentence.

Judgment of Lord Denning MR: "This is an interesting case. A warrant was issued for committing a widow, who was a debtor, to prison. Two bailiffs went to arrest her. She was not at her own home but at the home of her daughter and son-in-law looking after her grandchildren. The bailiffs opened the door and went in. The son-in-law (who was the householder) ordered them out. They did not go and he pushed one of them. He got hold of the lapels of his mackintosh and tried to get him to go. Eventually they did go. The money was paid by the debtor and all was well. But a summons was issued against the householder for assault on one of the officers, bailiff Southam, in the execution of his duty. The householder said that the bailiffs here were not acting in the execution of their duty. They were trespassers in that they entered unlawfully into the house ...

Bailiff Southam took out a summons before the county court judge complaining of the action of Smout in pushing him out or attempting to push him out of the house. It is quite clear on the evidence that Smout used no more force than was reasonably necessary in the circumstances. The judge held that it was an assault on the bailiff in the execution of his duty and fined Smout £10.

It must be remembered that this is a criminal case. The burden is on the prosecution to prove beyond reasonable doubt the guilt of the accused. At the end of the day the question must be asked: have the prosecution proved beyond reasonable doubt that it was an assault on bailiff Southam in the execution of his duty? and as the point being raised is that bailiff Southam was a trespasser, the burden is on the prosecution to show that he was not.

This question depends on the right of a sheriff's officer to enter a house to execute civil process. This order for the arrest of Mrs. McGuire is civil process and subject to the same rules as are writs of *fi fa*, and so forth. It was decided as long ago as 1797 that an attachment for non-payment of money is to be considered only as process to enforce payment of a debt and analogous to an execution.[22]

[22] *Harvey v Harvey* (1884) 26 ChD 644.

What is the law as to the entry of a sheriff's officer or a bailiff to enforce civil process? We go back to the leading case, *Semayne's Case*, in 1604. There the proposition was laid down that "the house of everyone is to him as his castle and fortress, as well for his defence against injury and violence, as for his repose" This is the basis of the classic passage of the Earl of Chatham: "The poorest man may in his cottage bid defiance to all the forces of the Crown. It may be frail - its roof may shake - the wind may blow through it - the storm may enter - the rain may enter - but the King of England cannot enter - all his force dares not cross the threshold of the ruined tenement." So be it - unless he has justification by law.

The question in this case is: what justification by law had the bailiffs to enter into this house? The most typical case of process, of course, is entry at the suit of the King, criminal process. In *Semayne's Case* it was held that: "In all cases where the King is party, the sheriff may break the house, either to arrest or do other execution of the King's process, if he cannot otherwise enter. But he ought first to signify the cause of his coming, and make the request to open the doors." This request was made in the customary demand: "Open in the name of the King." So at the King's suit the outer doors may be broken. But it is otherwise in civil process at the suit of an individual. It was always lawful for the sheriff to enter on civil process when the door was open. The fourth resolution in *Semayne's Case* said: "Where the door is open the Sheriff may enter, and do execution at the suit of a subject, and so also in such case may the lord, and distrain for his rent or service." That is, when the door is open. Then a further resolution goes on to say: "It is not lawful for the Sheriff, on request made and denial, at the suit of a common person, to break the defendant's house, scil. to execute any process at the suit of a subject." So in civil process the distinction is clear that if the door is open, the sheriff may enter to execute civil process: but he may not break in.

So far the law is simple; but the question which we have to decide in this case is: what is to happen where the door is shut but not locked, bolted or barred? For instance, where the door can be opened by lifting a latch, or turning a knob, or just by pushing? In the criminal law, for the purposes of a charge of burglary or housebreaking, it would be a breaking. Is it so in the civil law for executing civil process? In the days of *Comyn's Digest* it was said that a sheriff could not open the door when it was only latched. There is a passage in *Comyn's Digest* under "Execution", which says: "After a *fieri facias* delivered to him, the sheriff may enter the house of the defendant, when the door is open, and seize the goods of the defendant there found ...," and then it goes on: "But the sheriff cannot break a house to make execution upon goods, or body." Then there is this sentence: "Neither can he open the door, though it be only latched." If that represented the law of this country today, it would mean that a bailiff or sheriff's officer could not open a door which was shut.[23]

But that statement in *Comyn's Digest* fell to be considered by the Court of Exchequer in 1851 in *Ryan v Shilcock.* That was a case of a landlord distraining. It was a case not of a dwelling-house but of a stable. The door was kept closed by a padlock attached to a movable staple. The way people got in was not by unlocking the padlock, but pulling out the staple. It was held that an entry made by pulling out the staple was a lawful entry. Pollock CB said: "We think that he has authority by law to open the door in the ordinary way in which other persons could do it, when it is left so as to be accessible to all who have occasion to go into the premises." That is clear authority that when a landlord is making a distress, he can open a door when it is closed, even if it means lifting the latch or turning the knob. The court considered the passage in *Comyn's Digest* and at the conclusion of the judgment, the Chief Baron said: "We may observe that as to the passage referred to during the argument in *Comyn's Digest* 'Execution,' that the sheriff may not open a latch, there is no reference to any authority in support of it, and it is clear that the cases cited do not support that proposition. However, that passage applies only to a sheriff entering a dwelling house under an execution. Those observations clearly throw a good deal of doubt on the passage in *Comyn's Digest.* I fail to see any distinction in point of principle between a landlord, entering under lawful process to take a distress, and a sheriff's officer entering under his warrant to effect an arrest under civil process. In each case the officer comes by authority of the law. If it is permissible in the one case to lift the latch to walk in, so it must be in the other.

That seems to have been the view of the Court of Queen's Bench in the later case of *Nash v Lucas* in 1867, which was again a landlord distraining. Entry was made through a window, which of course was unlawful. But Lush J considered the earlier cases and he said in the course of argument: "The ground of holding entry through a closed but unfastened door to be lawful, is, that access through the door is the usual mode of access, and that the licence from the occupier to any one to enter who has lawful business may therefore be implied from his leaving the door unfastened." Sir Alexander Cockburn CJ said that the later authorities say you may open a door which is only fastened by a latch. He thought that was going a very long way, further than the American courts had done, but the authorities were limited to the case where the door is shut but can be opened without violence.

---

[23] Vol. 4, pp. 223-4 (c. 5).

It seems to me that the law now is that where a landlord enters under a right given by the law to levy a distress or a sheriff's officer enters by virtue of his warrant to effect civil process, he may not break the door, in the sense that he may not break it physically. If it is locked, bolted or barred, he must not open it: he is forbidden to do so. But if it is open and ajar, or if it is closed and can be opened by the peaceable means of lifting the latch or turning the knob or just by gently pushing, in those circumstances he can lawfully enter because there he is not breaking. The difference between the two cases is this, that in the case where a man locks, bolts or bars his door, he makes it clear that no one is to come in. Whereas if he leaves it open, or if he just shuts it and all that is needed is to turn the handle or lift the latch or give it a push, then he gives an implied invitation to all people who have lawful business to come in.

Such being the law on that part of the case, I would hold that bailiff Bland was not acting unlawfully when, as a result of his knocking at the front door, it fell open; and also when he went to the back door and opened it and let bailiff Southam in. It is just the same as if bailiff Southam had opened the back door himself. In both those cases it was simply opening a closed door; it was not forcing a door which was locked, bolted or barred. I would hold, therefore, that the mode of entering this house, being in pursuance of the process of the law, was lawful. It was not a trespass.

Then the second important question in the case is this. This was not Mrs McGuire's own house; it was Smout's house; it was his "castle." What right had the bailiff to go into his house when he was not going to arrest Smout or do anything to Smout's property? The law on this point seems to be now well settled that a sheriff's officer, when he goes into a *stranger's* house to execute process, enters at his peril, to this extent, that if the defendant's goods are *actually* there that he is to take, or if the person is *actually* there whom he is to arrest, then he is justified by the event. But if the goods are not there or if the person whom he seeks is not present, then he is guilty of a trespass. It seems illogical. It might be said that if he had *reasonable cause* to think the goods were there or *reasonable cause* to think the person was there whom he sought, that should be sufficient justification. But not so, as I read the authorities. It would be putting far too much power into the hands of sheriff's officers or bailiffs if it was open to them to excuse an entry by saying they had reasonable grounds. They might go and invade a person's house too easily without justification. Therefore the law has made it plain, to discourage them from any unwarranted intrusion, that they are only justified if they are sure the person is there or the property is there. They are only justified it that in fact proves to be the case. On this point there was no settled authority in the very early days. Perhaps the best discussion of the old authorities is given in the argument of Serjeant Bayley, as he was then, in

Ratcliffe v Burton, an argument which certainly had its impact on the later cases.[24] There was a series of cases in *Taunton's Reports*, to which we were referred, stretching from *Hutchison v Birch* through to *Cooke v Birt* and *Johnson v Leigh*.[25] But I need not go through them all now because the law seems to have been finally settled by *Morrish v Murrey*. It summarises the whole of the previous cases. Alderson B said "A party, however, who enters the house of a stranger to search for and arrest a defendant, can be justified only by the event."[26]

The reasoning of the law on this point, as counsel pointed out, is rather like the reasoning on the arrest of a felon. A civilian must not only have reasonable cause for believing that a felony has been committed, but he must prove in fact that a felony has been committed. So, here, if an officer is entering the house of a stranger on the ground that he has a warrant to arrest a person who is there, he is only justified if the person is *in fact* in the house. He enters at his peril unless the person sought is actually there. In this case Mrs. McGuire was there. So there was justification for entering even Smout's house to find Mrs. McGuire and to arrest her. Smout was not justified in ordering them out.

The final question which was raised was on the particular facts of this case. Assuming that bailiff Bland came in through the front door and arrested Mrs McGuire in the room, was there any justification for bailiff Southam to be let in through the back door? I think the answer to that point is this, that this was truly a joint operation. One can well see that if a bailiff went in the front door, the party sought might go out at the back; and if the person was not found there, it would be a trespass. In any case it was a difficult situation undoubtedly difficulties might arise. The presence of two might well be thought desirable and necessary. I think there was sufficient justification for the entry of bailiff Southam as well as bailiff Bland.

Those are really all the points in the case and it means this, that on the facts as found by the county court judge Smout was not entitled to order the bailiffs out: they were executing lawful process and were by authority of law in the house: they were executing their duty, and Smout, by pushing bailiff Southam out, was guilty of an assault on him in the execution of his duty. Those facts being established and the judge being satisfied of that, it is a case where the charge is made out.

---

[24] (1802) 3 B&P 223.
[25] Respectively (1812) 4 Taunt 619, (1814) 5 Taunt 765 & (1815) 6 Taunt 246.
[26] (1844) 13 M&W 52.

One further word. The judge said that, if necessary, he thought that s.165 of the County Courts Act 1959, was an answer to the case. I do not think I need read it. It says that an officer is not to be deemed to be a trespasser by reason of any irregularity or informality in the mode of executing the warrant. I suppose the judge must have thought that if anything went wrong in the procedure in this case, it was an irregularity in the mode of executing the warrant. Counsel for the bailiff very properly accepted the view that those words must not be given such a wide interpretation as to affect the common law rights which protect an Englishman's house as his castle. It seems to me that "irregularity or informality in the mode of execution" is something to do with reading out the warrant or some informality of that kind which does not affect the substance of the law at all. If Smout had been justified in ordering these men out because they were trespassers, they would not be protected by section 165.

One further matter. The judge imposed a fine of £10. Mr. Perry before us asked for leave to amend his notice of appeal so that that matter could be reconsidered. Counsel for the bailiff, I was glad to hear, submitted to us that perhaps in the special circumstances of this case, seeing that the law has been uncertain up to this moment, it is a ground upon which some extenuating consideration could be given. Who knows but that Smout may have been going by the law contained in *Comyn's Digest*? Whether he did so or not, the fact that the law has not been settled until this moment is a ground, it seems to me, for taking a lenient course in this case. But everyone must now know that after this case the law is settled. Bailiffs can enter by turning the handle of the door. In the circumstances of this case I would suggest reducing the fine of £10 to the sum of £2. I would, with this variation, dismiss the appeal."

Harman LJ: "In the course of the extremely interesting argument in this case I was reminded irresistibly of a poem by an eminent mathematician which is in these words:

> "And when I found the door was locked,
> I pulled and pushed and kicked and knocked.
> And when I found the door was shut,
> I tried to turn the handle but - ".
> 'Is that all?', Alice asked. 'That's all' said Humpty Dumpty."

That seems to me to describe the situation here. I do not say the judge was not right; I think he was right in his determination of the case and right for the reasons which my Lord has given, and I do not propose to say anything very much about it.

The original principle is very well stated in the judgment of Lord Ellenborough C.J., in *Burdett v Abbott* in these words: "Nothing is more certain than that in the ordinary cases of the execution of civil process between subject and subject, no person is warranted in breaking open the outer door in order to execute such process: the law values the private repose and security of every man in his own house, which it considers as his castle, beyond the civil satisfaction of a creditor."[27] One of the exceptions to that is next stated. This point, says Lord Ellenborough, "also has been settled, that where an injury to the public has been committed in the shape of an insult to any of the courts of justice, on which process of contempt is issued, the officer charged with the execution of such process may break open doors if necessary in order to execute it." Therefore, if this were properly to be treated as a process of contempt, breaking open the door would be justified, but it has been decided, as my Lord has said, that though arrest under the Debtors Act 1869 is not arrest for debt but arrest for disobedience to the court, it is nevertheless considered not as a process of contempt but process of an ordinary civil enforcement of a right. Therefore breaking open is not justified in a sheriff's officer seeking to arrest under the 1869 Act.

That having been said, you start with bailiff Bland who goes to the front door and who, without, according to what the judge found, anything but merely pushing upon it, opens it. I think it true to say that that did not involve a breaking and entering because the door was not fastened and there was therefore impliedly an invitation by the householder to anybody having lawful business in the house to come in. But even if it had been necessary to turn the handle, it would have been justified, as is shown in *Ryan v Shilcock,* cited by my Lord. Mr Perry sought to distinguish that case because he said it concerned goods and it concerned goods of the householder and was a case of distraint by a landlord. Speaking for myself, I do not feel that the fact that it was a case of distraint and that the goods being distrained on were those of the tenant makes any difference and I think the law as laid down in that case is, and has been ever since it was laid down, the law of this country.

The other and perhaps more interesting point was that this was not the debt of the householder but of somebody who, I suppose, for this purpose, being his mother-in-law, was a stranger to him. It was her debt and in that event it does seem an extraordinary thing that the officer is justified only if he do find the debtor in the house. It is a case of justification not by faith but by works. He may believe the debtor to be there but if the debtor be not there, he is not justified. He is only justified if it works, that is to say, if the debtor is within. Happily the lady here was. No doubt a bailiff was put at the back

[27] (1811) 14 East 1.

door as well as at the front in order that she should not run out of the back door and the bailiff be cheated of his prey and be liable for trespass. The bailiff at the back of the house, Southam, did not himself enter by turning the knob of the back door; he was let in by the bailiff at the front; and on that I must say I felt a little doubt. Counsel for the bailiff argued that it was just the same whether the handle was turned from inside or outside. But I do not like to put it on that ground. It seems to me that this was a combined operation and that Bland was justified in turning the knob inside if he felt, as I think he reasonably did, that in the delicate situation which confronted him, he needed the help of his superior and that a breach of the peace became thereby less and not more likely.

As for the appellant, who has the Shakespearian name of Smout, I am not surprised that when he found a man whom he knew to be a bailiff in his house for a debt he knew not to be his debt he was somewhat aggrieved. He does not appear to have misbehaved himself in any way, and therefore, although it is very necessary that the law should be vindicated, I assent to my Lord's proposal that that being done, we may reduce the fine in the way he has proposed. I, therefore, subject to that variation, would dismiss the appeal."

Pearson LJ: "I agree. As has been pointed out, in cases such as this there are two principles which need to be reconciled. The first is that an Englishman's house is his castle and must not be unlawfully invaded. The other is that it must be possible for bailiffs to do their duty by executing civil process, as it is in this case. It seems to me clear that it was lawful to have two bailiffs carrying out a combined operation. It is to be observed that the warrant under which they were acting, being a warrant of the Barrow-in-Furness and Ulverston County Court, was addressed to the registrar and bailiffs of the court and to other persons, and it contained this command: "You, the said registrar, bailiffs and others are therefore required to arrest the said defendant and to deliver her to the Governor of Her Majesty's Prison at Manchester." It was reasonable to have two bailiffs acting in that matter, and they were acting in combination, and it was reasonably arranged that one should go to the front door and seek entry there and the other should go to the back door and seek entry there. It so happened that bailiff Southam, who was at the back door, was admitted from the yard to the scullery or kitchen of the house by the other bailiff, Bland, opening the back door. In my view that makes no difference. Bailiff Southam gained admission to the house through the back door by virtue of the door being opened by ordinary means. I am not quite sure whether the evidence shows exactly what means were employed, whether there was the lifting of a latch or the turning of a knob. At any rate that back door was opened by ordinary means such as any person who wished to enter the house by the back entrance would employ for that purpose. In my view the position is exactly the same as if bailiff Southam himself had employed those ordinary means and opened that door.

So much for the facts. In this case there are two legal points involved and the first is that entry was made by the bailiffs to the house of a person who was not the person owing the sum of money involved. The money was owed by Mrs. McGuire and she was the person to be arrested and delivered to the Prison Governor under the warrant, whereas the house belonged to a different person, Smout, although he happened to be the son-in-law of Mrs. McGuire. The law is that a sheriff's officer or bailiff or person in a similar position may enter the house of a stranger for the purpose of executing a warrant and arrest of a person who is in fact there. It has been pointed out that there is the curious position that if the person sought is there, the entry is right and lawful: if the person sought is not there, the entry is wrong and unlawful. That is sufficiently clear from three cases which have been mentioned. There is *Cooke v Birt* decided in the year 1814. On this point the clearest passage in the judgments is that of Dallas J. He said: "The sheriff may enter the house of a stranger, if the door be open but it is at his peril whether the goods be found there or not; if they be not, he is a trespasser." There is also *Morrish v Murrey* in the year 1844. Alderson B in his judgment said this: "The plea amounts to no more than this, that the defendants had reasonable ground to suspect that the party sought to be arrested was in the plaintiff's house; but it turns out that she was not there. A party, however, who enters the house of a stranger to search for and arrest a defendant, can be justified only by the event." There was also the interesting argument in *Ratcliffe v Burton*, in which both the argument of Serjeant Bayley and the argument in answer of Serjeant Best tend to show the same position, that if the person entering to effect the arrest finds the person sought, his entry is lawful, but if the person sought is not there, the entry is unlawful.[28] In this case Mrs. McGuire was in the house and, so far as that aspect of the case is concerned, the entry by bailiff Southam as well as the entry by bailiff Bland was for that reason lawful.

The other question raised is as to the mode by which entry was effected, which must have involved on a reasonable view of the evidence turning the knob or lifting the latch or opening the door by some other ordinary means. Now "ordinary means" for this purpose would include such methods as that, or perhaps pushing a door that is merely standing ajar, or even more likely walking through the entrance to a door that was open in the ordinary sense, but it would not include going through a window, and would not include using physical force to break open the door and, if the door was locked, it

[28] (1862) 3 B&P 223.

would not include using a key if there was no authority from the householder to make use of the key. In my view the law is laid down for this purpose in, or can be sufficiently inferred from, two cases. The first is *Ryan v Shilcock*, where Pollock CB said in the course of his judgment: "the question resolves itself into this, whether a landlord, who on coming to premises for the purpose of distraining, finds the outer door closed but capable of being opened by lifting a latch, is justified in so doing. We think that he has authority by law to open the door in the ordinary way in which other persons could do it, when it is left so as to be accessible to all who have occasion to go into the premises."

The reason for that rule is explained in *Nash v Lucas*, where in the course of the argument Lush J. said: "If you are lawfully on the premises you may distrain. The ground of holding entry through a closed but unfastened door to be lawful, is, that access through the door is the usual mode of access, and that the licence from the occupier to any one to enter who has lawful business may therefore be implied from his leaving the door unfastened. Entry through a window is not the usual mode of entry, and therefore no such licence can be implied from the window being left unfastened."

Those two points of law having been resolved in favour of bailiff Southam in this case, the only question which remains is as to the amount of the fine that was imposed. I do wish to make it clear, in fairness to the county court judge and in regard to the exercise of this jurisdiction generally, that it seems to me that the amount which the judge assessed on the materials before him was a reasonable sum and that no complaint can reasonably be made that he assessed an excessive sum. But having regard to the attitude adopted on behalf of the prosecution on the hearing of the appeal, and having regard to the interesting and difficult points of law which were raised by the action of the defendant, Smout, in this case, and having regard to the fact that he did not use any more force than was needed for the purpose of removing the person whom he regarded incorrectly as a trespasser in his house, I agree with the decision that the amount of the fine should be reduced to £2. Subject to that variation, I agree the appeal should be dismissed subject to variation of fine from £10 to £2."

Commentary

As this judgment makes clear, it is perfectly lawful for a bailiff to gain entry to premises by 'normal' means- by the means that any occupier or visitor might use: pushing at a door or turning the handle. Unusual means are what are frowned upon. Thus the improper use of keys to gain entry would be illegal.[29]

The judgment shows the continuing relevance of *Semayne's Case* into modern times. It is also noteworthy that, as Harmon LJ stated, case law on rights of entry developed in the context of distress for rent will nonetheless lay down the law applicable to both distress and execution throughout England and Wales.

A bailiff who has entered lawfully and who has commenced a levy cannot be told to leave and cannot be expelled. It seems that the Court accepted that Mrs McGuire had already been arrested by the time Mr Smout ejected the bailiff. The evidence of the arrest may seem minimal- Bland said "I've come about the warrant for 25/- "but this was enough for the Court of Appeal in this instance. A bailiff who has started to seize goods will presumably also be protected from assault or expulsion, but as we will see in chapter 3 more evidence of the fact of a levy may be desirable.

Thirdly, the Court helpfully distinguished between what might be treated as an illegal or an irregular act. A mistake in reading out details of the warrant would constitute an irregularity; a forced or otherwise unpermitted mode of entry would be unlawful and the bailiff would be a trespasser who could quite lawfully be removed from the premises by the occupier.

Finally, the issue of the licence to enter is touched on by the judges in the course of their discussion. The following case examines this matter in far greater detail.

Robson & another v Hallett [1967] 2 QB 939

Facts Three police officers were making inquiries regarding an offence which had been committed. They came to the house where the defendants lived. The officers knocked on the door and questioned Thomas Robson. Shortly afterwards a police sergeant came to the door. Thomas permitted him to enter the house but not the other two officers, who remained outside. When Dennis Robson, the father of the defendant, saw the sergeant in his house he ordered him to leave. He began to do so and had reached the threshold when Thomas jumped upon his back and punched him. When the door opened the constables outside saw the sergeant fall forwards with Thomas on his back. They intervened and a fight developed. The justices convicted the Robsons of assaulting the officers in the execution of their duty. They appealed to

---

[29] *Alford v Thrupp* (1906) 67 EG 226.

quarter sessions, where the conviction of Dennis Robson for assault was quashed. Appeal was made against the further convictions.

Judgment of Lord Parker CJ: "... What is said in this case, and this is really the foundation of the argument, is that all three police officers were trespassers *ab initio*; having arrived at the garden gate, although up till then they were acting in the execution of their duty, making inquiries into an offence committed that night, yet the moment they set foot onto the steps leading up to the front door they were all three trespassers. It is no doubt true that the law is sometimes said to be an ass, but I am happy to think it is not an ass in this respect, because I am quite satisfied that these three police officers, like any other members of the public, had implied leave and licence to walk through that gate up those steps and to knock on the door of the house. We are not considering for this purpose the entering of private premises in the form of a dwelling house, but of the position between the gate and the front door. There, as it seems to me, the occupier of any dwelling house gives implied licence to any member of the public coming on his lawful business to come through the gate, up the steps, and knock on the door of the house.

The appellant has stressed the words used by Atkin LJ in *Great Central Railway Co v Bates.*[30] In that case a police constable, seeing the door of the defendants' warehouse open after dark, and in order to see that everything was right, entered the warehouse and injured himself. It was held that he had no legal right to enter, being neither an invitee nor a licensee. Atkin LJ in the course of his judgment said:

> "Now it appears to me that he had no right to enter these premises at all, and I think that counsel for the respondent has been a little hard put to it to defend the right of entry in these circumstances. It can hardly be suggested that the right exists in respect of a dwelling-house. If it did, the privacy of an Englishman's dwelling-house would be most materially curtailed. In view of the limitations that have been laid down over and over again as to the right of a constable to force a door, and as to the limitations of his powers unless he has a warrant, or in cases of felony, it appears to me quite impossible to suggest, merely because a constable may suspect there is something wrong, that he has a right to enter a dwelling-house either by opening a door or by entering an open door or an open window and go into the house. It is true that a reasonable householder would not as a rule object if the matter was done bona fide

[30] [1921] 3 KB 578.

> and no nuisance was caused. But the question is whether the constable has the right to enter."

I hope that nothing I am saying will be thought in any way to detract from what Atkin LJ said; but we are not here considering the right to enter the front door of the house but merely the right to go in at the garden gate and go up to the front door.

Lastly, under this head the appellant invoked *Davis v Lisle.*[31] It is unnecessary to go through the facts of that case in any detail, but there is no doubt that it did involve the right of a police officer to enter garage premises, and there are passages in the judgments in that case which in isolation might be taken to suggest that he had no leave or licence to enter onto those premises. But when one looks at the case, it is quite clear that the case was decided on the basis that a time came when the proprietor told the police officer to leave, and, as it was put, from that moment he became a trespasser and ceased to be acting in the execution of his duty. That case, in my judgment, is no authority for saying that a police officer on his lawful business making proper inquiries has no right to enter the front gate of private premises and to go up and knock on the front door.

Finally, it is to be observed that what I have said is fully in accord with a recent decision of this court in 1964 in *McArdle v Wallace.*[32] Again it is unnecessary to go into the facts of that case, though it is to be observed that the court there held that a constable who entered an adjacent yard and knocked on the rear door of premises in order to rouse the occupier and make inquiries came onto those premises with the implied authority of the occupier. The only question in that case was whether that implied leave and licence had been revoked by the occupier's son.

Accordingly, in my judgment all three police officers were lawfully upon those premises while they were outside the house. What happened then was, as I have said, that Sergeant McCaffrey was allowed to enter the house by the permission of the occupier's son. It was not suggested that the occupier's son had no authority so to do, and accordingly when Sergeant McCaffrey was in the house he was lawfully in the house and was still acting in the execution of his duty.

---

[31] [1936] 2 KB 434 - police officers entered without a warrant or permission. They failed to leave when asked and were assaulted. They were trespassers and not in execution of their duty.

[32] (1964) 108 Sol Jo 483 - a police officer was asked to leave a café by the owner's son. He failed to do so and was assaulted by the son.

What the appellant says in regard to Sergeant McCaffrey is this, that the moment Mr. Robson, senior, said "Get out" he at once became a trespasser and at once ceased to be acting in the execution of his duty. That proposition, which I confess sounds remarkable, is based as I understand it on the last sentence but one in the judgment of Goddard J in *Davis v Lisle* Goddard J said: "He had no right to be on the premises once he had been asked to leave." In my judgment it is quite wrong to read those words as words of a statute; they were in relation to a case where the police officer, having been plainly told to leave, was remonstrating and asserting his right to stay. In the present case Sergeant McCaffrey was doing all he could to leave, and was not asserting any right to stay.

It seems to me that when a licence is revoked as a result of which something has to be done by the licensee, a reasonable time must be implied in which he can do so, in this case to get off the premises; no doubt it will be a very short time, but he was doing here his best to leave the premises. Looked at in a slightly different way, it is argued that he was acting in the execution of his duty up to the very moment he was told to get out, and one asks oneself what was he doing when he was assaulted? He was surely carrying on his duty, which was a duty to get out.

In my judgment, therefore, the prosecution's cross-appeal in regard to the assault on McCaffrey succeeds. In regard to the two remaining assaults, those by Dennis and Thomas on Police Constable Paxton, the appellant's case is really based on the fact that they were throughout and remained trespassers. As I have already said, I think they were lawfully on those premises when they entered them; they, as opposed to McCaffrey, had never been told to get out, their implied licence to be there had never been revoked, and accordingly there they were in this little garden seeing McCaffrey set upon by Thomas, and a general mêlée developing. It seems to me quite impossible in those circumstances to say that they were not acting in the execution of their duty in coming to the assistance of Sergeant McCaffrey, and also avoiding any further breach of the peace.

It is really unnecessary to go further, but even if they had been outside the gate, it seems to me that they would have abundant right to come onto private property in those circumstances. Accordingly I would dismiss the appeal by the defendants Dennis and Thomas Robson, but I would send the case back to quarter sessions with a direction that they should dismiss the appeal by Dennis Robson against his conviction by the magistrates for assaulting Sergeant McCaffrey.

Diplock LJ: "I agree. These appeals raise three simple points on the law of trespass to land which affect all members of the public as well as the police officers with whom this appeal is concerned. The points are so simple that the combined researches of counsel have not revealed any authority upon them. There is no authority because no one has thought it plausible up till now to question them. The first is this, that when a householder lives in a dwelling-house to which there is a garden in front and does not lock the gate of the garden, it gives an implied licence to any member of the public who has lawful reason for doing so to proceed from the gate to the front door or back door, and to inquire whether he may be admitted and to conduct his lawful business. Such implied licence can be rebutted by express refusal of it, as in this case the Robsons could no doubt have rebutted the implied licence to the police officers by putting up a notice on their front gate "No admittance to police officers"; but that was not done in this case.

The second proposition is this, that when, having knocked at the front door of the dwelling-house, someone who is inside the dwelling-house invites the person who has knocked to come in, there is an implied authority in that person which can be rebutted on behalf of the occupier of the dwelling-house to invite him to come in, and so licence him to come into the dwelling-house itself. In the present case it was the son, and not the father who was the occupier, who invited Sergeant McCaffrey to come in. In those circumstances Sergeant McCaffrey, whilst in the dwelling-house on the invitation of the son, was no trespasser. The licence, however, could be withdrawn by the father, who was the person entitled to give it. He withdrew it and, upon its being withdrawn, the sergeant had a reasonable time to leave the premises by the most appropriate route for doing so, namely, out of the front door, down the steps and out of the gate, and, provided that he did so with reasonable expedition, he would not be a trespasser while he was so doing. That is sufficient to give the reasons for allowing the appeal of the prosecution in the case of the attack upon Sergeant McCaffrey.

As regards Police Constables Paxton and Jobson, it does not seem to me to matter whether, when they were denied entrance at the front door, they were trespassers in remaining in the garden, if they did remain in the garden after that, because there are two ways in which a person who enters land of another person may fail to be a trespasser. One is leave and licence of the person entitled to possession, to which I have already referred; the other is in the exercise of an independent right to proceed on the land. In the case of police constables Paxton and Jobson, once a breach of the peace was taking place under their eyes, they had not only an independent right but a duty to go and stop it, and it matters not from that moment onwards whether they started off on their journey to stop it from outside the premises or from inside the premises. They were entitled, once the breach of the peace occurred, to be on the premises for the purpose of preventing it or stopping it. I agree with the order proposed by my Lord.

Commentary

The main reason for including this case report is for the light that is shed upon the development and implementation of the concept of the licence to enter. This judgment (and most of the other recent authorities cited on the subject) relates to police officers investigating criminal offences. The point is, if a constable detecting crime enters premises only subject to a licence, is it likely that a bailiff enforcing a civil debt has any greater right? Most enforcement agents act only on warrants issued by individual creditors, without court intervention, and in the absence of any greater authority it may be best to assume that what the higher courts have said for the police will also apply (until a specific decision on bailiffs' rights is made).

The key point of interest in this particular case is what happens if a licence is revoked. The police officer (or bailiff) *must* then leave the premises, but at the same time s/he must be given reasonable time physically to do this. In fact, as may have been noted, Diplock LJ even suggested that an implied licence could be withheld in advance by means of a prominent notice or locked front gate. This would, in its effect, be akin to a closed door but would prevent an enforcement agent even setting foot on the front path or drive. This is important because, as *Robson* states, lawful visitors otherwise have a right to enter into gardens, entrance ways, common stair wells and the like.[33] The effectiveness of such a notice in terminating an implied right of entry was endorsed by Donaldson LJ in *Lambert v Roberts* (1981).[34] He said that "there can be no doubt that, in the absence of a locked gate or some other notice such as "Police keep out," police officers, like all other citizens, have an implied licence to enter upon a driveway and to approach the door of a dwelling-house if they have, or reasonably think that they have, legitimate business with the occupier. But it is a licence which is revocable without prior notice."

Lambert v Roberts was also concerned with the entry rights of police officers. This time they were investigating a possible offence of drink driving and entered premises to take a breathalyzer sample from a suspect. Roberts refused to provide a sample and declared that he was on private property and that the police officers were trespassing. This was treated as notice revoking their licence to be there. As a result the magistrates' court found that Roberts was not guilty of any offence because the police officers had acted unlawfully in requiring a sample when they were trespassers. Once their licence was revoked, the police officers were under a duty to withdraw from Roberts' property with all reasonable speed and, as they did not do so,

---

[33] *Knox v Anderton* [1983] Crim LR 115; *R v Leroy Roberts* [2003] EWCA Crim 2753.
[34] 72 Cr App R 223.

they were not thereafter acting in the execution of their duty.[35] Mr Roberts' subsequent arrest was unlawful.

If a police officer investigating a suspected criminal offence cannot remain once permission to be on premises has been withdrawn, and if any steps taken after that are likewise rendered unlawful, it may be prudent to assume that the same will be the case for a bailiff and that any levy will be invalidated by a trespass.

Part Two: Police involvement & resistance

Skidmore v Booth (1834) 6 C&P 777

Facts This case involved a levy of distress for rent. The plaintiff rented warehouse premises in East London from the defendant. In June 1834 the tenant informed his landlord that he would be away in Liverpool on business for a few days, but upon his return would pay the quarterly rent that was about to fall due. The landlord stated that he was content with this and so the plaintiff departed, leaving a boy aged about 14 to look after the warehouse. The next day the landlord met the boy outside the warehouse and assaulted him, demanding the key to the premises. Two days after that the landlord entered the warehouse with two other men and declared he had come to distrain. They set about making an inventory, but as the boy still refused to give up the keys, the landlord called a police officer. The youth was threatened with arrest by the landlord and the boy began to cry whilst a crowd assembled outside. The men conducting the levy remained about two hours; after they left the constable remained outside the door for about half an hour. The landlord also put up a 'to let' notice in the window of the warehouse and, when a customer of the tenant came to collect some goods, initially refused to release them to him. When the tenant returned to London he settled the rent immediately, but then issued a claim for trespass and damage to reputation.

Judgment of Tindal, CJ (summing up for the jury): "... the defendant comes and says, "I am come to seize these goods"; and you will have to say whether what took place on that day satisfies your minds that a distress for rent was taken at that time. There is no doubt that there was rent due... The difficulty I feel in the case is upon what the policeman has said. Circumstances may arise which may require the presence of a peace-officer. But it must be

---

[35] *Morris v Beardmore* [1980] 71 Cr App 256.

shown, to justify such a proceeding, that it was necessary, either from the apprehension of violence, the threat of resistance, or some similar circumstance. It does not appear that either of the men remained in possession. If the policeman was introduced other than as an assistant in taking the distress, you must find your verdict for the plaintiff, and give him such damages as you think he is entitled to. It appears that people assembled on the outside, and asked what was going on. The landlord cannot justify under this form of pleading for anything but a distress. You may, therefore, consider whether he intended what he did as a distress, by seeing whether he confined himself to it. Now, it seems, that he did more, for he put up a bill in the window. I think that, being in to make the distress, he might put up the bill without creating a new trespass. If you are not perfectly satisfied that the intention was to make a distress, and that the policeman was introduced for the purpose of the distress, and was necessary for that purpose, you must find your verdict for the plaintiff." The jury awarded the plaintiff damages (of 1/-).

Commentary

All too often, it seems, police officers are called to premises *not* because a breach of the peace is genuinely feared by a bailiff but for psychological reasons. The constable's presence can further intimidate a recalcitrant debtor who is legitimately refusing entry and can thereby facilitate a levy. This is what happened in *Skidmore* - the landlord summoned the officer to further scare the boy. The judge though was very clear: to justify a bailiff in calling a police officer, it must be shown that his presence was made necessary either by threats of resistance or by the fear of violence. Conversely, for the occupier of premises, if a person enters and makes a noise or disturbs the peace it is lawful for the occupier to eject him if he refuses to leave or the police may be called.[36]

A number of other cases have elaborated on the nature of breaches of the peace and how the police should respond. If a breach of the peace occurs within an officer's sight he is bound to intervene immediately.[37] What constitutes a breach can include refusing to leave a property and resisting expulsion when causing a disturbance.[38] Also wrongful would be an attempt at forcible entry to premises, despite resistance.[39] However, mere trespass is *not* a breach of the peace, so that simply refusing to leave a property and

---

[36] *Green v Bartram* (1830) 4C&P 308; *Shaw v Chairitie* (1850) 3 C&K 21.
[37] *Anon* (1593) Poph 12.
[38] *Howell v Jackson* (1834) 6 C&P 723.
[39] *Ingle v Bell* (1836) 1 M&W 516.

creating a disturbance does not justify an arrest[40] - nor does ringing on a door bell and making a noise in order to gain entry.[41]

Vaughan v McKenzie [1969] 1 QB 557

Facts The case concerns an assault upon a county court bailiff. The judgment debtor was prosecuted by the victim bailiff in the magistrates' court for assault upon a county court officer in the execution of his duty (see now section 14 of the County Courts Act 1984). The case was dismissed by the magistrate and was appealed to the High Court.

Judgment of Lord Parker CJ: "This is an appeal by way of case stated from a decision of the stipendiary magistrate for the City of Leeds, dismissing an information preferred by the appellant against the respondent for that she, on May 22nd, 1967, did assault the appellant, an officer of the Leeds county court, while in the execution of his duty as such officer, contrary to section 30 of the County Courts Act, 1959.

The short facts giving rise to this case, and a case which raises an important principle, are these: on May 5th last year a warrant of execution against the goods of the respondent was issued by the Leeds county court, which was for some £91 in respect of costs. The appellant, who is a bailiff of the Leeds county court, went with another bailiff on May 22nd to the house where the respondent lived. When they got there, the house was closed, the respondent being away. The bailiffs waited, and later the respondent returned with her child. Outside the front door, the appellant and the other bailiff told the respondent that they were bailiffs, and had come to levy execution on her goods. It is true that no warrant was produced to her, but it is quite clear that she knew full well who they were, and what they had come about, because she immediately told them that she had written to the county court and the Lord Chancellor regarding these costs, and she said she would not admit them to the house.

What happened then was that she and the child entered the house and immediately attempted to shut the door, but the other bailiff, Richmond, got his foot in the door and pushed against the door, the respondent on her side pushing to keep him out. The appellant came to the assistance of Richmond, and both of them forced the door open with the object of gaining entry to the house, whereupon the respondent, finding a milk bottle handy, picked it up and struck the appellant on the head with the bottle of milk, whereby he

---

[40] *Green v Bartram* (1830) 4 C&P 308; *Jordan v Gibbon* (1863) 8 LT 391.
[41] *R v Bright* (1830) 4 C&P 387; *Grant v Moser* (1843) 5 M&G 123.

sustained a one-inch long cut requiring three stitches. Those are the short facts of this case.

The magistrate stated his opinion in this form:

> "That the appellant and Richmond were not justified in law for the purpose of gaining entry to execute a civil warrant, in attempting to push open the door which the respondent was endeavouring to close against them and that they were accordingly trespassers; (b) that, in any event, the appellant and Richmond, not having shown or read the warrant to the respondent, were not acting in the execution of their duty."

So far as that latter reason is concerned, I am quite satisfied that the magistrate was wrong. This was a case where she plainly knew that they were bailiffs, and plainly knew the object with which they had come, and the fact that the warrant was not produced was not, in the circumstances, fatal to these proceedings.

The real question here is whether the bailiffs were justified in attempting to push open the door by force against the will of the respondent. I confess that in the course of the argument my own feeling was that the magistrate had come to a right conclusion. It is to be observed that in *Southam v Smout* concerning the mode of entry which is lawful,[42] a passage occurs in the judgment of Lord Denning MR where, after referring to *Nash v. Lucas*,[43] he said:

> "Sir Alexander Cockburn CJ said that the later authorities say you may open a door which is only fastened by a latch He thought that was going a very long way, further than the American courts had done, but the authorities were limited to the case where the door is shut but can be opened without violence."

I confess I find it difficult to see what the real difference was here between a door which is momentarily opened but sought to be closed and can only be fully opened by violence, and a door which is shut and which can only be opened by violence.

---

[42] [1964] 1 QB 308.
[43] See earlier.

However, in the course of the proceedings Winn LJ, with his usual industry, found the case of *Broughton v Wilkerson.*[44] The facts of that case were almost identical with the present; there the bailiff went to the respondent's house, he knocked at the outer front door, which was locked; the respondent came to the door, opened it and held it until they had an altercation; the appellant then took hold of the door, put his foot between it and the door post and shoved his shoulder against it to obtain entry; he did not produce the warrant or tell the respondent what his business was, but the respondent knew him well and said: "You, you shan't come in" and shoved him out. Sir Alexander Cockburn CJ said:

> "The justices seem to give a wrong reason for their decision, but the decision was right. The officer had no right to force his way into the respondent's house, which was the respondent's castle. Whether the officer was known or not this was illegal, and therefore he was not in the execution of his duty at all when he was assaulted. He seems to have provoked the assault. I think as he was clearly not in the execution of his duty our judgment must be for the respondent."

Lush J said:

> "Every man's house is his castle. That has been settled long ago, and a bailiff cannot force his way inside to lay execution for a debt. It is impossible to read this case and say that the bailiff was in execution of his duty."

Further industry, this time on the part of Mr. Bridge, has found that that case has been approved in *Rossiter v Conway.*[45] That case differed in certain immaterial respects; it was a constable executing a warrant of distress; that does not affect the matter, and instead of a foot between the door and the door post it was an arm. The court in that case held that the constable was not acting in the execution of his duty, and relied upon and approved the earlier case of *Broughton v Wilkerson.* Both those cases are binding upon this court, and I have no doubt in those circumstances that this appeal must be dismissed.

Winn LJ: "I agree. It seems to me that the essential criterion in any such situation is whether the householder has left a means of entrance available for me without the employment of any degree of force. As Lord Parker CJ

---

[44] (1880) 44 JP 781- this case was also cited in argument in *Lewis v Owen* (1893) *The Times* November 6th p.3b (QBD): it was argued that it was not contempt to assault a county court bailiff who tried to climb over a locked gate after entry had been refused.

[45] (1893) 53 JP 350.

has said, this is a case where a foot was interposed between the door post and the door itself. In the other two cases arms were thrust in, but it is perfectly clear that whilst in those cases some force was used, in neither of them was entrance being sought *vi et armis*."[46]

Commentary

The appeal court conducted a review of bailiffs' rights of entry and debtors' rights of resistance. Bailiff Vaughan's barrister argued that a bailiff executing civil process had a legal right of entry conferred by law and wholly independent of the debtor's consent. As soon as his foot was placed in the door, he had made a legal entry and any attempt to evict him was unlawful. However, on considering *Semayne* and the two Victorian cases uncovered by the Court, the unanimous conclusion was that Ms McKenzie was perfectly entitled to resist entry being made against her will and that, if force was used, she could oppose it with reasonable force. The case is quite conclusive on the matter, but it still appears to be a widespread belief within the enforcement sector that obstructing a door with a foot is not somehow 'forcible entry' in the same way that kicking it open or picking the lock might be. This is plainly mistaken. A bailiff placing a foot in a door is a trespasser- and any levy attempted after this will be invalidated whilst the entry to the premises may be resisted.

The difficult issue arising from this case is the limit to be placed upon 'reasonable' force. What is acceptable will depend upon what amount of force is used by the person trying to gain entry. Whilst the debtor or occupier cannot initiate the use of violence, the degree of resistance may be matched to the force being used to try to get in.[47] Excessive force must be avoided.[48] If the entry is peaceable, albeit unpermitted, a request to leave should always be made first.[49] It seems that the debtor, another occupier of the premises or an employee may all take these steps.[50]

We may lastly note the decision as to the warrant. Ms McKenzie had argued that, by failing to produce it, the bailiffs had ceased to be execution of their duty. The court did not agree- they felt that she knew perfectly well who they were and why they were there from their words alone; nor did she ever demand to see the warrant. This position is confirmed by other cases (see *Andrews* in chapter 7)

[46] " *Vi et armis*" means "with force and arms" and was a key element in any claim of trespass.
[47] *Weaver v Bush* (1795) 8TR 78; *Simpson v Morris* (1813) 4 Taunt 821; *Polkinhorne v Wright* (1845) 8 QB 197.
[48] *Gregory v Hall* (1799) 8 TR 299; *Oakes v Wood* (1837) 2 M&W 791.
[49] *Tullay v Reed* (1823) 1 C&P 6.
[50] *Hall v Davis* (1825) 2 C&P 33.

Lesley Bibby v The Chief Constable of Essex Police

(2000), Court of Appeal, April 2000

Facts This case concerned the correct use of the police's power to intervene in levies of distress in order to prevent a breach of the peace. A shop owner owed business rates. The bailiff wished to remove goods previously levied and impounded subject to walking possession. He was opposed by a group of four people who threatened to call for help. Tempers quickly became short and the police were called. The police concluded that the group would come to blows, that the bailiff was being intimidating and that he was being unreasonable by refusing to leave, even under threat of arrest. Accordingly Mr Bibby was arrested for breach of the peace and was removed from the premises.

Judgment of Schiemann LJ: "This appeal concerns the conflict between the rights and duties of certificated bailiffs and policemen in circumstances where the bailiff is confronting a judgment debtor who does not wish to part with his assets and is uncooperative with the bailiff. What happened was that policemen were called by both the bailiff and the debtor to the debtor's shop and went to a room where the bailiff and the debtor were; temperatures and tempers in that room were raised, the policemen thought there would be a breach of the peace, told the bailiff to go, and, when he refused, arrested him and led him away to the police station in handcuffs. They released him about an hour later without charge, taking the view that at that time there was no longer any risk of a breach of the peace. The bailiff sued the police for assault and wrongful imprisonment...

It was conceded in the court below that PC O'Hare honestly believed that a breach of the peace was likely. The assistant recorder proceeded on the following legal basis. It was for the defendant to prove that PC O'Hare's honest belief was based on reasonable grounds. The test was whether a reasonable man, assumed to know the law and possessed of the information which was in fact possessed by PC O'Hare, would have believed on reasonable grounds what PC O'Hare in fact believed. He asked himself whether the decision to arrest the bailiff rather than the debtor was unreasonable on *Wednesbury* grounds [51] and in particular whether the PC had taken into consideration matters irrelevant to the exercise of his discretion...

The bailiff contended before the assistant recorder that he was entitled to remove the goods scheduled to the walking possession agreement, that his refusal to leave without either money or goods was reasonable and that in

[51] From *Associated Picture Houses v Wednesbury Corporation* [1947] - is a public body's decision so outrageous that no sensible person could have arrived at it?

those circumstances the arrest for failure to leave was unlawful and that in any event his handcuffing was unreasonable.

The assistant recorder's conclusion from the facts which he found was that they entitled the PC to arrest the bailiff and take him off to the police station in handcuffs. He stated:

> "Mr Bibby ... had placed himself in a position where his arrest was inevitable. I do not suggest that he had committed any criminal offence but his arrest, for the reasons given, was inevitable. He can not now complain of the use by the police of handcuffs to restrain him. If they need justification for it, it is amply contained within s.3 of the Criminal Law Act."

That section provides:

> "A person may use such force as is reasonable in the circumstances in the prevention of crime ..."

The courts have frequently had to consider what constitutes a breach of the peace. This court stated in *R v Howell (Errol)*:[52]

> "... there is a breach of the peace whenever harm is actually done or is likely to be done to a person or in his presence to his property or a person is in fear of being so harmed through an assault, an affray, a riot, unlawful assembly or other disturbance. It is for this breach of the peace when done in his presence that a constable, or anyone else, may arrest an offender without warrant."

It had stated on the previous page:

> "We entertain no doubt that a constable has a power of arrest where there is reasonable apprehension of imminent danger of a breach of the peace; so for that matter has the ordinary citizen. We hold there is a power of arrest for breach of the peace where (1) a breach of the peace is committed in the presence of the person making the arrest, or (2) the arrestor reasonably believes that such a breach of the peace will be committed in the immediate future by the person arrested although he has not yet committed any breach, or (3) where a breach has been committed and it is reasonably believed that a renewal of it is threatened."

The present case, if it falls into any of these categories, falls into the second. On the facts of the present case, the assistant recorder did not find, and there was no material upon which he could have found, that the bailiff had any intention of assaulting the debtor, absent a prior threatened assault by the

---

[52] [1982] 1 QB 427.

debtor. So far as the debtor is concerned, the assistant recorder found that the debtor had forcefully told the bailiff to leave and stated that he and his wife would call friends to prevent the removal of the goods.

In substance the assistant recorder found that PC O'Hare reasonably considered that the bailiff was acting lawfully but provocatively and that, as a result of that provocation a breach of the peace was likely to result; that any attempt on the part of the bailiff to remove the goods scheduled to the walking possession agreement would be resisted by the debtor and that violence by one on the other or each on the other would most probably result; that in those circumstances it was reasonable of the PC to ask the bailiff to go and unreasonable of the bailiff to insist on staying until he had either the money or the goods.

Beldam LJ, with whom the other members of the court agreed, pointed out in *Foulkes v Chief Constable of Merseyside Police*, a case decided in this court, that:[53]

> "... there are many of cases in the books in which conduct not obviously illegal has nevertheless been held to be sufficient to justify an arrest if persisted in or provocatively done."

But Beldam LJ went on to say:

> "... the common law power of a police constable to arrest where no actual breach of the peace has taken place but where he apprehends that such a breach may be caused by apparently lawful conduct is exceptional. Many of the instances in which such a power has been upheld in the past are, as a result of the enactment of the Public Order Act 1986 , unlikely to give rise to difficulty since for offences under that Act, and particularly under ss. 4 and 5, statutory powers of arrest without warrant are conferred on a constable ... although I am prepared to accept that a constable may exceptionally have power to arrest a person whose behaviour is lawful but provocative, it is a power which ought to be exercised by him only in the clearest of circumstances and when he is satisfied on reasonable grounds that a breach of the peace is imminent ... there must ... be a sufficiently real and present threat to the peace to justify the extreme step of depriving of his liberty a citizen who is not at that time acting unlawfully."

[53] [1998] 3 All ER 705 - there must be very good reasons for arresting a person on the grounds that a breach of the peace might take place. Only a serious and imminent threat will justify an arrest.

Simon Brown LJ in *Nicol & Selvanayagam v DPP*, a case decided in the Divisional Court , addressed the problem in these terms:[54]

> "Before the court can properly find that the natural consequence of lawful conduct by a defendant would, if persisted in, be to provoke another to violence, it should ... be satisfied that in all the circumstances it is the defendant who is acting unreasonably rather than the other person ... some clear interference at least with the rights ... of others is bound to characterise any conduct of which it can properly be said that it would naturally provoke violence in others. Putting it another way, the court would surely not find a s.115 [of the Magistrates' Courts Act 1980] complaint proved if any violence likely to have been provoked on the part of others would be not merely unlawful but wholly unreasonable- as, of course, it would be if the defendant's conduct was not merely lawful but such as in no material way interfered with the other's rights."

Sedley LJ in *Redmond-Bate v DPP*, another Divisional Court case, pointed out that:[55]

> "The ... critical question for the constable, and in turn for the Court, is where the threat is coming from, because it is there that the preventative action must be directed ... It is only if otherwise lawful conduct gives rise to a reasonable apprehension that it will, by interfering with the rights or liberties of others, provoke violence which, though unlawful, would not be entirely unreasonable that a constable is empowered to take steps to prevent it ... Mr Kealy for the prosecutor submitted that if there are two alternative sources of trouble, a constable can properly take steps against either. This is right, but only if both are threatening violence or behaving in a manner that might provoke violence."

Beldam LJ in the passage which I have cited stated that the common law power to arrest for apprehended breach of the peace caused by apparently lawful conduct is exceptional. Simon Brown LJ and Sedley LJ, in the passages which I have cited seek to make more precise the nature of that exception. They considered that a person who is engaging in or threatening to engage in lawful actions which are likely to result in a breach of the peace can only be arrested on the basis that a repetition of those lawful actions is likely to result in a breach of the peace if his lawful actions, actual or threatened are wholly unreasonable and in some way interfere with the other person's rights. I express my general agreement with the views set out in those passages.

---

[54] (1996) 160 JP 155.
[55] *The Times* July 28th 1999.

Counsel for the defendant did not suggest that those passages conflicted with authority but submitted that police officers are under a duty to prevent breaches of the peace and that there is a greater public interest in preventing violence than in the bailiff obtaining the goods and that if there is a conflict between these two desiderata then the quest for peace must prevail.

Counsel for the claimant submitted the case law justified the following. In order to exercise the now exceptional common law power of arrest certain conditions must be met in relation to the person who is to be arrested and his conduct:

1. There must be the clearest of circumstances and a sufficiently real and present threat to the peace to justify the extreme step of depriving of his liberty a citizen who is not at the time acting unlawfully - *Foulkes*;
2. The threat must be coming from the person who is to be arrested- *Redmond-Bate*;
3. The conduct must clearly interfere with the rights of others - *Redmond-Bate*;
4. The natural consequence of the conduct must be violence from a third party- *Redmond-Bate;*
5. The violence in 4 must not be wholly unreasonable- *Redmond-Bate*; and,
6. The conduct of the person to be arrested must be unreasonable - *Nicol.*

I consider that this accurately states the law. Of course I accept that it is desirable that violence be prevented. It is also desirable that citizens who are neither doing nor threatening any wrong are not deprived of their liberty. The problem in this type of case is the conflict between these two desiderata. The police are given various special powers under various acts to arrest without a warrant but none of these are relied on here. Mr Johnston relies on common law powers of arrest for apprehended breach of the peace which are possessed not merely by police officers but also by every other citizen.

If counsel for the defendant's submission were right it would make the police's own job difficult. Take this situation. A policeman is about to arrest a man who threatens violence to the policeman if the policeman touches him. A passer-by tells the policeman to go away because otherwise there will be a breach of the peace. Is the policeman bound to obey at the risk of himself being arrested by the passer-by (or indeed the man threatening violence) for provoking a breach of the peace? That can not be right. It would be a charter for anyone who threatens violence.

It has not been suggested that the bailiff was not entitled to take the goods away in the absence of payment. He was acting lawfully. He was not threatening to commit any crime. He was not threatening to interfere with any right which the debtor had in the scheduled goods. Nor in my judgment was he acting unreasonably in explaining to the debtor that the latter must either produce what he owed or let the bailiff remove the goods. It was the debtor who was not acting reasonably when he told the bailiff to leave and threatened to call friends to prevent the removal of the goods. There may be room for the assertion that the bailiff was not tactful and that his firmness and size intimidated those in that room. It may well be that the bailiff was at the end of his tether and did not want to have a discussion as to how it came about that he wished to exercise his rights in relation to the goods. It may be, though there seems no reason to believe it, that if the bailiff had engaged in reasoned argument with the debtor the latter would have voluntarily handed over the money or the scheduled goods. It may well be that if the bailiff had left and come back on some future occasion, either in half an hour or the next day, the debtor would have been persuaded by the police to see the error of his ways. But even if all that be so it does not justify the bailiff's arrest. For the debtor to react by violence to such behaviour as the bailiff was likely to engage in would have been unreasonable.

I have sympathy for the constable faced with an explosive situation which required fast judgments. No one criticises him for coming to the conclusion that a breach of the peace was imminent. I am prepared to accept that he came to that conclusion on reasonable grounds. But as it seems to me PC O'Hare made the same mistake as the constable in Redmond-Bate. He failed to consider where the threat was coming from. True it is that had the bailiff not been seeking to exercise his rights there would have been no threat to the peace. But in circumstances such as these the threat, in so far as there was one, of violence should have been perceived as coming from the debtor rather than the bailiff. I am prepared to proceed on the basis that the debtor was not verbally threatening violence as such. He was however threatening to prevent the bailiff from doing what he could lawfully do and which did not interfere with any of the debtor's rights. Implicit in that was a threat to use violence if the bailiff went ahead.

In my judgment the assistant recorder fell into error in bringing the *Wednesbury* case into his consideration. That case is concerned with the limits of discretions in administrative law. The court is not in the present case reviewing a discretion. It is deciding whether a constable was justified in arresting a citizen. The mere fact, if it be a fact, that the constable reasonably thought that a breach of the peace was likely did not in my judgment justify the arrest of the bailiff.

Various other grounds were relied on by Mr Johnson in support of the submission that the arrest was unlawful and the detention was too long. In the circumstances it is not necessary to consider them and I do not do so. I only add that, as it seems to me, the use of handcuffs in the circumstances was not reasonable.

I would allow this appeal...

Pill LJ: Mr Leslie Edward Bibby is a certificated bailiff. He questions the lawfulness of his arrest by police officers on January 13th 1995 at business premises occupied by Mr and Mrs E Brannan. He was attempting to enforce a liability order made by the Chelmsford Magistrates under reg.12 of the Non-Domestic Rating (Collection and Enforcement) (Local Lists) Regulations 1989. Regulation 14 empowers the authority which applied for the order, in this case Chelmsford Borough Council, to levy the appropriate amount by distress and sale of the goods of the debtor against whom the order was made, in this case Mr and Mrs Brannan. The bailiff was attempting to levy distress on behalf of the authority.

In his judgment, Schiemann LJ has set out the sequence of events. The bailiff told the debtors that he required cash if they were to avoid the removal of their goods and they quite forcefully told him to leave saying they would call friends to prevent the removal of goods as they had done before. Both parties called the police. The police officer has sought to justify the arrest on the ground that a breach of the peace was imminent. The bailiff had refused his request to leave the premises. It was not suggested that the bailiff had been violent towards anyone else at the premises or had threatened violence. The bailiff had himself said in evidence, however, that there was a serious risk of imminent violence. Constable O'Hare described the bailiff's conduct in this way:

> "He just didn't appear to me to be a person who would be reasonable. I actually asked Mr Bibby at some stage to calm down, and he wouldn't. He remained loud and he seemed to be channelled in one avenue, so to speak, and he didn't seem to be prepared to be flexible."

The constable said that he found Mr Bibby to be "quite threatening just by his mere physical presence". Mr Bibby said that he wanted to stand his ground and stay where he was entitled to be. That was his job. He said that Mr Brannan threatened violence to him. There was no finding of fact that the bailiff was likely to strike anyone present. Such a finding would not have been tenable on the evidence. Indeed, the suggestion was not even put to the bailiff when he gave evidence.

This type of situation was considered by this court in *Foulkes v Chief Constable of Merseyside Police*. A man was locked out of the matrimonial home which he owned jointly with his wife, following a family dispute. The police told him, as was the fact, that his wife and children did not want him to re-enter the house and the police suggested that he leave the vicinity of the property until tempers had abated. He was arrested when he refused to leave and insisted that he wished to enter the house. It was held that the arrest was not justified.

Beldam LJ stated that "... the common law power of a police constable to arrest where no actual breach of the peace has taken place but where he apprehends that such a breach may be caused by apparently lawful conduct is exceptional ... In the circumstances of this case, although I am prepared to accept that a constable may exceptionally have power to arrest a person whose behaviour is lawful but provocative, it is a power which ought to be exercised by him only in the clearest of circumstances and when he is satisfied on reasonable grounds that a breach of the peace is imminent."

Beldam LJ continued:

> "In the present case PC McNamara acted with the best of intentions. He had tried persuasion but the plaintiff refused to be persuaded or to accept the sensible guidance he had been given but in my judgment that was not a sufficient basis to conclude that a breach of the peace was about to occur or was imminent. There must, I consider, be a sufficiently real and present threat to the peace to justify the extreme step of depriving of his liberty a citizen who is not at the time acting unlawfully."

In *Redmond-Bate v Director of Public Prosecutions* Sedley LJ, in the Divisional Court, contemplated a possible situation in which the conduct of a group of persons was "so provocative that someone in the crowd, without behaving wholly unreasonably, might be moved to violence [so that the officer] was entitled to ask them [the group] to stop and to arrest them if they would not."

The bailiff in this case was acting lawfully. Indeed, he was attempting to enforce an order of the court. The task of a bailiff is often a difficult one, as the Assistant Recorder rightly acknowledged. In this case the bailiff's behaviour towards others present was thought by the police officer to be unreasonable and inflexible. It was not found, and could not on the evidence properly have been found, that the bailiff was likely to initiate violence by striking anyone. Insofar as there was a fear of violence, the inference must be that any violence would have come from another source.

Nothing the bailiff did, in attempting lawfully to levy distress, could have begun to justify a resort to violence by another person present. In those circumstances, the police officers were not justified in arresting the bailiff on the ground that he declined to accede to their request that he should leave the building he had lawfully entered. I do not of course exclude the possibility that a bailiff, or someone in a similar position, might behave so outrageously, short of violence, that he was likely to provoke a not wholly unreasonable violent reaction from others, thereby justifying his arrest. The unreasonableness and inflexibility which the officers believed to exist in this case fell far short of conduct justifying arrest.

In agreeing with Schiemann LJ that the appeal should be allowed, I add that placing the bailiff in handcuffs and taking him in handcuffs through a public place and on the journey to the police station in a police car was in my view wholly unjustified. Even if the arrest had been justified, which it was not, the situation did not require that further indignity."

Commentary

Police officers are often called to attend levies of distress. The proper circumstances of their attendance were discussed in *Skidmore* earlier. In this case there seems little doubt that the police were summoned appropriately. How they dealt with the situation they found was the source of the dispute. The court decided that a lawful levy by a bailiff cannot justify a breach of the peace by another person because the bailiff is not acting in an unreasonable manner and is not interfering with the other person's rights. In itself, exercising one's rights and duties as a bailiff is not a breach of the peace. A bailiff who is lawfully enforcing a lawful liability is entitled to remain on premises and to remove goods. Accordingly the arrest of Mr Bibby could not be justified and the handcuffing especially could not be excused.

In general, violent opposition to a lawful levy will be unreasonable. However, the matter does depend on where the threat of violence is coming from. In some circumstances violence in response to a purported levy may not be unreasonable if it is the bailiff who is behaving unreasonably.

Conclusion

Bailiffs' rights of entry can appear extensive at first glance, but consideration of the long-evolved case law will demonstrate these rights to be considerably more provisional and transitory than might have been supposed. The rights to refuse and to resist are well established, if not always as well known as they should be. Lastly, it seems likely that the concept of the licence still has scope for significant further development in the context of bailiffs' law.

Chapter 3

LEVYING ON GOODS

Introduction

The correct conduct of the levy is central to the process of distress and execution. Regrettably, the accumulated case law on the subject is complex and often difficult to apply to modern experiences. In large measure, this is a result of the fact that developments in bailiff practice and in social circumstances have not been matched by a modernisation of the law. The two stage process of seizure and impounding is, by and large, unchanged since the sixteenth century. Innovations in procedure made for the convenience of the bailiff, or debtor, or both, and in response to technological advances, sit uncomfortably with older principles. This will remain the case until a thorough reform of the law takes place.[1]

To understand the arguments, and to avoid the pitfalls, an in -depth understanding of the present law is essential. A complete comprehension of the levy process is a necessity for many reasons: for example, to determine whether the bailiff is entitled at all to remove and sell;[2] to decide whether interference by a debtor constitutes an offence;[3] or, to resolve whether the creditor is entitled to try other remedies.[4]

A ready apprehension of the process is inhibited by its evolved complexity. It is further complicated by the fact that there is no settled meaning for many of the basic terms: for example - 'to levy' and 'to execute' have been held to have an identical meaning, denoting seizure, but not necessarily sale, of

---

[1] For more discussion see *Law of Seizure of Goods* c.8; *Powers of Distress* c.3 Part 1 and A lawful trespass c.8.
[2] *Brintons v Wyre Forest DC* - see later.
[3] *Lavell v O'Leary* [1933] 2 KB 200; *Abingdon RDC v O'Gorman* - see chapter 7.
[4] *R v Burnley* JJ *ex. p. Ashworth* (1992) 32 RVR 27; *Re: A Debtor* (No.340 of 1992) [1994] 3 All ER 269.

goods.[5] Similarly interchangeable are 'distraining' and 'levying' and 'levied' and 'impounded' according to Holt CJ in *Alton v James* (1708).[6]

M.21 Hen.VII fo.39b pl.55

Facts A tenant brought replevin against his landlord for taking his shocks of grain. The defendant lord avowed that he took the tenant's shocks of grain in distraint for rent in arrears. The plaintiff tenant replied that defendant had made a pound on the same land held by tenant.

Judgment that the lord cannot distrain shocks of grain for rent (in) arrears from his tenant, because the tenant cannot have replevin for this, nor return of the shocks of grain, because he is not certain to have cognisance of this, but for damage feasant on his land one can distrain shocks of grain well enough.

All the Justices agreed that if one distrains his tenant in fee simple - or his tenant for life or for years - for rent in arrears, he cannot make a pound on the same land for this distraint, but if he distrains for damage feasant on his own land, he can make a pound on the same land well enough. This distinction was admitted by the Justices. Serjeant Keble argued: "When the lessor distrains his tenant at will for rent, and then makes a pound on the same land, this making of the pound is a discharge of the lease, and so he can make a pound well enough on the same land."

Commentary

This *Year Book* case is very important, but is a slight puzzle for us. It is dated 1505, but Serjeant Keble (one of the barristers in court) is mentioned and he died in 1500. At the same time an apparently identical case is reported as H.11 Hen.VII fo.14 pl.8 - a report of 1496 which seems probably to be a more authentic date for the case.

This judgment is concerned with two separate matters. The main issue (at the time) was whether grain or other loose produce could be distrained. This was not permitted at common law because some of the goods might be lost in transit and some might become mixed with other hay or straw and become unrecognisable so that the owner could not recover it through payment or replevin (this is the meaning of "he is not certain to have cognisance").[7]

The second issue, which is still of current concern, is the question of *where* impounding might take place. As will be seen, unless a levy of distress

[5] *Cheston v Gibbs* (1843) 12 M&W 111.
[6] (1708) 11 MR 144.
[7] See detailed discussion in *Bailiffs' law*, vol.1, *A lawful trespass*, c.5, pp.140 -142.

damage feasant was involved, an immediate removal to a pound had to take place. This was why there was such concern about the landlord having seized stooks of corn. Impounding on the land in instances of distress damage feasant was presumably lawful as it was the distrainor's own land and no trespass on another's property would be involved. In other cases, impounding away from the site of the levy had to occur. The suggestion of Serjeant Keble which closes the report indicates the importance of the issue. He argued that, if a landlord chose to impound on the tenant's land, it would count as a termination of the lease.

This was the situation for distrainors in the late fifteenth/ early sixteenth century. It continued to be good law after that time. In *Dod v Monger* (1704) Holt CJ confirmed that the common law required the landlord to remove goods within a convenient time to a pound (a matter of days at most it would seem).[8] Likewise in *Griffin v Scott* (1726) the court affirmed that the common law did not permit impounding on the premises and that goods had to be removed to a pound as soon as reasonably possible.[9] Leaving goods eight days on the premises after seizure as in this case was held to be unreasonable. As seen in chapter 1, section 10 of the Distress for Rent Act 1737 confirmed the common law rule but overrode it for landlords levying distress for rent.

In other cases, the law was not altered and the common law principle continued to apply into the nineteenth century. See, for example, the case of *Peppercorn v Hofman* (1842).[10] This concerned a levy of distraint for rates. The plaintiff argued that "the defendant had no right to put a man in possession of goods on the premises, as it was not like a distress for rent, but a species of execution." Remaining five days on the premises was presented as an unlawful act and, on appeal, a new trial was ordered. In respect of executions, we should also note the comments of Hilbery J in *Watson v Murray & Co* [1955]. He observed that "At common law the sheriff's duty is to remove the goods to some place where they can be kept safely until they are sold..." This conclusion is confirmed by *Reed v Harrison* (1778). The judges were concerned with the practice of the Court of Record in Newcastle under which a *fi fa* was executed by leaving a man in possession for six months. The custom of this court was clearly unfamiliar to the bench in Westminster and they considered it to be a trespass, remarking that whilst

[8] 6 MR 215; see too *Nevill v Packman* (1697) 1 Ld Raym 121.
[9] 2 Ld Raym 1424.
[10] 9 M&W 618; see too comments made in *Piggott v Birtles* (1836) 1 M&W 441 and in *Scott v Denton* (1906) 121 LT 95 - a fee for a man in possession was unlawful in part because it was not possible to impound on the premises in distress for rates.

the common law rules on impounding had been altered for distress for rent, they had *not* for executions.[11]

The conclusion seems to be clear: in respect of levies of execution and statutory forms of distraint, the common law rule remained in force for another four centuries after the *Year Book* cases and was only altered by statutory intervention for rent. We must expect the rule still to be effective at present unless again Parliament has changed the law for a particular debt.

Lumsden v Burnett [1898] 2 QB 177

This case was known at the time as the "walking possession case." It is primarily concerned with the charges that may lawfully be made for a man in possession, but there is also a useful analysis of the nature of impounding by means of a walking possession agreement. The case report and analysis are in chapter 6.

Jones v Biernstein [1900] 1 QB 100

Facts The plaintiff landlord distrained on premises for rent in arrears. This took place on a Wednesday, and a man was left in possession. On the Saturday night this man left the premises, and did not return until Monday. During his absence the defendant, who was the true owner of some of the goods, entered the house and seized and removed his possessions. The plaintiff brought an action for damages for pound breach in the county court. The judge found that the goods had been impounded within the meaning of s.10 of the Distress for Rent Act 1737 (see chapter 1); that the man in possession had no reasonable necessity for his absence, and that he had therefore abandoned possession; but that as he had intended to return he had not abandoned the distress, and might be considered as remaining in constructive possession. He held, however, that real possession was necessary, and entered judgment for the defendant. The landlord appealed.

Judgment of Lawrance J: "The question raised in this case which we are called upon to decide is whether, as against the true owner of goods taken in distress, real possession is necessary. The county court judge finds that everything required by the statute of George II (i.e. the Distress for Rent Act 1737) was done to make a good distress, but that the man who was left in possession abandoned possession though he did not abandon the distress, and he decides that real possession is necessary. I think that the county court judge came to a wrong conclusion. I cannot see that the true owner of the goods stands in any different position from the tenant on whose premises the goods were seized. I

---

[11] [1955] 1 All ER 350 at p.359G; (1778) 2 W Bla 1218.

do not think it was necessary that notice of the distress should be given to the true owner of the goods, but as a matter of fact - there is no dispute about the facts - such notice was given. The only question we have to decide is whether it was necessary that the man should remain in real possession of the goods after they had been seized and impounded. I do not think so. After the goods had been seized and impounded it seems to me, on the authority of *Bannister v. Hyde*,[12] to which my brother Channell has called my attention, that it is not necessary that any one should remain on the premises on behalf of the landlord at all. As to that there seems to be plenty of authority. It is not necessary for us now to decide what acts will amount to an impounding, since the county court judge finds as a fact that these goods were impounded. I have therefore no hesitation in saying that the county court judge was wrong in holding that, where goods had been impounded on the premises in accordance with the statute of George II, physical or real possession on the part of the landlord was necessary to sustain an action for pound breach. There must, therefore, be judgment for the plaintiff.

Channell J: I am of the same opinion. The action is brought for pound breach, and therefore, in order to succeed, the plaintiff must show that the goods, at the time that they were taken away by the defendant, were in *custodia legis* (i.e. in legal custody). The question raised at the trial in the county court was whether it was necessary, in order that the goods should be kept in *custodia legis*, that the party interested - that is to say, the landlord - should retain actual possession of them. It appears to me to be quite clear from the authorities that when once the goods are in *custodia legis* the actual retention of possession by the party distraining on them is not necessary. If the distress is abandoned, of course the custody of the law ceases. The case of *Bannister v. Hyde* states clearly that where goods have been impounded and a man has been left in possession, his subsequent withdrawal is evidence, but evidence only, of an intention to abandon the distress.

When the goods have once been impounded, as the county court judge finds was the case here, there is, I think, no difficulty. The question, however, of what amounts to an impounding is a difficult one, and one which we are not called upon now to decide. Considering the length of time that has elapsed since the Act was passed, there are very few decisions upon it. Although there may be some cases where taking possession and not retaining possession without anything more is insufficient, I should think that in the general way the mere fact of taking possession of the goods is sufficient for the purposes of the statute. As has been pointed out, the seizing of goods is an act done once for all, and when notice of possession is given that may be

---

[12] (1860) 2 E&E 627.

sufficient to constitute an impounding within the statute of George II. But, as I have said, that question is not left to us, as the county court judge has found as a fact that these goods were impounded, and that there was no abandonment of the distress. In *Kemp v. Christmas* it is worthy of note that it was assumed that, notwithstanding that the man in possession had gone out of possession, an action for pound breach could be maintained. It was not discussed, it is true, but it was assumed.[13] I agree, therefore, that judgment must be entered for the plaintiff."

Commentary

This case paved the way for the acceptance of walking possession and, as a result, has continued to be cited in such cases as *Lloyds & Scottish Finance, National Commercial Bank* and *Evans* (see later). Whether possession is retained and whether the levy has been abandoned depends on the circumstances of the case. In *Bannister v Hyde,* the case discussed by the judges, going out of possession briefly was decided not to be abandonment. Possession may be maintained by the bailiff by physically remaining on the premises (see *Lumsden v Burnett* in chapter 6*)* or it may be retained by agreement (see *Abingdon RDC v O'Gorman* in chapter 7).

Lloyds & Scottish Finance Ltd. v Modern Cars & Caravans (Kingston) Ltd [1966] 1 QB 764

Facts The sorry tale of this case is rather tortuous because so many parties were involved and the motor caravan in question changed hands so many times in quick succession. Briefly, Mercantile Credit got a judgment against Frederick Wood in the High Court. He did not pay and so a writ was issued and sheriff's officers levied on a motor van. That levy will be described in detail later. After the levy by the sheriff, Wood sold the van to the defendants, Modern Cars and Caravans. They removed it and, despite being told about the judgment and writ by the sheriff, they sold the van on to the plaintiffs, Lloyds & Scottish, who in turn sold it on HP to a Mr Worsfold. The sheriffs recovered the van from Worsfold whose reaction was to refuse to pay Lloyds & Scottish. They in turn sued Modern Cars for selling them goods they were not entitled to sell because of the pre -existing sheriff's levy. Modern Cars tried to defend the claim on the basis that there was either no effective levy or that the seizure had been abandoned. The analysis of taking possession and abandonment which followed is the part of the judgment of interest to us.

The details of the levy are as follows. The sheriff called at the caravan site where Wood lived in the van with his family on April 14th 1961. The sheriff

[13] 79 LT 233.

could not remove the van, nor try to remain in close possession of it along with the family of four, so he tried to get Wood to sign a walking possession agreement. Wood refused to do so, in large part because his wife was claiming ownership of the van. She would not agree to signing walking possession either, so the sheriff had little option but to depart, leaving the following documents with the family:

- Details of his employer's address;
- A note of the judgment details; and,
- Details of the judgment creditor's solicitors as Wood said he wanted to arrange payments on the judgment with them.

Mrs Wood had signed a formal claim to the van and on May 4th interpleader proceedings were begun. The bailiff revisited the caravan site on April 18th, 24th and 27th and on May 4th, 5th and 8th. He saw the van was still there and spoke to the Woods about their negotiations with the judgment creditor's solicitors. On May 10th, 12th and 15th he visited but found no-one at home. On May 19th he visited and found that the van had gone (Modern Cars took it the day before).

Judgment of Edmund Davies J: "... I turn to the first issue - namely, did Allison (the sheriff's officer) ever seize the caravan in execution before the sale by Wood? Whether seizure has occurred is a question of fact, turning upon the circumstances of each particular case, but certain guiding principles have been evolved over the years, and these are conveniently summarised in *Halsbury's Laws of England* in this way:

> "For an act of the sheriff or his bailiff to constitute a seizure of goods, it is not necessary that there should be any physical contact with the goods seized; nor does such contact necessarily amount to seizure. An entry upon the premises on which the goods are situate, together with an intimation of an intention to seize the goods, will amount to a valid seizure, even where the premises are extensive and the property seized widely scattered, but some act must be done sufficient to intimate to the judgment debtor or his servants that a seizure has been made, and it is not sufficient to enter upon the premises and demand the debt. Any act which, if not done with the authority of the court, would amount to a trespass to goods, will constitute a seizure of them when done under the writ."[14]

---

[14] 3rd ed. (1956), vol.16, p.55. These principles are derived from several judgments, including *Gladstone v Padwick* [1871] 6 Exch 203 in which a claim to have seized all goods, coupled with a warning not to remove anything and the presence of a man left in possession, was held to be

In the light of the authorities cited in support of this passage, I hold that on April 14th there was a seizure by the sheriff's officer of the caravan and its contents as against the judgment debtor. He did not merely demand payment of the debt (as was done in *Nash v Dickinson* but,[15] having entered and told the debtor that he had come to levy execution and read out his warrant, he handed him the written intimation already referred to. Furthermore, he proffered for signature a "walking possession" agreement, and he warned Wood and his wife that the caravan must not be moved. It is said that he should have done more: that he should have asked the Wood family to leave the caravan, and then locked it up or towed it away. Such a submission is unrealistic, for the Woods' refusal to sign the agreement indicated clearly that they would not have consented to the much more drastic course of leaving; and had the officer proceeded to move the caravan with the Wood family still inside, and after Mrs. Wood had laid claim to its ownership, he would have run a grave risk of involving the sheriff in liability to pay damages for wrongful execution, wrongful imprisonment and trespass against the person, as occurred in *Cave v Capel*.[16] It would have been highly inconvenient (though, it seems, physically possible) for him to have remained in the caravan with its four occupants, and he had no legal right to camp outside on the caravan site. Having done what he did, he went away. In my judgment, he departed after having effectively seized the caravan and its contents. It has been submitted that to do so after he had been refused consent to "walking possession" indicates that he never seized at all. But I interpret this incident in quite a different way, for in my view the fact that he requested such a consent supports the view that he was then levying execution.

Where, as here, a judgment debtor concurs in the adverse claim of a third party to the goods, it would in most cases be impossible to get the debtor to agree to walking possession. Then does it follow that, in every such case, there can be no seizure and no continuance thereof unless the sheriff's officer remains throughout on the premises? I think that question must be answered in the negative. In *Lumsden v Burnett* (see chapter 6), a case relevant mainly to the issue of abandonment, distress was claimed to have been levied on eight pairs of trousers which were never actually taken into possession by the

---

'actual seizure.' Bramwell B said "it is clear that it is not necessary for the sheriff to lay his hand on a single article. If the sheriff goes and makes known ... that he is come to seize and does, so far as words and intention can go, seize all the goods ... he has done enough." See also *Bird v Bass* (1843) 6 Scotts NR 925 - an entry with the intention of seizing and retaining possession, combined with notice of his purpose, amounted to valid seizure. Contrast *Balls v Pink* (1845) 4 LTOS 356/ 9 Jur 304 in which the court decided that a levy on goods on third party premises was ineffective when an officer merely declared the goods were seized, warned against removing them and then went away, failing to maintain absolute or constructive possession (see too *Blades v Arundale* (1813) 1 M&S 711).

[15] [1867] 2 CP 252.

[16] [1954] 1 QB 367.

sheriff's officer, he merely having obtained the signature of the debtor's 13 - year-old daughter to a "walking possession" agreement, which was manifestly worthless. The child had no authority to sign this document, but it was nevertheless held that the officer had effected execution and that it had not been abandoned, although the most that the officer did thereafter was to visit the premises occasionally to see whether the goods had been removed.

In *In re: Cooper* a sheriff's officer, intending to levy execution on two caterpillar tractors, went to the debtor's farm and there handed to an employee two forms stating that execution had been levied on the two tractors, although they were not removed, and he also handed him two forms inviting the debtor to agree to walking execution and then left. Danckwerts J held that this constituted a levying of execution.[17] But the citation of authorities could proceed indefinitely. I hold on the facts of this case that on April 14th, 1961, the sheriff's officer seized under the writ the caravan and its contents.

Then was that seizure abandoned before the defendants bought the caravan from Wood? This is again a question of fact, and it is agreed that the answer depends upon the intention of the sheriff's officer, which is a matter of inference to be deduced from the evidence as & whole. For the defence, it is submitted that if a sheriff's officer leaves the debtor's premises for any reason, he abandons possession, and, certainly as against a third party, the debtor's goods are thereafter free from any encumbrance. More particularly, it is submitted that, as far as outsiders are concerned, seizure cannot be continued even by a "walking possession" agreement signed by the debtor.

Reference must here be made to *Bower v Hett,* where Lord Esher MR said: "In this case there was a seizure of goods by the bailiff; but he went out of possession under an arrangement with the judgment debtor that he might at any time come in again and retake possession of the goods. He was therefore out of possession."[18]

I do not think that these words can be interpreted as meaning that whenever an officer leaves the debtor's premises he must in all cases be regarded as having abandoned his seizure of the debtor's goods, in so far as third parties are concerned, and the decision must turn, as I think, on the wording of the arrangement entered into between the parties. In *Ackland v Paynter* Graham B said: "I do not mean to lay down the general proposition, that a sheriff can

---

[17] [1958] Ch 922.

[18] [1895] 2 QB 337 - a mere letter from a debtor acknowledging possession and a right to re - enter and retake possession was not enough to prevent abandonment.

in no case quit possession without any qualification; but I should consider, that to show it not an abandonment, he ought to be able most clearly to account for it, as being caused by some urgent necessity, and to give very satisfactory evidence of that."[19]

Bagshawes v Deacon affords an example of failure by the sheriff to produce such satisfactory explanation of going out of possession.[20] It is to be observed that A. L. Smith LJ gave the leading judgment both in that case and in *Lumsden v Burnett* to which reference has already been made, where possession was held to continue notwithstanding that the sheriff's officer had left the premises.

Counsel for the defendants, relying upon *Blades v Arundale* has submitted that, to be effective, the seizure must be maintained by continued personal possession.[21] He submits that even a "walking possession" agreement signed by the judgment debtor would not serve to avert abandonment of the seizure as between the creditor and a third party. *Swann v Earl of Falmouth* is relevant to this latter submission as well as to the question of what constitutes seizure.[22] There a landlord's agent entered the tenant's premises (a wharf), walked around them and gave a written notice that he had distrained certain goods lying there for arrears of rent, and that unless the rent was paid or the goods replevied within five days, they would be sold, and he then went away. Littledale J, after holding that there had been an original seizure and no abandonment thereof, continued:

> "The case might have been different, had the question arisen between the landlord and an execution creditor, or a purchaser for valuable consideration without notice, for the landlord might, perhaps, be considered to have lost his right as against third persons if he neglected to give reasonable notice of it."

But in these days when "walking possession" agreements are such a common feature and have even been encouraged in the case of county court bailiffs by the Lord Chancellor's Department (see *Mather on Sheriff and Execution Law*)[23] it is difficult to see why, if abandonment turns on intention, any distinction should be drawn between the judgment creditor and third parties,

---

[19] (1820) 8 Price 95.
[20] [1898] 2 QB 173 - the sheriff withdrew on promise of payment and being allowed to re -enter, meanwhile permitting the seized goods to be sold.
[21] (1813) 1 M&S 711 - possession was abandoned when the writ was locked in the drawer of a seized table and the sheriff then left with the key.
[22] (1828) 8 B&C 456.
[23] 3rd ed. (1935), pp.118 -119.

and there are several reported cases where no such distinction has been made. In my judgment, it is one which cannot validly be made. There was either abandonment of the seizure, or there was not.

In the present case, did the sheriff ever intend to abandon the seizure made by his officer on April 14th? The evidence indicates that he did not. The nine visits paid by his officer between that date and the disappearance of the caravan, his reporting of Mrs. Wood's claim to the judgment creditor, and his action in taking out the first interpleader summons, all point unmistakably, in my view, to the conclusion that at no time did he intend to abandon the seizure. On the body of evidence I hold that in fact no abandonment took place."

Commentary

This case creates both opportunities and problems for High Court enforcement officers and bailiffs:

- A valid levy can be conducted, and effective possession taken, without a signed walking possession agreement. This gives a bailiff considerable leeway in the procedures they can follow and facilitates a successful levy in even the most unpromising of circumstances. As long as the agent's purpose and intention are made clear, the warrant will be executed;[24] however,
- The levy must be protected from abandonment. Whether or not possession has been abandoned will depend on the intention that can be inferred from the facts. Here, over a period of five weeks, the bailiff called ten times - once very three or four days on average. This was held to be sufficient to sustain the levy until the illegal removal took place. Seizures without a signed possession agreement are therefore possible, but the bailiff must work at them diligently, making contact with the debtor at least once during the working week and ideally more frequently than that. Visits to inspect the premises would seem to be essential to ensure that goods remain on site, although the occasional text or phone call might be permissible.

  The courts have taken different views over how strictly they should construe abandonment. For instance, in *White v Chapple* (1847) a sheriff's officer went out of possession of seized goods for a very

[24] By way of example, see the case of *Hervey v Alexander* (3 Ontario Digest 6905) in which the defendant presented the sheriff with a list of his goods. No actual seizure took place, but the court refused to allow the defendant later to bring a claim for trespass.

short while in order to get food and drink.[25] He left his son on the premises with a copy of the warrant. During his absence another bailiff entered and levied. The Court of Common Bench was not prepared to overturn this second seizure as contempt, even though it was their own writ which was ousted. Fortunately for most enforcement agents, it seems very unlikely that such a strict interpretation of the rules would now be applied.

National Commercial Bank of Scotland v Arcam Demolition & Construction Ltd & others & Hatherley Hall Ltd [1966] 2 QB 593

Facts Judgment was entered by the plaintiff against several defendants including a Mr Campbell. A sheriff called to enforce a writ at Campbell's home. He would not sign walking possession as Hatherley Hall Ltd claimed ownership of his household contents. The sheriff revisited several times over the next month and then on January 24th 1966 managed to persuade Mrs Campbell to sign the possession agreement. The next day her husband wrote to the sheriff's officer stating that his wife had no authority to sign. The sheriff initiated interpleader proceedings so that the Court could decide Hatherley Hall's claim to the household contents. They argued that possession had been abandoned when the wife signed the agreement, but the Court dismissed the claim. Hatherley Hall appealed.

Judgment of Lord Denning - The sheriff could not, of course, sell the goods until the claim had been determined. So he had to take out an interpleader summons to determine the issue. Meanwhile, he had to remain in possession of the goods: because if he abandoned possession, the goods would cease to be in the custody of the law: and the company, Hatherley Hall Ltd., would be able to take possession of them as purchasers, free of the claim of the judgment creditor; see *Blades v. Arundale*; *Bagshawes Ltd. v. Deacon.*[26] Accordingly, the sheriff, by the bailiff, was under a duty to retain possession. He invited Mr. Campbell to sign a document agreeing to "walking possession." But Mr. Campbell refused to sign it. So the bailiff had to remain in possession. He did not actually stay in the house. But he did what was, I think, sufficient to retain possession. He visited the premises frequently and made sure that the goods were safely there and not removed. He did this from December 14th, 1965, to January 24th, 1966. But then something happened which is said to amount to an abandonment of possession.

[25] (1847) 4 CB 628.
[26] (1813) 1 M&S 711; [1898] 2 QB 173.

It happened in this way: On January 24th, 1966, the bailiff went to the house. He saw the wife, Mrs. Campbell. She had a houseful of children there and did not want the bailiff about the place. The bailiff told her that she could avoid it by signing a paper agreeing to give him "walking possession." She said she ought to speak to her solicitors, and then the bailiff said that it did not matter so long as the furniture was not going to be moved. She said that she did not want to move the furniture as she was using it all. She read the paper and signed it. The bailiff left a copy with her and went away. When Mr. Campbell came home, he repudiated what his wife had done. He said that she had no authority from him to sign the paper: and he wrote and informed the bailiff. Hatherley Hall Ltd. wrote to the sheriff's solicitors saying that Mrs. Campbell had no right to sign anything.

It was at one time thought that, in order to retain possession, the bailiff, as the sheriff's officer, must actually remain in the house with the goods. He used to sit down in the kitchen and make himself at home. But that has long since been regarded as unnecessary. It is sufficient if he visits the house frequently to make sure that the goods are safely there and not removed. He then still retains possession. But he need not even do as much as that - he need not visit the house - if he gets an agreement by some responsible person in the house to see that the goods are not removed. After getting such an agreement, he is said to take "walking possession."[27] This has become so universal a practice that a form has been prescribed for "walking possession" such as to entitle the sheriff to fees: see the Sheriffs' Fees (Amendment) Order 1956. This form is so framed as to be signed by the judgment debtor, who would be the person usually in charge of the goods. It is in these words:

> "I hereby request that you will not leave a bailiff on my premises in close possession of the goods which you have seized under the above warrant of execution. If this convenience is allowed to me, I undertake, pending the withdrawal or satisfaction of the warrant: - (a) not to remove the said goods or any portion thereof nor to permit their removal by any persons unauthorised by you in that behalf; (b) to inform any county court bailiff or other persons who may enter my premises for the purpose of levying any other execution or distress that you are already in possession of my goods under the above warrant; (c) to inform you immediately at your office of the visit of any such county court bailiff or other persons for the purposes of levying as aforesaid."

---

[27] *Lumsden v Burnett* [1898] 2 QB 177; *Watson v Murray* [1955] 2 QB 1 - in the latter a signed walking possession agreement was said to retain a 'notional' possession.

But I do not think it necessary, in point of law, for the agreement to be made by the judgment debtor himself. It is sufficient if it is made by any responsible person in the house. Take the simple case where the only person in the house is a caretaker. It would suffice if the caretaker signed a form saying that he would not permit the goods to be removed and would inform the bailiff if anyone tried to remove them. It would not be necessary for the caretaker to have the authority of the judgment debtor. So here it was sufficient for the wife to agree that the goods would not be removed. She was a responsible person in the house. She could see to it that the goods were not removed: or, if anyone attempted to remove them, she could tell the bailiff. She did not need her husband's authority for the purpose. The agreement signed by her was good enough to give "walking possession," even though the judgment debtor did not authorise it, or even objected to it. Once the agreement was signed, there was no need for the sheriff's officer to visit the premises every day. He could rely on it as giving "walking possession."

In my judgment, the sheriff has never abandoned possession. The interpleader was properly taken out and heard and determined: and the sheriff retained possession meanwhile. The master so held. He went on to hear the claim of Hatherley Hall Ltd and decided in favour of the judgment creditor and barred the claimant, Hatherley Hall Ltd. I think the master was quite right and I would dismiss this appeal."

Davies LJ: "I agree. In *Mather on Sheriff and Execution Law* there is reproduced a circular issued by the Lord Chancellor's department to registrars and high bailiffs of county courts. The principles adumbrated in that circular apply with equal force to the sheriff, and the relevant part of that circular is in these terms:

> "The Lord Chancellor considers that it is to the public advantage that walking possession should be adopted by high bailiffs to the utmost possible extent, goods being removed or a possession man being put into close possession only in cases where it is considered that the course is necessary to safeguard the goods."[28]

That being the principle, it seems to me that the course followed by the sheriff in the present case was eminently proper. What he did was to take the undertaking from Mrs. Campbell, who was a responsible person in the house where the goods were. That course would, of course, be most convenient to her and her family. It would save embarrassment and, not only that, it would save expense which might ultimately have to be met either by the judgment

[28] 3rd ed. (1935), pp.118 -119.

debtor, her husband, or the claimants, Hatherley Hall Ltd. In one sense it might be said that the sheriff took the course of constituting Mrs. Campbell his agent to safeguard the goods and to remain in possession of them as some sort of bailee.
The argument put forward forcibly by Mr. Lewis in this case seems to be that the only person who could sign the undertaking which is scheduled to the Sheriffs' Fees (Amendment) Order, is the judgment debtor. But if that be right, walking possession in this case would have been impossible, for the judgment debtor, Mr. Campbell, refused to give the undertaking on the ground that he was not the owner of the goods. If it be only the judgment debtor who can sign such an undertaking, then the claimants, Hatherley Hall Ltd, could not do so. That would give rise to such an impasse that the sheriff would have to remain in close possession.

The further point which is, I think, of great importance in this case as showing what the intention of the sheriff was and what the realities of his actions were is that on the day after he had received this undertaking from Mrs. Campbell, he put the matter in the hands of the court in the sense that he issued his interpleader summons. On those facts and in the light of those principles, the contention that the sheriff abandoned possession is quite an impossible one, and I agree, therefore, that the appeal fails.

Russell LJ - "I also agree. It is admitted that the sheriff never intended to abandon possession. But it is said that the fact, which seems to have been accepted, that between January 24 and the hearing of the interpleader summons the sheriff did not actually visit the premises constituted abandonment. But this failure to visit is explicable in a manner inconsistent with abandonment, because the wife, who was as much in actual control of the furniture in question as anyone, had signed this particular document. Here was, I should have thought, ample factum to add to the admitted intention. It is, of course, very rarely that the occasion could occur when the person signing the walking possession agreement is not both the judgment debtor and also the owner of the goods. I am happy that one can arrive at a decision which I think it consistent not only with due process of law but also with common sense. I venture to read two sentences from the evidence of Mrs. Campbell herself: "I was signing on behalf of myself, not on behalf of my husband. He said" - that is, the sheriff's officer - "it would save him leaving someone in the house. I had a houseful of children and did not want that."

Commentary

This is a significant case for our understanding of walking possession, as well as providing a useful short summary of its development. The essential conclusion is that any 'responsible person' can sign (a spouse in this case, though a caretaker is also suggested) without the authority of the judgment debtor. This is quite correct - the opinion of the debtor is wholly irrelevant as it is the bailiff who chooses the fit person to be in possession. The main function of the role is to prevent seized goods being removed and the only essential to perform this is that the person is 'responsible' i.e. an adult. Today we might wish to elaborate this principle further. Clearly in Mr Campbell's objection there was a measure of obstructiveness but also a good degree of sexism that would not be tolerated in the twenty first century. We may accept that a spouse or partner might sign, as might an adult child still living with the household, an elderly relation or a lodger also resident in the property or an employee. We should also ask if a person should be excluded because of mental disability or even certain mental illnesses and whether the fact that a person does not speak English as their first language might exclude them.

Brinton's Ltd v Wyre Forest District Council [1977] QB 178

Facts This is a case of distress for rates which raises important questions about the nature of a levy. A discussion about the debt and costs took place between the debtor and the council representatives. Payment was received without any paperwork being prepared or other work done, but levy fees were charged. This was standard practice not before questioned but was found not to be lawful when Brintons sued to recover the charges.

Judgment of Donaldson J: "Sir Tatton Brinton, the chairman and managing director of Brintons Ltd, manufacturers of carpets (the plaintiffs), set out to protest against the increase in the rates demanded by the Wyre Forest District Council. With this in mind he withheld £83,000. The council took out a summons before the local justices and Sir Tatton made his protest. Whether it was effective as a protest, I know not, but the justices were bound to issue a distress warrant and did so.

The plaintiffs' intention was to pay the rates the next day, but the council moved with a speed which is unusual in a local authority. No doubt they had it in mind that the non -payment of these rates was costing the general body of ratepayers £24 a day by way of interest. That afternoon Mr Williams, the council's chief rating assistant, and Mr Dallow, a bailiff, went to the plaintiffs' offices and met Sir Tatton. They were invited into the boardroom and the bailiff told Sir Tatton that they had come to levy distress for the outstanding rates and for costs. Sir Tatton said that a cheque for the rates had been prepared but it required a further signature. It was at this stage that the bailiff informed Sir Tatton that as he had come to levy distress under a warrant, the plaintiffs would have to pay not only the amount of the rates, but also the cost of levying distress. This amounted to some £1,255.28. The plaintiffs, having little alternative, drew a further cheque for this sum which they delivered under protest. I am told that any bailiff would have acted in the same way and that the correctness of this course never seems to have been challenged. However, the plaintiffs take the view that the demand for £1,255.28 cannot possibly be justified. If they are right, this case is of considerable importance to all local authorities and the plaintiffs' second protest has probably been more effective than their first.

The council does not seek to contend that it can retain the money if it was not entitled to demand it in the first place, nor does it contend that in the circumstances of this case the delivery of the plaintiffs' cheque did not amount to a tender of the rates and of the costs demanded. The plaintiffs, for their part, do not seek to challenge the arithmetic involved in arriving at a figure of £1,255.28.

Mr. Shaw for the council puts his claim to be entitled to this sum in two ways. First, he submits that on the facts the bailiff levied a distress and thereupon became entitled to the appropriate fee under paragraph 3 (1) (ii) of the Distress for Rates Order 1972. Second, he submits that if the bailiff did not get as far as levying a distress, the council is entitled to a like sum under section 105 (2) of the General Rate Act 1967.

The claim to have levied a distress for rates

In *Mortimer v Cragg* (1878) Brett LJ defined the stages in the execution of a writ of *fieri facias* and the sheriff's entitlement to poundage as follows:

> "Where an execution issues the transaction may be divided into four parts (1) the delivery of the writ to the sheriff; (2) seizure; (3) the possible payment of money after seizure; (4) if no payment, sale. The first step does not entitle the sheriff to poundage and if he does not seize *Nash v. Dickenson* (1867) is an authority that he is not entitled to poundage.[29] Although he seizes, nothing may be realised because the seizure may be wrongful. It may be withdrawn by direction of the law, and then the sheriff would receive no poundage. Then comes the case after seizure. The money may be paid by the execution debtor either directly or indirectly: directly by virtue of the seizure to the sheriff; indirectly where payment is made by means of a compromise which is the consequence of the seizure. In either of those cases the sheriff is entitled to poundage."[30]

[29] [1867] 2 CP 252.
[30] 3 CPD 216.

It is not suggested that any different principle applies to the execution of a distress warrant for rates. The issue is thus whether the bailiff in fact seized any goods. In my judgment he did not. As counsel for plaintiffs has pointed out, the bailiff was not entitled to seize the whole of the goods present in the offices and factory. He had to select sufficient goods to cover the rates whilst ensuring that the distress was not excessive. This involved some process of selection before seizure and the bailiff never started on this process. Nor did he ever say that all or any of the goods were seized or do anything which amounted to taking possession.

In relation to the execution of a warrant of *fieri facias* the dividing line between what is and what is not a seizure is shown by comparing *Nash v. Dickenson* (1867) which seems to me to be indistinguishable from the present case and *Bissicks v Bath Colliery* (1877) which is distinguishable because the sheriff's officer threatened to leave a man in possession of the goods and both parties treated the action of the sheriff's officer as having amounted to a seizure.[31] The claim to poundage on this basis therefore fails.

The claim under section 105 (2) of the General Rate Act 1967

Section 105 is in the following terms. The side note reads: "Abatement of proceedings on payment of rate and costs." The section provides:

> "(1) If after proceedings have been taken under this Part of this Act against a person to compel payment of any sum for rates, but not after he has been imprisoned in default of a sufficiency of distress, that person pays or tenders to the rating authority, or to some other person authorised to receive the rates, the sum sought to be recovered together with the amount of all costs and charges up to that time incurred in the proceedings, the rating authority or other person shall accept the amount so paid or tendered and no further proceedings shall be taken for the recovery thereof. (2) If after the issue of a warrant of distress under this Part of this Act for a rate the person against whom it is issued tenders the amount of the rate before any levy is made, he shall nonetheless be liable to pay the cost of the warrant and of any person for his attendance to make the levy."

Subsection (1) is concerned with the stage between the issue of a summons for a warrant of distress and the issue of that warrant. Payment or tender of

[31] [1867] 2 CP 252; [1877] 2 Ex 459 &, on appeal, [1878] 3 Ex 174. In *Nash* the court said that merely producing the writ and demanding payment, without doing any more, was not seizure whereas in *Bissicks* attending the premises, showing the writs and demanding payment or else a man would remain in possession was adequate seizure.

the rates and the costs and charges of the authority to date operates as an immediate stay of all further proceedings. Subsection (2) is concerned with the stage between the issue of the distress warrant and the seizure of the goods. If the ratepayer tenders the amount of the rate before any seizure is made his remaining liability is to pay the cost of the warrant and the cost of any person, and I quote, "for his attendance to make the levy." The question is what is this cost.

Counsel for the plaintiffs suggests that it is an apportioned part of the bailiff's salary and pension, together with his travelling expenses, but this seems to me to be an unlikely construction. Counsel for the local authority submits there is so little difference in point of time and expense between attending to make a levy and actually levying a distress that Parliament must have meant to refer to the fees payable on the making of the levy itself. I do not agree. If this had been what had been intended the section would have read, "He shall nonetheless be liable to pay the costs of the warrant and the minimum fees, charges and expenses which would have been payable if the levy had been made." In my judgment the intention of Parliament is clear. It contemplated that the Minister would make an order under section 101 of the Act which would specify the costs recoverable for attending to levy a distress. Section 101 (1) provides:

> "The Minister (now the Secretary of State for the Environment) may make an order regulating the charges in respect of, and incidental to, the levying of distress for rates; and a warrant of distress under this Part of this Act may provide that the charges attending the distress, to the amount authorised by the order, shall be levied under the warrant."

For one reason or another, perhaps due to an oversight, he has not done so. As it has not been contended that in the absence of such an order "reasonable costs" are recoverable, no costs are recoverable and the plaintiffs are entitled to be repaid the sum of £1,255.28. No doubt the Minister will wish to consider amending the Distress for Rates Order 1972, as a matter of urgency."

Commentary

This case continues to be of relevance. It is surprising how often it seems to happen that a bailiff gains entry to a debtor's premises and then fails to conduct a levy, instead merely discussing how the debt will be repaid. The judgment in *Brinton's* makes clear that such a discussion is *not* a levy. Levying distraint involves some process of inspecting and selecting goods sufficient to cover the debt and costs (see *Rai & Rai v B'ham City Council* in chapter 4) combined with some clear declaration or indication that this is being done (see *Davies v Property & Reversionary* in chapter 4). In *Brinton's*

no such process took place and, in its absence, there was no levy and no entitlement to levy fees. This will still be the situation today: if the bailiff fails to levy during a visit he cannot add fees for a seizure nor - of course - would he have any rights to force entry and remove goods at a later time.
The alternative argument was made that, in the absence of a specified charge for a visit on the fee scale then in operation, some sort of general staff overhead could be recovered. This was not accepted. Bailiffs should always be careful to stay within the strict form of the applicable scale (see chapter 6). It is also interesting to note how the court was content to apply law developed on the context of executions to levies of statutory distraint. In many respects, the basic practice is identical in all forms of seizure of goods and rules of fundamental procedure are transferable.

Evans v South Ribble Borough Council [1992] QB 757

Facts A liability order was made against Mrs Evans for unpaid community charge. When the bailiff called at her home she was at work. After speaking to her on the telephone he posted through her letter box a notice of distress and a draft walking possession agreement which he had signed. She challenged the validity of this purported levy by issuing a complaint under reg.40 of the Community Charge (Administration & Enforcement) Regulations 1989. The justices held that the authority had validly distrained on the complainant's goods; Mrs Evans appealed to the High Court.

Judgment of Simon Brown J: "Historically distress was a common law remedy available to landlords to recover arrears of rent. The landlord had to remove the goods from the tenant's premises and hold them in a pound as security. By the Distress for Rent Act 1689 he was empowered to sell the goods if the arrears were not paid within five days and by the Distress for Rent Act 1737 he was authorised to secure the goods otherwise than by impounding them. The complainant's first submission is that these statutory provisions relate only to distress for rent and that later powers of levying distress - for rates, for taxes, to enforce fines and to recover unpaid community charge, each introduced by a separate statute - are only exercisable in accordance with the original common law rule; with the result that no distress is effective save only when the goods seized are actually impounded.

This is not an argument which was advanced before the justices nor were steps taken to alert the authority to it in advance of the hearing. Differences plainly do exist between distress for rent and distress under reg.39 - under the latter, for instance, there is no requirement to allow the debtor five days or any other period of time to satisfy the debt, nor indeed for a notice of distress although, as will be noted, this particular authority, and doubtless others, choose to adopt those particular features of the rent recovery procedure when distraining for unpaid community charge. For the purposes of this appeal, however, I propose to assume, in the absence of full argument upon the point, that the question of what constitutes an effective levying of distress must receive the same answer irrespective of the particular statutory provision authorising the remedy. It certainly seems to me improbable in any present day context that nothing short of impounding will constitute proper distress. and clearly such a contention is difficult to reconcile with the express provisions of the regulations, referring as they do to both close and walking possession agreements.

I therefore shall consider, as did the justices, whether the bailiff's action here constituted lawful distress by reference to the principles established in relation to rent recovery, the context in which virtually the whole of the law of distress has developed. That those principles present difficulty enough in themselves is plain from the following words in the Law Commission's Working Paper on *Distress for Rent*: "The present law of distress for rent is riddled with inconsistencies, uncertainties, anomalies and archaisms."[32] That paper's statement of the present law of distress went wholly uncriticised through the subsequent consultation process and has been included as an appendix to the recent Law Commission Report, *Landlord and Tenant Distress for Rent* on this topic, a report, be it noted, whose central recommendation is that distress for rent should without exception be abolished.[33]

What then is the present law? Having regard to the Law Commission's statement, *Halsbury's Laws of England* and the several authorities cited to me, I take the basic principles to be essentially as follows.

1. The process of distress consists of three stages: the entry into the premises, the seizure there of goods, and the subsequent securing of the goods (generally called impounding).

2. Although a right to distrain necessarily involves a right to enter, this can only be exercised lawfully, i.e. without breaking into the premises. There is no right to forcible entry although in certain circumstances there is a right to forcible re -entry.

3. Seizure may be actual or constructive. Actual seizure involves identification of the goods distrained coupled with a declaration that they are

---

[32] (1986) no. 97, p.145, para.5.1(1).
[33] (1991) Law Com. no.194.

being taken for distress. Precisely what constitutes constructive seizure is unclear. The Law Commission suggest that it occurs when the landlord's intention to distrain particular goods is made apparent by his actions. *Halsbury's Laws of England*, states:[34]

> "A constructive seizure may occur in various ways. It is enough that the landlord or his agent interferes to prevent the removal of the article from off the premises on the ground that rent is in arrear, and he does this when he declares that the article shall not be removed until the rent is paid"[35] - "and it is immaterial that the article is in fact subsequently removed."[36] "Any acts indicative of an intention that antecedent steps should be treated as a distress . . . will be sufficient evidence of a seizure. Thus . . . if the bailiff after intimating his intention to distrain walks round the demised premises and without touching anything gives written notice that he has distrained, that will amount to a seizure."[37]

4. Impounding can take a number of forms. It is this which places the goods in the custody of the law and paves the way for their sale. Goods may be impounded on the premises or removed to a pound. What constitutes impounding on the premises is again unclear as also is the effect of a walking possession agreement, in particular whether it operates as a form of, or a convenient substitute for, impounding. As to this the Law Commission's Working Paper on *Distress for Rent* stated:[38]

> "This uncertainty makes the consequences of the breach of the agreement unclear. In *Abingdon RDC v O'Gorman* [1968][39] the owner of a television set hired to the tenant took back his property without knowing that the tenant had entered into a walking possession agreement with the landlord's bailiff. The landlord claimed treble damages against the owner for poundbreach. Lord Denning MR was prepared to hold that, as against strangers, goods were not validly impounded unless they were secured in such a way that it was manifest that they should not be taken away. He said that walking possession might be sufficient against the tenant who agreed to it, but not as against a stranger who knew nothing of it. Davies LJ thought that the true analysis was that there had been no actual impounding (which, technically, would preclude poundbreach), but that the agreement

[34] 4th ed., vol.13, p.156, para.308.
[35] *Cramer v Mott* [1870] 5 QB 357.
[36] *Werth v. London and Westminster Loan Co.* (1889) 5 TLR 320.
[37] *Swann v Earl of Falmouth* (1828) 8 B&C 456.
[38] (1986) (No. 97) p.58, para.2.53.
[39] 2 QB 811 - see chapter 7.

prevented the tenant from saying so. Russell LJ, however, was firmly of the view that walking possession did amount to an impounding on the premises, even though a stranger ignorant of that impounding would not be guilty of poundbreach."

5. Once the goods are impounded the distress is complete subject only to its not thereafter being abandoned. *Halsbury's Laws of England* states:[40]

> "When the landlord impounds the goods upon the premises, leaving them there without anyone in possession, that is sufficient custody, for they are in the custody of the law."[41] "If he abandons them, then the possession reverts to the tenant. Whether or not his acts amount to an abandonment is always one of fact when the point arises. If he puts a bailiff in possession it is not necessary that the bailiff should retain continuous physical possession:"[42]

From that brief and necessarily simplified overview of the law it will readily be seen that the respondent authority here face a number of difficult hurdles. In the first place their bailiff failed to gain actual entry to the complainant's premises. Second, and directly consequent upon their failure to gain entry, they could not seize her goods save only by referring in the documents to the general contents of the premises. Third, their only act of "impounding" the goods was to claim in the posted documents that they had done so and to state that unless payment were made within five days (or longer if a walking possession agreement was entered into) the goods would be sold. Implicit, although nowhere I think stated explicitly, in the posted documents is the authority's assertion that the complainant is not entitled to dispose of the goods: they are in the custody of the law. Whether, of course, that is so depends upon the resolution of this present issue. As to the threat to sell the goods after five days, that threat, however the present issue is resolved, is necessarily an empty one unless the complainant were to admit the bailiffs to her premises upon some later visit. If she keeps the premises locked against them they cannot gain lawful entry. Although counsel for Mrs Evans submits to the contrary - assuming that is, this appeal were to fail - the authority, to my mind plainly rightly, do not themselves so contend. Rather they submit that the sole effect of the process of distress thus far achieved is to prevent the complainant from disposing of her goods and, less importantly, third parties from levying distress or otherwise executing against them. One can of course readily see that the mere threat of sale, unenforceable though it be

[40] 4th ed., vol.13, p.160, para.316.
[41] *Swann v Earl of Falmouth* (1828) 8 B&C 456.
[42] *Bannister v Hyde* (1860) 2 E&E 627; *Jones v Biernstein* - see page 70.

without a subsequent peaceful entry, would generally prove a highly effective way of encouraging debtors to discharge their liabilities. But these proceedings are not concerned with practical considerations of that nature; only with the question whether any effective distress has been levied.

How then does the authority seek to overcome the obstacles apparent in his path? As to the requirement for entry to the premises, he relies primarily upon *Cramer and Co Ltd v Mott.* In that case the tenant occupied a room in the landlord's house. In the room he kept a piano hired from a third party. When the third party sought to remove the piano they were met by the landlord's wife in the passage outside the tenant's room. She said, "The piano shall not be taken away till our rent is paid." Cockburn CJ said:

> "She was not, perhaps, actually on the demised premises, being outside the door of the room; but she was close to the door, the tenant being at the door, and she was so close that if the men had persisted in attempting to remove the piano, she could have at once interfered and prevented the removal. . . . I think there need not be an actual seizure to create a distress; it is enough that the landlord or his agent takes effectual means to prevent the removal of the article from off the premises, on the ground of rent being in arrear; and he does this when he declares that the article shall not be removed till the rent is paid."[43]

The other main decision upon which the council relies in this connection is *Werth v London & Westminster Loan Co.* There the tenant's goods were actually removed by a loan company who had no right whatever to levy execution in that fashion. The loan company were sued by the landlord whose claim depended upon whether or not there had been a distress previous to the removal. Huddlestone B said:

> "The landlord had exercised his right to distress by giving notice to the depredators (they deserved no other description) of his claim to distress, and by his trying to detain the goods for his rent."[44]

By the same token that *Cramer v Mott* had turned upon the landlord's wife's ability to intervene physically to prevent the removal of the tenant's goods, in *Werth*'s case the landlord succeeded by virtue merely of trying to stop the removal of the tenant's goods albeit the defendants, acting unlawfully even as against the tenant, in fact succeeded in removing them.

---

[43] In *Cramer v Mott* [1870] 5 QB 357 the ability physically to seize goods (or to prevent any interference with them) was key to there being an effectual seizure.

[44] In *Werth* (1889) 5 TLR 320 the landlord had his tenant distrain on his behalf by means of a letter and a verbal declaration. This was valid.

Although the direct question in both cases was whether the landlord's distress was good against a third party, there had first to be, as counsel for the local authority submits, a valid distress in respect of the tenant. In my judgment both decisions are explicable upon the footing that the distress became valid and effective against the tenant at the point immediately before the third party attempted (in *Werth*'s case successfully) to remove the goods. That cannot, as it seems to me, assist the authority in the present case. There was here, after all, no attempt beyond the mere posting of documents to prevent removal of the complainant's goods. Not merely, indeed, did the authority never gain entry to her premises; they never even made physical contact with her at the door. Had they done so, and had she or a third party at that time been attempting to remove her goods, this case would have borne a close resemblance to those cited. As it is, however, the differences seem to me more substantial than the similarities.

Nor is the authority's argument to my mind advanced by *Swann v Earl of Falmouth.* There the Earl distrained for rent outstanding from Swann in respect of a wharf by entering upon the wharf, examining the goods stored there, leaving a notice of distress in respect of various identified goods, and departing. Swann was prevented by this distress from carrying on his business. When eventually he sued for damages on the ground that excessive distress had been levied, the Earl's somewhat unattractive defences were first that there had been no seizure and second, that even if there had, distress had been abandoned. These defences failed. But the striking difference between that case and this is, of course, that entry there was made upon the tenant's premises even though it is true the subsequent seizure and impounding can clearly only be described as "constructive." Had the complainant in the present case left her door unlocked whereby the bailiffs were able to gain lawful entry, and had they then, having examined her goods, left their notice of distress inside, that might well have been an effective distraint and not only would Swann's case so suggest; so also would *Jones v Biernstein* in which Channell J said:

> "It appears to me to be quite clear from the authorities that when once the goods are in *custodia legis* the actual retention of possession by the party distraining on them is not necessary. . . . I should think that in the general way the mere fact of taking possession of the goods is sufficient for the purposes of the statute. As has been pointed out, the seizing of goods is an act done once for all, and when notice of possession is given that may be sufficient to constitute an impounding."

Lloyds & Scottish Finance v Modern Cars & Caravans (Kingston) Ltd [1966][45] seems also to like effect. There the sheriff's officer went to a caravan occupied by the judgment debtor to execute a writ of *fieri facias*. Having gained admission, he read out the warrant of execution and told the debtor that the caravan must not be moved. That was held to be an effective and continuing seizure of the caravan and its contents notwithstanding the debtor's refusal to sign a walking possession agreement and notwithstanding that the officer left the caravan.

In short, it appears to me plain on the authorities that whereas, once entry is made, little in the way of seizure and impounding is required to preclude the debtor, even without a walking possession agreement, from disposing of his goods, there must in the first instance *be* an entry - save only in the wholly exceptional situations arising in *Cramer v Mott* and *Werth*'s case where the goods sought to be distrained were on the point of removal and the distrainer directly confronted the removers.

The authorities therefore point to the insufficiency of a mere posting of documents as here to constitute a distraint of goods. Is there then anything in the directly applicable legislation which suggests a different conclusion? In my judgment there is not. On the contrary, the language of regulation 39 tends to support the conventional view that entry is required. Paragraphs (3) and (4) each make express reference to seizure and paragraph (4) further provides in terms that, if the debt is discharged before sale, "the sale shall not be proceeded with and the goods shall be made available for collection by the debtor." All that appears to presuppose at the very least prior entry and, indeed, that no further co -operation is needed on the part of the debtor (in particular by allowing peaceable entry prior to sale such as is clearly still required in the present case) before the sale can be proceeded with. Paragraph (5), moreover, requires the distrainer to carry a written authorisation and to show it to the debtor if so requested. What point in that if the distraint is effective merely by posting documents through the door? and Schedule 5 in turn defines and provides for close and walking possession agreements, which again point strongly towards a direct meeting between the debtor and the person levying distress.

I do not suggest that any of these provisions are decisive of the point. They are not - and I reject the council's submission that Sch.5 necessarily implies that the only effective impounding of goods, absent a close or walking possession agreement, is by removing them from the premises. Sch.5, I repeat, is concerned solely with the charges exigible in connection with

[45] See earlier.

distress. Nothing in it is in my judgment inconsistent with the impounding of goods by, for instance, close possession without an agreement (although no charge can be made for that), or perhaps even without any continuing act of possession at all. But all that said, there is clearly nothing in the legislation from which the authority can draw any comfort in the particular circumstances of this case.

I have some considerable sympathy with this authority (and indeed others) concerned to recover outstanding community charges from errant householders and I recognise the difficulty in which an adverse ruling here will place them. Their solicitor's affidavit highlights it thus:

> "In a large number of cases in which distress is levied, bailiffs employed by local authorities find it impossible to gain entry to the debtor's premises, either due to the absence of the debtor or the refusal of the debtor to allow the bailiff access. In such cases it is the practice of bailiffs to levy 'constructive distraint' on the debtor's goods by making such an inspection of goods as is possible from outside the premises and posting a written notice of distraint through the debtor's letter box. This method is the only practical course of action open to the bailiff."

So it may be - and apparently still more when distraining for rent, since process then is confined to the period between sunrise and sunset and is forbidden on Sundays. But it is my clear conclusion that external inspection and posting through the letter box is a course of action insufficient to bring about any of the legal consequences of distress.

If Parliament wishes to provide for distraint of goods merely by posting documents in this fashion (and if that, why not merely by sending them registered delivery?) then it will do so by further legislation - although perhaps, following the Law Commission report, it is more likely that distress will instead be abolished entirely. Any further legislation, indeed, to be truly effective - effective, that is, otherwise than as an unenforceable threat - would need also to provide for forcible entry since, as stated, the debtor can in any event always prevent sale by denying peaceable entry. In the meantime I hold that the action thus far taken by the authority has achieved nothing in the way of securing the complainant's goods or precluding her from dealing with them as she wishes. The answer to the question posed by the justices is, in a word, "No." That being so, and having regard to the threatening nature of the documents posted, the complainant is clearly someone aggrieved by this attempt to levy distress against her goods.

There is perhaps one final authority to which I should briefly refer, *Brown v. London Borough of Haringey* (1986).[46] The question there was whether the appellant was a "person aggrieved by a distress" for the purposes of s.99(5) of the General Rate Act 1967. The bailiff had been let into the premises by the debtor's wife and had left behind a draft walking possession agreement. That agreement being unsigned and ineffective, and the bailiff not having purported to take other than walking possession, the court held that there was no "completed distress" sufficient to found the statutory right of appeal to the Crown Court. It is not suggested by Mr. Garside that that decision operates to deny this complainant her right of appeal under reg.40; on the contrary, he strives to distinguish it on the substantive question as to what action is required for the making of an effective distress. I find it unnecessary to reach any conclusion as to whether Brown's case is properly distinguishable on the issues of seizure and impounding; my judgment rests squarely upon the requirement for entry to be made in the first place. At least in Brown's case the bailiff gained entry. Here he did not.

In the result this appeal succeeds. The case must be remitted to the justices with a direction that they uphold the complaint and set aside the award of costs previously made against the complainant. I decline the council's invitation to indicate what, short of entry and removal of the goods, are the minimum steps which would constitute distraint sufficient to put the goods in the custody of the law. Helpful to bailiffs though I recognise that might be, this field of law is altogether too unclear and problematical to venture unnecessary and unappealable *dicta* of that kind."

Commentary

The judgment in *Evans* continues to be of considerable relevance in bailiffs' law. On the specific method of levying attempted in this case, Simon Brown J concluded that "external inspection and posting through a letter box is a course of action insufficient to bring about any of the legal consequences of distress." However, the judgment has developed wider relevance than that. It is a very useful summary of the essential stages in the levy process and it emphasises that, for a bailiff to be able to claim to have levied, he must get into a position where - if needs be - goods could be physically removed. This will rarely be necessary, and it is envisaged that something far less than physical possession will be needed effectively to place goods in the custody of the law. Nevertheless, for household goods to be seized and impounded, the bailiff *must* have gained access to the house.

---

[46] Unreported, 3 October 1986, a decision of the Divisional Court (Watkins LJ and Kennedy J).

Evans is not only important for its ruling on levies made by posted documents. It exposes and prohibits a range of practices which have grown up since. It seems plain that the procedure discussed in *Evans* was an attempt to maximize bailiff productivity by permitting the maximum number of warrants to be executed in the least possible time. The approach taken in *Evans* is (surprisingly perhaps) still followed today along with analogous forms of levy:

- *Levies of household goods* carried out at a bailiff's office or other premises;
- *Levies of cars* or other goods conducted merely by driving past premises;
- *Levies on vehicles* conducted in communal car parks at blocks of flats and with notices of seizure left by communal entries;
- *Levies based on 'generic' lists* of goods without any detailed inspection of premises;
- *Two stage levies* which rely in part on the use of 'global seizures' of goods by 'catch -all' phrases on inventories (see *Ambrose v Nottingham City Council* in chapter 4); and,
- *Doorstep levies* without full entry.

All of these must be scrutinised to verify that they comply with the essential elements of a levy as laid down in the *Evans* judgment.

A few other minor points may be noted:

- *Impounding off premises* - the judgment acknowledges that, before the Distress for Rent Act 1737 changed matters for distress for rent, the common law required impounding off the premises (see earlier);
- *"Impounding"* - to begin with Simon Brown J creates a false opposition between 'impounding' in the sense of taking to a pound and possession in the sense of impounding on the premises. This does not seem to be sustained throughout the judgment and readers must beware his slightly inconsistent use of terminology; and,
- *Schedule 5* - the fee scales for local taxes define the nature of close and walking possession. Simon Brown J emphasises that this is done for the sole purpose of regulating "the charges exigible in connection with distress." It is sometimes believed that only the debtor can sign a local taxes walking possession agreement. This is incorrect: any responsible person can sign (see *Arcam* earlier) but only the debtor's signature will do if the statutory fee for possession is to be recovered.

Conclusions

The 'pound' is central to the process of enforcement against goods, yet the nature and consequences of legal custody are ill -understood and, indeed, seem to evolve some distance behind developments in practice. This is problematic, to say the least, when so much depends on the successful creation and continuance of a pound. It is clear, though, that in trying to find harmony amongst the discordant authorities, the courts have lagged behind the innovations of practitioners and often seem to be seeking a legal justification after the event, endorsing that which is already widespread.

The legalisation of impounding on the debtor's premises has led to as many problems as advantages. Removal to a pound was a clear and unequivocal act, separate in space and time from the seizure of goods. The merging of the two stages of the levy into one has effaced vital distinctions and introduced uncertainties that the courts have struggled to eliminate. Clear words and actions, expressing the bailiff's intentions, will serve to seize goods. Similar clarity of action and intent is required to retain possession of those goods. A full levy must be conducted properly to secure the creditor's rights, however difficult it might prove - for instance, because of resistance or obstruction by the debtor.[47]

Implementation of the Tribunals, Courts & Enforcement Act 2007 will alleviate some of these problems by creating a statutory one stage process of "taking control" of goods. Even so, this will not guarantee that everything goes smoothly in practice, any more than now, and questions of the validity of seizures and subsequent abandonment of possession are still likely to tax the courts.

---

[47] *Jones v Davies* (1892) 40 EG 372.

Chapter 4

GOODS AND INVENTORIES

Introduction

It is in respect of the goods distrainable by bailiffs that there has perhaps been the greatest statutory interference over the last two hundred years. More and more items have been exempted, whether for the commercial benefit of society or for the welfare of the individual. In most forms of distress and execution the categories of protected goods, vehicles and household items are now quite extensive and very subjective, borrowed ultimately from the Insolvency Act 1986. Judicial guidance as to their interpretation and application is surprisingly sparse, despite two decades of use. It is clear that the burden of proving exemption lies with the debtor or owner. This is especially the case when it is necessary to demonstrate *personal* use of tools and equipment. Moreover, the claimant should act with honesty and reasonable promptness. In the case of *Moffatt v Lemkin,* heard by the High Court in November 1993, a claim to photographic equipment as essential tools of the trade was dismissed, in part because it was delayed for more than a year after the levy and in part because it was preceded by claims on the part of the debtor that the items in question were owned by third parties.

In instances of genuine claims, there is no reason why considerable amounts of goods and chattels might not be protected. In *Brookes v Harris* (1995), a "very substantial" collection of records, tapes and CDs worth £10-20,000 (according to its owner) was claimed as tools of the trade.[1] Mr Robert Harris, "a well known broadcaster and presenter of musical programmes on radio and television" applied to the High Court for release of his goods from seizure in execution of a judgment entered against him by Mr Bruno Brookes. Mr Brookes was owed £134,000 and valued the collection at a significantly higher figure than the judgment debtor. The High Court master

[1] (1995) *The Times,* April 22nd, p.17 (Ch D).

nonetheless accepted that all these items constituted the tools of Mr Harris' trade and should not have been taken in execution.[2]

Bishop v Bryant & others (1834) 6 C&P 484

Facts The plaintiff was a pipe maker and was tenant of a Mr Bryant. In April 1833 the landlord was owed one quarter's rent, totalling £10, and he therefore instructed a bailiff, Mr Chuck to levy distress. Chuck and his two sons distrained goods at the premises on April 19th and left a man named Chassey in possession. Six days later all three called again, on which occasion the plaintiff was asked by Chuck senior to pay his expenses. He did this and the Chucks then went away, taking the possession man Chassey with them. Chassey stayed away all night. The next day the Chucks came again, accompanied by two others, and began to remove the goods. They took away virtually all the contents and so negligently handled the pipes that a great many were broken. It further appeared, that, after the distress and delivery of the inventory, the bailiffs found a cupboard in which were a quantity of pipes, a sofa bedstead, an electrifying machine, and a model of a ship, all of which they also removed. It was also complained that the goods were not properly appraised before removal (as required under the Distress for Rent Act 1689) and that the tenant had been unable to obtain a copy of any valuation of the goods since.

Judgment of Tindal CJ: "... If these goods which were taken from the cupboard were not included in the original distress, an action of trover will lie for them. It is not pretended they were included in the inventory, because it was not known at the time that they were there... It seems to me that the landlord constitutes the bailiffs his agents when he sends them in to make this distress; and if they wrongfully or negligently take away anything they ought not, he is liable for their acts...

(*to the jury*) It appears to me that there are three points which must be submitted to your consideration; first, whether the defendants were guilty of selling the goods without having previously appraised them by two sworn brokers, as required by the statute? Secondly, whether any damage was done to the goods by want of proper care in the removal of them? And, thirdly, what damage has been occasioned by the sale of those articles which were not in the inventory? According as you find the counts relating to these matters sustained or not by the evidence, you will find your verdict for the plaintiff or the defendants. On the first point you must say what damage the

[2] See further in *Powers of distress* c.3 Part IV, *Law of Seizure of Goods* c.9, *Persons of no value* cc.7 & 8 and *A lawful trespass* c.5.

owner of this property has sustained by reason of its not having been appraised. There is no evidence of the time at which the sale took place; and if the appraisement was made before the taking for the purposes of sale, all would have been done that was necessary as far as the time was concerned. Then you will consider whether the necessity of the appraisement was dispensed with by the plaintiff; for, if you are satisfied that it was, then he cannot bring an action for the neglect of that which he has himself dispensed with. I recommend you, if you find for the plaintiff on any of the three grounds I have mentioned, to find the damages separately on each, as it may prevent the parties from coming here again."

The jury found for the plaintiff—damages on the first ground, £85; on the second, £10; and on the third, £5.

Commentary

Because this case was determined by a jury, we do not have extended reasoning from the judge as to the law. Instead, we have his interjections to counsel and his summing up for the jury, which indicate clearly enough that removing goods not initially distrained will be wrongful. A similar case was heard earlier the same year.[3] It was unusual as it involved a distress for rent which was collusive between landlord and tenant: the tenant asked his landlord to distrain in order to defeat another creditor's execution. The landlord distrained as requested- and then sold the goods. The tenant sued to recover them but the court refused to assist *except* in so far as a number of pairs of boots and shoes not included in the inventory had been sold. This part of the levy was confirmed by the court to be wrongful.

Reference may also be made to the judgment in the case of *Clooney v Watson* (1851).[4] The Irish Court of Exchequer held that trover would lie in cases where a landlord levied a second time having failed to seize all the available goods on the first occasion. Pigot CB remarked that "there was other distress on the land at the time, and not of a character to escape observation, or such as the landlord could not have found, had he chosen to seek for it." Accordingly, the second seizure was unquestionably wrongful.

The significance of these three cases is how they relate to modern practices of 'two stage' or partial levies that depend on 'catch-all phrases' in inventories. The latter are discussed in the next case and in detail later, but it will be clear from the last three judgments that bailiffs cannot simply add on other goods discovered during a later visit to premises. What is on the inventory is what

[3] *Sims v Tuffs* (1834) 6 C&P 207.
[4] (1851) LR Ir 2 CL 373.

has been levied once and for all and cannot be amended. Especially pertinent to this point is the decision of the Queens Bench Division in *Gray v Cole* (1856). An individual claimed for illegal and excessive distress. Two machines he owned were seized for arrears of rent due for premises at which he worked. He kept the machines there but they were not used by the business and, in fact, had never been used. Initially the bailiff agreed not to include the machines on the inventory but when he returned to remove items for sale, the bailiff prepared a second inventory including the two. They were then sold for a fraction of their worth. Lord Campbell CJ felt that the sale was illegal as, being absent from the first inventory, the goods were never the subject of a lawful levy.[5]

Davies v Property & Reversionary Investments Co Ltd [1929] 2 KB 222

Facts The plaintiff was tenant of a flat of which the defendants were the landlords. Because rent was in arrears, distress was levied by a certificated bailiff, and a notice of distress was served on the plaintiff. This read: "Take notice that by virtue of an authority to me given I have this day seized and distrained the goods and chattels specified in the following inventory .... Sitting room [various articles - e.g., carpet, 2 bookcases, sideboard] Bedroom [various articles, e.g. four pictures, wardrobe] and all other goods upon the premises (unless specially exempt) sufficient to satisfy the amount of this distress and expenses." Goods not specifically named in the notice but coming within the concluding words of the notice were sold. The plaintiff brought an action against the defendants claiming damages for illegal distress which was referred to an Official Referee.[6] The Official Referee held that the sale was illegal on the ground that the above notice was insufficient. The defendants appealed.

Judgment of Talbot J: "The point raised in this action is that, so far as relates to the goods not mentioned by name in the notice, that sale was illegal, because no notice of distress, so far as those goods are concerned, had been given to satisfy the requirements of the Act of William and Mary. Of course it is well known that that Act was passed in the interest of landlords, to add to their facilities for recovering rent by enabling them to do that which, before the Act was passed, they could not do - namely, sell goods taken in distress. Before that Act, all the right they had was to detain them as pledges, as the preamble says, for enforcing the payment of the rent; and the preamble goes on to add that "persons distraining have little benefit

[5] *The Times,* February 11th 1856 p.11a.

[6] Under the Judicature Act 1873 a judge could refer a case to a referee for an investigation of the facts, an examination of the evidence and a decision.

thereby"; and it was in order to give them more benefit that this Act was passed. It enacts by s. 2 that: "where any goods or chattels shall be distrained for any rent reserved and due upon any demise, lease, or contract whatsoever, and the tenant or owner of the goods so distrained shall not within five days next after such distress taken, and notice thereof (with the cause of such taking) left at the chief mansion house," and so on. Then: "after such distress and notice as aforesaid, and expiration of the said five days, the person distraining shall and may" - then various formalities. Then: "cause the goods and chattels so distrained to be appraised," and after such appraisement shall and may lawfully sell them to the amount specified of the rent for which the said goods and chattels shall be distrained, and charges, and so on. It is obvious, therefore, that it is a condition precedent to the right of the landlord to avail himself of the indulgence given by this statute, that he should have done what the statute requires, the object of which is perfectly plain - namely, that the goods shall not be sold until the owner of the goods or the tenant of the premises shall have had an opportunity of replevying and giving proper security. The question therefore is whether the notice which has been given in this case, the material parts of which I have read, is a notice of distress (the words of the Act being "notice thereof") within the meaning of the Act of Parliament. The learned Official Referee has decided that as to goods which are only covered, if they are covered at all, by the words at the foot of the notice "and all other goods upon the premises (unless specially exempt) sufficient to satisfy the amount of this distress and expenses," this is not a good notice within the statute of the goods taken, which is what the statute requires it to be a notice of.

It is obvious that if this matter were being decided afresh this is a question which might permit of very considerable debate, and it might well be said that there are two alternative meanings which can be given to the statute: firstly, that every article distrained and intended to be sold or as to which the power of sale is claimed or reserved, must be specified in the way in which things are specified in a detailed inventory. I gather from that that was so decided at *nisi prius*,[7] in two cases before the case of *Wakeman v Lindsey*, to which I will come in a moment.[8] That would be one alternative. Of course that would be the most complete and businesslike way of giving the tenant or the owner of the goods, as the case might be, exact notice of what goods of his, or what goods on the premises in the case of the tenant, were in peril.

The other alternative would be that it is not necessary to give a detailed inventory or a detailed description of anything, but that it is enough to say:

[7] A trial of a civil case under the old court rules.

[8] See *Sims v Tuffs* and *Bishop v Bryant* earlier.

"I have distrained all the goods on the premises, and they will be sold if you do not replevy them." That is a matter that has not been argued and one which may arise some other time. It might be said those are the two alternatives and that one must adopt one or the other, and it is obvious that there are arguments for and against both, both on the actual wording of the statute (perhaps the only thing that can be considered) and on the convenience and reasonableness of the matter.

The embarrassment which has been caused here is that there are two cases in which this precise point was dealt with, that is, the meaning of the words "notice thereof" in the statute of William and Mary. There are two cases in which the Courts - both Courts of great authority - have had to consider whether a notice very much resembling in general form the notice in this case was a sufficient compliance with the statute.

The cases are *Wakeman v Lindsey* and *Kerby v Harding.*[9] In *Wakeman v Lindsey* the action was, as it is here, for an illegal sale of goods distrained, and on the ground, as here, that the notice did not cover the goods sold. The form of the notice is set out in the report. [22] After a very short inventory, the whole of which was this: "Tap room, one clock and weights, etc., etc.," it went on: "and any other goods and effects that may be found in and about the said premises"; then there is a comma, for what it may be worth; then: "to pay the said rent and expenses of this distress." The case was tried by Erle J and it was submitted that the notice was defective and legally no notice, and on that point the learned judge is recorded to have agreed with the counsel for the defendants, and to have held that the notice was sufficient in law. As has been pointed out in the argument which we have heard from the learned counsel for the appellant, it was assumed by the Court of Queen's Bench, in which the rule was moved and granted, that the intention was to distrain everything on the premises. But the Court evidently felt very great difficulty about the case, and I should gather from the judgments that it was new and surprising to them that a notice in this form should be adopted. Patteson J, who, of course, was a judge of very great experience and learning, uses the expression, "The wording of this form is extraordinary," and he criticises it. Then he says: "Perhaps the fair interpretation may be, all that are there; and, if in fact the broker has taken everything without exception, the practice may be very bad and loose, but I cannot say that it vitiates the sale." Coleridge J. is perhaps still more doubtful about it. He says: "I have felt doubt, and decide with reluctance." He says: "The object of [the] statute Distress for Rent Act 1689 was that the party distrained upon should have notice of what was taken," and he says that in his opinion the language of

[9] (1850) 14 QB 625; (1851) 6 Exch 234.

the notice in that case was not fair notice. He goes on, as did Patteson J, to say that the landlord distraining "may assume that the tenant knows sufficiently what [the goods distrained] are, and that to say 'all' is enough. I do not feel justified in laying down that, in such a case, there must be a specification." He decided with very great hesitation and evidently with great disapproval of the form which had been adopted. Erle J, who had originally tried the case, gave the last judgment, and he also expresses his dislike of the form of words. He says: "There is evil in the use of such forms; yet there may be more if a landlord is held liable to an action for the use of words somewhat too general, and if it is rendered necessary that at the time of making a distress every thing must be brought out for the purpose of being described and numbered." Then his final words are very material, I think, because they illustrate or define the difference between *Wakeman v Lindsey* and the case of *Kerby v Harding*. He says: "The word 'all' does give a description; so far that, if all be more than is required, the landlord is in peril for having taken too much." It is, of course, perfectly true in a sense that the word "all" does give a description; that is to say, however tedious the process may be, if one says one has taken all the goods on the premises, then it is only a question of going through them one by one and one finds exactly what has been distrained.

Then we come to the other case: *Kerby v Harding*. It is upon this that the learned Official Referee has decided the present case, and in his opinion - and perhaps there are not many opinions on such a point which are entitled to more weight - it is indistinguishable from the case which is now before the Court. That was an action, in substance, for selling goods without a proper notice under the statute. The words of the notice are not unlike the words of the notice in *Wakeman v Lindsey*, but they are different. They are general words after some particular chattels enumerated and described - namely, "and all other goods, chattels, and effects on the said premises that may be required in order to satisfy the above rent, together with all the expenses." This case was tried before Parke B. It is needless for me to say anything about the authority of Parke B. He had tried the case in the first instance, and he also gave the considered judgment of the Court upon the rule. What happened at the trial was this. The defendant said that *Wakeman v Lindsey* was an authority in favour of the sufficiency of the notice and that it was precisely in point; and so fine is the distinction between the two cases that Parke B, upon that authority being cited to him, ruled that the notice was sufficient; and it was upon that ground that the rule nisi for a new trial on the ground of misdirection was obtained, the jury having found a verdict for the defendant.

From the report of the argument, it appears that the same points were discussed there as have been discussed here. The learned counsel who appeared in support of the rule had to deal, of course, with *Wakeman v Lindsey*, and he said this: "The case of *Wakeman v Lindsey*, when examined, will be found very distinguishable from the present. The notice there included all the goods on the premises, whilst the present notice leaves the particular goods seized in uncertainty." That was the argument, and that, in substance, is the ratio of the decision given by the Court.

I pause for a moment to call attention to the very great authority of *Kerby v. Harding*, a decision on the precise point which is raised in the present appeal. We have the decision in *Wakeman v Lindsey* on facts so similar that Parke B accepted that judgment as decisive of the case before him. His ruling was challenged before the Court of Exchequer, of which Parke B, I gather, was President, for the report does not say that the Chief Baron was present - and he delivered the judgment. Having heard this matter fully argued, and of course there having been much more opportunity of considering it than there had been at *nisi prius*, he came to the conclusion that he had been wrong in following the case of *Wakeman v Lindsey*, and that that case was distinguishable from the case then before the Court. One can hardly imagine a stronger decision, because not only is there the great authority of the Court of Exchequer of 1851, but there is the fact that Parke B, certainly one of the most learned and accurate judges who ever sat in an English court, came to the conclusion, on argument, that he had been wrong in his direction at *nisi prius*, and gave judgment making the rule absolute for a new trial. I think the grounds upon which he did that are stated, as they always are in Parke B's judgments, with perfect lucidity and freedom from ambiguity. He had to deal there with the words which I have already read: "and all other goods, chattels, and effects on the said premises that may be required in order to satisfy the above rent, together with all the expenses."

I will read three or four passages from the judgment which show, I think, perfectly clearly what the decision was. Parke B says: "Upon consideration, we think that the terms of this notice are too vague, and do not point out any certain goods, chattels, or effects, except those which are before enumerated, which are the subject of the distress." Then he calls attention to the statute, and a little lower down he says: "It appears to us the statute not only requires the cause of taking to be mentioned, but also a notice to be given 'thereof,' that is, of the distress taken, which must include every thing taken." Then he refers to the fact that before the statute no notice at all was necessary, and he goes on: "This statute clearly requires some notice of the taking; and we think that, according to the reasonable construction of the statute, the notice ought to inform the tenant or the person whose effects are taken, by expressing what are the goods taken, and also what is the amount of rent in arrear. The general description, 'any other goods, chattels, and effects on the premises, or in and about the premises,' according to the decision of the Queen's Bench, is sufficient."

That is, I think, a perfectly accurate description of the decision in *Wakeman v Lindsey.* Whether the Court were right or wrong in reading the notice there as having that meaning is another matter and quite unnecessary for us to consider here, but it is quite clear that they decided that it was a good notice because they construed the notice as meaning that all the goods were taken; and if it did mean that, then, in the words of Erle J, the word "all" does itself give a description which covers everything that is on the premises; and that, Parke B says in *Kerby v. Harding* was the decision in *Wakeham v Lindsey.* He continues: "But this notice does not impound all the goods on the premises, but only the goods, chattels, and effects that may be required in order to satisfy the rent mentioned in it. This notice leaves it uncertain what goods are taken; and therefore we think that it is not sufficient, and that the subsequent sale of any of the articles not included by name in the inventory itself is an illegal sale, for which the defendants are responsible." Parke B meant that the tenant or the owner of the goods would be unable to put his hand on any particular chattel and say: This is taken, or is not taken.

There is no doubt - it is sufficiently obvious from the argument to which we have listened - that these two cases leave the law in a somewhat unfortunate and inconvenient condition; but if the ordinary principles upon which cases are to be weighed are to be observed it is impossible to see how light can be more decisively obtained from a decision than from the decision of *Kerby v Harding.* Not only, as I have said, is it a case of the very greatest authority, but it deals specifically with *Wakeman v Lindsey*, which is compared with it, and which appears on its face to be in conflict with it, and states in perfectly clear terms what the difference between them is.

In my opinion, it being quite clear that we ought to follow *Kerby v Harding*, the only question is whether it can be distinguished from the case before us. Of course, unless the words are absolutely the same, one can always suggest some ground of distinction, but the question is whether there is any real ground of distinction. The words in *Kerby v Harding* are: "All other goods, chattels, and effects on the said premises that may be required in order to satisfy the above rent, together with all the expenses." The words here are: "And all other goods upon the premises (unless specially exempt) sufficient to satisfy the amount of this distress and expenses." The words are not the same, but for my part I can see no distinction in meaning between "all ... goods ... that may be required in order to satisfy the above rent" and "all ... goods upon the premises ... sufficient to satisfy the amount of this distress." They mean precisely the same thing; and if it be true, as the Court of

Exchequer said, that the notice in *Kerby v Harding* left it uncertain what goods were taken, so, in my opinion, does the notice here.

I should like to add that the fact that the learned Official Referee considered that the case was absolutely indistinguishable from *Kerby v Harding* adds greatly to the confidence which I feel in coming to the same conclusion. In my opinion the learned Official Referee was perfectly right. I think I agree with every word of his judgment; I certainly do so with the whole of the substance of it, and the appeal must be dismissed with costs."

Humphreys J: "I concur, and I do so upon the ground stated in the judgment of the learned referee, where he says: "I confess, having considered the form of this notice and the form and the reasoning in the case of *Kerby v Harding*, as expressed in Parke B's judgment, I cannot differentiate the notice in this case from the notice in that case." If the decision in *Kerby v Harding*, which was a considered decision of the full Court, consisting of some of the most eminent judges who have graced the Bench of England, is to be reconsidered, it having been delivered in the year 1851, at least it cannot be by this Court today. I entirely agree with my Lord that we are bound to follow that case. Therefore the only question that I think we are at liberty to consider, in spite of the exceedingly able argument of Mr Eddy, is: Is it possible to distinguish the notice given in this case from the terms of the notice which was decided to be a bad notice in *Kerby v Harding*? My view of the two cases, which are certainly the two most important cases which have been referred to here, quite shortly is this. In *Wakeman v Lindsey* it was assumed that the person who distrained intended to distrain upon all the goods that were upon the premises, and as between the landlord and the tenant the Court came to the conclusion, though with considerable hesitation, that the expression, "any other goods and effects that may be found in and about the said premises," was an indication that all the goods which in fact were upon the premises were then seized; and the Court held - and, I think, this is the only decision in that case - that if a notice states sufficiently clearly that the seizure is a seizure of all the goods upon the premises, it is not necessary to set out the goods in detail in the form of an inventory or otherwise. Then came the case of *Kerby v Harding*, and the distinction which was drawn by Parke B in his judgment and taken by all the judges who agreed in that judgment, between the notice in that case and the notice in *Wakeman v Lindsey*, consisted in the introduction of four words in the notice in the later case. Those four words are the words, "that may be required," so that the notice read as being a notice that there had been taken in distress "all other goods, chattels, and effects on the said premises" - so far it was clearly an intimation that the distress extended to all the goods, but it continued, "that may be required in order to satisfy the above rent." The decision of *Kerby v Harding* is a decision, as I read it, to the effect that because of those words the notice in that case was not a notice which made it sufficiently certain what goods were taken; to use the language of the judgment itself: "This notice leaves it uncertain what goods are taken; and therefore we think that it is not sufficient."

In the present case it has been pointed out by Mr. Eddy, and I was struck by his argument, that the four words in the notice in *Kerby v Harding* are not to be found. The material words of the present notice are, "all other goods upon the premises (unless specially exempt) sufficient to satisfy the amount of this distress and expenses." I have endeavoured to distinguish the words in this case from the words in the notice in *Kerby v Harding*, but, like my Lord, I have found myself unable to do so. The words, of course, are different, but the language seems to me to be the same. I, therefore, agree with the learned Official Referee that it is impossible to distinguish *Kerby v Harding* from this case."

Commentary

As the judgment in *Davies* makes clear, inventories have a dual purpose. One is (of course) to indicate what goods have been levied. The inventory is seen as forming part of the notice of seizure which is presented to the debtor at the end of the levy, providing "tangible evidence" of *what debt* is being enforced and by the seizure of *what goods* this enforcement has been effected. It should be precise and *not* vague.[10]

Secondly, it is worth emphasising the point that taking an inventory also amounts to the first stage of the levy process as it is conventionally analysed.[11] The levy involves 'seizure' followed by 'impounding.' The document listing goods constitutes a 'constructive seizure' of items; they are identified as being allocated or appropriated to cover the debt and costs due. Nevertheless, a separate act (usually a separate document) is required to impound the goods, securing them in legal custody. Typically, that document is a walking possession agreement. Alone, therefore, an inventory does not complete the levy process- something more must be done or said by the bailiff. Making a list, in itself, does not change the status of the goods, this is why drafting an inventory which includes goods which are not leviable is *not* an illegal act for which a damages claim could issue. This is because the inventory alone does not interfere with the goods' disposition and does not constitute possession of them.[12]

---

[10] *Wilson v Nightingale* (1846) 8 QB 1034; *Skene v Midland Railway Co* (1911) *The Times*, February 28th, 3b, KBD.

[11] See the judgment in *Evans v S.Ribble BC* in chapter 3.

[12] *Ward v Haydon* (1797) 2 Esp 553.

To appreciate fully the role fulfilled by an inventory, it is necessary to return to some of the basic principles of distraint. Before 1689 distress could not be sold, so the goods seized had to be items which could be returned to their owner in exactly the same condition as they were taken. This accordingly excluded from seizure:

- Loose goods such as corn, unless in a cart (this was altered by the Distress for Rent Act 1689 s.2);[13]
- Perishable produce such as fruit and vegetables; and,
- Loose money (unless contained in a purse or cashbox) because the identical goods had to be restored to the tenant.[14]

For the purposes of the present discussion, the ability to identify the separate items distrained is the crucial provision here.[15] As the legal writer C. J. Jones explained, the duty to be able to enumerate specific goods means that inventories should be precise and that vague terminology and phrases should be avoided as "objectionable."[16] A clear and exact inventory specifying which goods are subject to legal custody is therefore vital to all those involved. This is for the benefit of several parties:

- *The debtor* - it informs the debtor exactly what has been levied, should s/he wish to challenge this or apply for replevin. It informs the debtor exactly what has been levied, so that s/he knows what should not be disposed of or removed. If goods *not* included on the inventory were later to be removed, it would enable the debtor to take court action;[17]
- *The creditor* - it protects the creditor by showing the items against which the debt is now secured. These can eventually be sold, if needs be, whilst in the meantime these goods have protection against interference by the debtor or others;
- *The bailiff* - it is part of the evidence that a levy has taken place and acts as confirmation that the bailiff has carried out a levy and that it is legitimate to make charges for that task. It guides a bailiff later sent to remove what goods may lawfully be removed. It enables a bailiff later sent to remove whether or not there has been poundbreach; and,
- *Third parties* - it enables third party claimants to seized goods to initiate interpleader or some other remedy and it tells other bailiffs who may

---

[13] See chapter 1 a& also my *Bailiffs' law*, vol.1, *A lawful trespass*, c.5, pp.140-142.
[14] 22 Ed.IV 50b/ Bro Abr Distress 58; 1 Roll Abr 666-667, H4; 2 Bac Abr Distress B.
[15] *Wilson v Ducket* (1675) 2 MR 61; 11 Hen.VII 14/ Bro Abr Distress 100; 21 Hen VII 39/ Bro Abr Distress 30.
[16] Jones, *On the collection & recovery of rentcharge*, 1849, p.96.
[17] See *Sims v Tuffs* and *Bishop v Bryant* earlier.

visit what is already impounded in the custody of the law and therefore cannot be impounded again,

Older writers provided their readers with recommended forms of inventories, which listed individual chattels building by building, room by room around the debtor's premises. Indisputably, this format achieves the purpose of ascertaining which particular items are involved. Baron Gilbert went as far as to suggest that a witness should also be present at the time of drawing up the document.[18] The preferred wording describing the goods levied upon should be either:

- Everything; or,
- An individualised list.

The former option was endorsed in the case of *Wakeman v Lindsey*. However, there are several problems with the practice, as the court itself stressed:

- It is potentially *excessive*;
- It is *bad practice*. The claim to 'all goods' was variously described by the judges as shameful, bad and loose, careless, extraordinary and as being inconsistent with good sense. The court felt that it was unfair for the bailiff to evade his duty under the Distress for Rent Act 1689 to give a clear notice of seizure to the tenant and it was with great reluctance that they endorsed the form of words. However, if the bailiff genuinely intends to seize all the goods, in such cases "all" will provide a succinct and clear description of what has been taken; and,
- The decision predates the Law of Distress Amendment Act 1888. Section 4 of this Act introduced the basic categories of exempt goods (tools and household effects). As a result, the decision in *Wakeman* may no longer be good guidance as to the law.

The decision in *Wakeman v Lindsey* can hardly be read as an enthusiastic endorsement of the 'all goods' inventory. The better course of action for enforcement agents must be to prefer the detailed, exact list which the weight of case law supports. Many readers will also be aware that the CIVEA code of conduct also discourages members from using such all-encompassing phrases on their inventories.[19]

---

[18] Bradby, *The law of distresses,* 1808, p.219, Gilbert, *The law & practice of distress & replevin,* 1823, p.230; Bullen, *Practical treatise on the law of distress for rent,* 1842, p.134; Jones p.96.
[19] See www.civea.co.uk, *Code of conduct & good practice guide,* p.8.

There is a potential element of doubt introduced into the judgment. *Davies* postdates the Law of Distress Amendment Act 1888 which exempted basic clothing, bedding and tools and the wording of the inventory alludes to these exemptions. Nonetheless, only £5 of goods were protected. Arguably the reason for the court not commenting on the reference to goods "specially exempt" in the inventory was that it was considered clear by all parties what would be denoted. Whilst there may not have been great scope for doubt in the late 1920s, the situation must be very different now the highly subjective and personal categories of exemption used to day are in operation. This issue was considered further in *Ambrose* (see later) but it is a further argument for avoiding any phraseology remotely resembling that condemned here.

In conclusion, therefore, the ideal is that goods are fully and accurately identified, showing make, model and serial number. Vague and catch-all phraseology on inventories are never likely to be acceptable. This conclusion is neatly underlined by two judgments of the Lord Chief Justice, Lord Tenterden. In *Streek v Gill* in 1829 he told the jury that "it was certainly the duty of brokers [bailiffs] to specify in the inventory the whole of the articles distrained..." A year later in *Green v Chapman* he repeated that "in the inventory of goods distrained every article ought to be particularised and not included under any such general head as sundries."[20]

Rai & Rai v Birmingham City Council (1993)

Unreported, before Mr J P Kieran, deputy stipendiary magistrate, Birmingham Magistrates' Court

Facts The complainants were indebted to the city council for unpaid community charges of £252.93, £302.84 and £315.50 for the years 1990-93 respectively. Liability orders were issued and Crilleys were instructed to levy. On July 21st 1993 two bailiffs called at the Rais' home, in which the complainant Mrs Rai and her 17 year old daughter, Mrs Bassi, were present. Mrs Rai had been advised by her neighbourhood office to refuse entry to the bailiffs and she did just that. She stood in the doorway and held the door slightly open but would not permit entry. The bailiffs asked to use her phone; she lied and said she did not have one. She was about to go out to speak to them when one bailiff put his foot in the door and then both pushed their way in, forcing her out of the way.

The bailiffs began to remove goods to two vans. They were told that some were Mrs Bassi's wedding presents but the removal continued. Staff from

[20] *The Times,* July 13th, 1827, 3c, KBD & February 20th, 1830 6a, KBD.

Crilleys office confirmed that calls were received on the day of the levy from Mrs Rai and from one of the bailiffs and that the Rais had complained of the removal of third party goods. Subsequently Mrs Bassi applied for return of certain items of property seized as they belonged to her (these included a television, VCR, stereo system and food blender).

On July 28th 1993 Mr and Mrs Rai laid a complaint of irregular distress against Birmingham City Council under regulation 40 of the Community Charge (Administration and Enforcement) Regulations 1989. At the hearing the bailiffs who attended denied forcing entry and also said that Mrs Rai told then that certain goods later claimed by Mrs Bassi were actually hers.

Judgment of Mr Kieran: "As far as any determination of facts is concerned, in this case I find in favour of the complainants. I had the benefit and the facility of observing all witnesses who testified before me. I was impressed by Mrs Rai. Her account was detailed concerning the events at the front door of her property. I have no reason to disbelieve her in regard to that particular account. More probably than not, I find that she was primed, via advice from the neighbourhood office, into not admitting the bailiffs to her house. I find it unlikely in that event that she would have left her front door wide open and this a gaping and inviting entry for those bailiffs. Moreover, I have no reason to disbelieve the quiet but measured way in which Mrs Bassi testified upon those opening events. As far as events inside the house as concerned, it is consistent with Mrs Rai's version of the facts that she had indeed occasion to speak by telephone to Crilley's office concerning the issues of the wedding presents and wanting the bailiffs out of her home. I find it improbable that Mrs Rai, when asked about the TV, the stereo and the Moulinex, would have stated that the items belonged to her and her husband. Those items clearly did not belong to her and the subsequent proof by Mrs Bassi of ownership and the reclamation of those goods tends, in my judgment, to establish the point perfectly.

I now need to consider the application of the facts to the regulation referred to in argument addressed to me by both counsel in the case. Mr Wise for counsel for the complainants had three main strands to his argument. Firstly, there was a forced entry to the property. Secondly, there was a removal from the property of goods not belonging to the debtors. Thirdly, proper documentation under regulation 39(5) of the 1989 Regulations was not left at the premises and not presented to Mrs Rai.

As far as the first point in concerned- the mode of entry to the house- that is plainly a levy that was irregular. It would be facile to place any other construction upon that method of entry. The bailiffs overstepped the mark. Perhaps through over zealous and frustrated feelings the bailiffs believed that they were being thwarted from what otherwise would have been proper execution of their powers.

In regard to the second point, the removal of the goods (not the debtor's goods) again, in my judgment, the levy was irregular. The bailiffs do have a duty of care to exercise. They must act with discernment and judgment. The power to distrain is not a dragnet trawling all within it. If the bailiffs are put on notice- as I find they were in this particular case- that certain goods do not allegedly belong to the debtor, then the bailiffs must act with due caution and circumspection.

In regard to the third point- a breach of regulation 39(5)- I believe that it is important to remind myself of the precise wording of this particular subsection of the regulation. The subsection states "The person levying distress on behalf of the authority ... shall hand to the debtor or leave at the premises where distress is levied a copy of this regulation and schedule 5 and a memorandum setting out the appropriate amount and shall hand to the debtor a copy of any close or walking possession agreement entered into." The regulation is couched in strict and mandatory terms. It imposes obligations upon the bailiff. In many respects, this particular regulation and the compunction that it imposes on the bailiff is analogous to the responsibilities attaching to police officers who effect warrants to search property in accordance with PACE. Certain copy notices simply must be served upon the appropriate party. In my judgment, the defendant's submission fails despite its attractive, albeit specious, presentation. It simply will not do to abbreviate the statutory obligation under reg.39(5) by somewhat obliquely trying to circumvent this requirement by reference to a letter which, says the defence, was despatched to Mrs Rai an appreciable period before July 21st 1993- that is, on September 16th 1992. In my judgment, it is plainly the intention of the legislation that schedule 5 and its terms should be served upon the debtor at the time when the levy for distress is taking instant effect. I therefore uphold the submission made to me in this respect by Mr Wise.

And so, I find that there has been a threefold commission of irregular levy. What remedy applies in so far as these complainants are concerned? In accordance with regulation 40(3) I order that the goods distrained shall be discharged if they are in the possession of the authority, as I believe to be the case."

Commentary

The Rai case, although only a magistrates' court decision, is instructive in several ways:

- It is a positive example of a complaint to a magistrates' court regarding an 'irregular' levy of distraint. The stipendiary magistrate found that the levy was irregular on all three of the points argued and accordingly ordered return of the goods removed. In fact the forced entry and seizure of third party property were illegal and could have rendered the distraint trespass *ab initio* but no award of damages was made;
- The duty to leave the documents required by the Regulations (now reg.45(5) for council tax) is mandatory. The debtor needs to know what is due, what the charges are, what has been levied, so that payment may be made or challenges may be brought or notice may be given to third parties who may wish to make claims to the goods listed. Failure to supply these documents was an irregularity but no special damages seem to have been claimed (see *Ambrose* and *Wilson* later); and,
- Far more important is the ruling on the conduct of the levy. In emphasising the bailiff's duty of care and his obligation to deal with claims of ownership made during the levy, the judge underlined the fact that distraint is increasingly a dialogue between enforcement agent and debtor. The bailiff needs to be thorough in his examination of a property and, equally, thorough in listening to debtors' responses to a proposed levy: what is owned by strangers; what is a basic necessity?

The validity of the magistrates' decision on the bailiff's obligations is underlined by the recent High Court decision in *Huntress Search v Canapeum Ltd & DSI Foods* [2010].[21] This was an appeal against a decision made in interpleader proceedings. The High Court enforcement officers unsuccessfully tried to overturn an order of the High Court permitting DSI Foods to bring a claim for substantial damages against them.

The case arose as follows. Huntress Search obtained a county court judgment for £4872 against Canapeum. This was transferred to the High Court for enforcement and a writ was issued for execution at Canapeum's business premises. In the meantime, Canapeum went into administration. An officer was directed to levy at Unit 8, Victoria Industrial Estate, Acton. He called instead at Units 5/6, the premises of DSI Foods. DSI had purchased from the administrators various assets of Canapeum, such as the lease for the units, all business equipment and even the business name. DSI did *not* assume liability for the company's debts.

When the HCEO called, DSI's accountant tried to show him copies of documentation relating to the purchase of the assets. The officer refused to inspect them; he refused to speak to the administrators and he acted in what

[21] EWHC 1270 (QB).

the High Court master called a 'heavy handed manner' by starting to remove goods. DSI's staff were told to leave the premises because the HCEO wished to seize the machinery and equipment they were using. DSI produce in-flight meals for airlines. Despite vigorous protests from company staff, the HCEO insisted on entering the production area without a white coat or hairnet. This led to contamination of all the food produced during that shift, which had to be thrown away.

The High Court master agreed with DSI that the HCEO had acted in a high handed and unprofessional manner. On appeal, although the HCEOs argued that DSI's proper conduct on the day would have been to initiate an immediate interpleader claim on the basis that the goods were not the property of the judgment debtor, Mr Justice Eady was not prepared to reverse the master's decision or to protect the HCEO from court action.

This was a case of execution dealt with in quite a different manner by the courts, but the essential guidance for enforcement agents seems to be the same. Any bailiff levying is under a duty to act with care, caution and common sense. Plausible claims to goods *must* be considered. Whilst it may be the legally correct procedure, insisting on formal proceedings and refusing to inspect any evidence made available at the time of the levy, may seem overly formal and inflexible and may serve only to aggravate a situation.

Toseland Building Supplies Ltd v J Bishop trading as T Bishop (Groundworks) [1993] Court of Appeal, October 28th 1993

Facts A writ of *fieri facias* was issued to the Sheriff of Bedford for execution against the defendant and a JCB digger was levied upon. Mr Bishop claimed that this machine should have been exempted from execution as it was necessary to his business. It was, he asserted, protected as a "vehicle ... necessary to [him] for use personally in his employment, business or vocation."

The sheriff made an application for relief in the local district registry. The district judge found in favour of the defendant but the matter was appealed to the High Court. The evidence submitted to the Court was that Bishop generally hired out the digger with himself as driver but that occasionally he allowed subcontractors to drive it and, indeed, the judgment creditors had hired the machine from him to be driven by another person. The judge concluded that the JCB was not for use personally by Bishop alone and was therefore not exempt from seizure. Mr Bishop appealed to the Court of Appeal.

Judgment of Steyn LJ: "Here it is important to bear in mind what the correct approach is in a case like this. The general principle is that, *prima facie*, all the judgment debtor's goods are liable to seizure under a writ of *fieri facias.* If a judgment debtor claims to the benefit of a statutory exemption, the burden of showing that exemption resist squarely on him."

Turning to the appellant's evidence, Steyn LJ observed that "this affidavit accepts that other employers are allowed to drive the JCB. It may well be that he allows his employees to use it- in which case, it is not for his personal use." He repeated: "It must be said that, when the sheriff seizes goods he seizes all the goods, and if the judgment debtor maintains that some are tools of trade then the burden is on him to raise this as an issue." In conclusion therefore "In this case the judgment debtor ran a business and, in the course of that business, he used the JCB mainly by himself but also hired it out on contracts in which it was driven by his employees. For this reason the JCB was not something for use personally by him." Accordingly, the appeal was dismissed.

Commentary

This case is significant because it is almost unique in dealing with the precise interpretation of the modern category of exemption for basic tools of the trade. Unfortunately for Mr Bishop, the Court of Appeal applied a strict reading of the exemption and concluded that any evidence of use by third parties would be fatal to the claim of privilege.

The other case of significance is the Queens Bench Division judgment in *Thompson v Bertie* [2007].[22] Mr Thompson challenged seizure of his motor bike under a writ of *fi fa* on the grounds that he used it to get to his part-time job as a university lecturer and also to travel to private lectures and martial arts classes that he taught. His main argument was that it was more economical for him to travel by bike than by public transport. Teare J did not accept this interpretation of the exemption. A vehicle required for "business, employment or vocation" is one that is directly necessary for performing that work. As a sociology lecturer, using the bike to travel to and from where he exercised his vocation, Mr Thompson did not satisfy the condition. Certainly, the fact that it was cheaper for him to travel this way did *not* mean that the bike was used *for* his employment. In reaching this conclusion, Teare J is wholly in line with the reasoning of Canadian cases described in *Law of Seizure of Goods.*[23]

---

[22] [2007] EWHC 2238 (QB); see too *Moffatt v Lemkin* & *Brookes v Harris* in the *Introduction.*
[23] *Law of Seizure of Goods*, 9.10.

It will also be noted from the *Toseland* judgment that the burden of making and proving the claim falls squarely on the debtor. In this latter judgment the Court merely followed the older authority of *Gonsky v Durrell* [1918].[24] In this the Court of Appeal interpreted the terms of the then County Courts Act very strictly and insisted that the aggrieved person fully make out their case in line with the terms of the statutory protection. Earlier decisions on these exemptions tended to impose a greater responsibility on the bailiff and more recent judgments, such as *Ambrose* and *Rai*, generally have preferred this approach. In *Taylor v Ashworth* (1910) Parry J expressed the opinion that the bailiff's duty was to consider the interests of the debtor as well as those of the creditor. Although no claim for exemption might be made during the levy, the bailiff ought to make "reasonable and proper enquiry" as to tools of the trade on the premises and should enquire "properly and carefully" about basic household items. If any doubt exists, erring on the side of the debtor was the best course of action. Failure to make enquiries about exempt items could endanger a certificate. In *Atkinson v Lyons* (1905) Emden J warned against seizing tools of the trade unless (at least) the debtor signed the inventory to confirm that an item was not an essential tool and that sh/e consented to its seizure. In *Singer Manufacturing Co v Butterfield* (1902) the judge suggested that the debtor be invited to select the items to be treated as exempt.[25] The reason for this detailed advice was the frequency with which the courts saw cases of basic tools and household items being illegally distrained.[26] A callous and negligent attitude on the part of the bailiff to the basic protection afforded to debtors may lead to the loss of a certificate.[27]

Finally, in the *Toseland* case an attempt was made by the appellant to challenge the form of proceedings adopted by the sheriff in the district registry. The sheriff's application had been by way of interpleader under RSC Order 17. The Court rejected this argument by Mr Bishop, stating that the form of proceedings was irrelevant: if there was an important question to be resolved by the courts the manner in which it was brought before them was unimportant. It may be noted that, since 1993, it has been widely accepted that interpleader proceedings are an acceptable forum in which to raise claims of exemption from execution.

---

[24] [1918] 2 KB 71.

[25] (1910) 129 LT 578; (1905) 13 PMR 963; (1902) 114 LT 39.

[26] *Haines v Adams* (1889) 33 EG 476; *Levy v Robins* (1891) 38 EG 60; *Brown v Atkins* (1894) 2 PMR 491; *Bushbridge v Harvey* (1897) 49 EG 254; *Jones Sewing Machine Co v Porter & Sons* (1897) 49 EG 955; *The Times* February 2nd 1906 3f.

[27] *Smith v Thomas & Wilberforce* (1899) 53 EG 710; *Black v Moore & Thompson* (1908) 59 Property Owner's Journal 4.

Ambrose v Nottingham City Council (2004) District Judge Morris Cooper, Nottingham Magistrates' Court, October 2004

Background A liability order was made against Mr and Mrs Ambrose for unpaid council tax. In September 2004 a bailiff employed by Rossendale Ltd attended their home to levy distraint. The detailed conduct of that levy, and the practice on levying operated by the company, were the subject of the case.

Rossendales operated a 'two tier' levy system. The first tier was a 'first call bailiff' making contact. He operated alone in a car and his role was to assess the situation, conduct a levy and prepare and leave behind the necessary documentation (inventory, walking possession agreement, application to pay by instalments and so on). The company policy was to try to include at least 7 items on the inventory, supported by a pre-printed claim to "all other goods on the premises unless exempt or specially exempt by statute." The second tier of the system was the 'van bailiff' who actually removed goods for sale. Where walking possession was agreed, removal only occurred if payments were not made. The company always sought to agree walking possession where some goods of value were available. Mrs Ambrose agreed to pay £30pm subject to walking possession. However, she felt that a levy should not have been made at all because she did not have sufficient goods to cover the outstanding council tax, let alone additional charges on top. She sought advice from a local law centre and as a result took court proceedings.

Mrs Ambrose issued a complaint to the magistrates' court under regulation 46 of the Council Tax (Administration & Enforcement) Regulations 1992 on the basis that the levy had been irregular. Her argument was that:

- Exempt goods and third party goods were included in the levy;
- The bailiff had failed to conduct an adequate inspection of the premises to satisfy himself that only a sufficient quantity of goods was being seized. He was invited to do this in order to impress upon him the absence of seizable goods on the premises, but declined to do so as it was not company policy for the first call bailiff to undertake such an inspection; and,
- The notice of distress was too vague to inform Mrs Ambrose, or other bailiffs who might visit, what had or had not been levied.

Judgment After outlining the facts and the relevant law the district judge continued:

"Mrs Ambrose's appeal raises quite fundamental questions concerning the nature of the process of levying distress and is clearly intended to mount a legal challenge to the so-called 'two tier' procedure used by Rossendale Ltd on behalf of a very large number of local authorities. I am aware, therefore, that the outcome of these proceedings could have very significant consequences. However ... the decision in this case will be confined to the issues arising on the facts of the case.

Most of the law of distress has developed in the context of distress for rent. A convenient statement of the law is contained in the judgment of Simon Brown J in *Evans v South Ribble Borough Council* [1992]. [The district judge then summarised the conclusions of the *Evans* case as to the nature and elements of the levy process- see chapter 3- and its application to the case of Mrs Ambrose. He noted that *Evans* was concerned with entry, whereas *Ambrose* was concerned with levying.]

The extent of the bailiff's powers, in relation to council tax, is subject to the clear wording of reg.45(1) of the 1992 Regulations. Thus, he can levy 'the appropriate amount' ... by distress and sale of the 'goods of the debtor', the interpretation of which arises in this case in relation to hired goods. An important limitation on the bailiff's powers is contained in reg.45(1A) which deals with goods that are in effect exempted from distraint [i.e. the exemptions that apply to basic tools of the trade and basic household items].

It is important to note that, although reg.45(5) of the 1992 Regulations requires that certain documents are to be given to the debtor by the bailiff, nothing in those regulations requires a notice of distress or an inventory of goods seized or exempted. This is in contrast with the rules relating to distress for rent, which do require a notice of distress, including an inventory of the goods distrained, to be given.

[The judge then discussed *Davies v Property & Reversionary Co Ltd* [1929]- see earlier. He continued:] "The Davies case is, undoubtedly, an important authority, but it is concerned as I have already said, with what can amount to an adequate notice of distress (under the Distress for Rent Act 1689), something which the statutory provisions do not require in respect of the enforcement of council tax, albeit that in the case I am dealing with there was, in fact, a notice of distress that included an inventory incorporating a global seizure of un-itemised goods. However, a notice of distress, whether or not required by statute, merely records the distraint that took place. The issue in the present case is whether there was an irregular distraint....

There are no issues in this case concerning entry into the premises, the first stage of the process of distress. It is common ground that the bailiff entered the home of Mrs Ambrose lawfully, by invitation. The issues concern the second and third stages, seizure and impounding. It follows from my findings of fact that the bailiff seized furniture that was necessary for satisfying the basic domestic needs of Mrs Ambrose and her family. There were three people living in the house, although the bailiff did not investigate the fact. By seizing the sofa, footstool and four dining chairs, on his own evidence, the bailiff left only the chair he was sitting on and possibly one other to satisfy domestic needs. I do not think that the defendant can rely on the words "unless exempt or specially exempt by statute" on the notice of distress as qualifying the seizure of articles that the bailiff has specifically itemised, when, on my findings, he was told that there was no other seating in the house. Those words can only qualify "and all other goods on the premises." Under the two tier system used by Rossendale Ltd, the function of the van bailiffs can only be to take away for sale goods already distrained upon or to abandon the whole or part of the levy. The prohibition in reg.45(1A) of the 1992 Regulations applies at the point of seizure and if proscribed articles have been identified and seized the bailiff has exceeded his authority.

The word 'irregular' in reg.46(3) of the 1992 Regulations is not defined or explained and I have not been referred to any authorities as to what it might mean. The case has been argued on the basis that the levy was not unlawful, but is alleged to have been irregular within reg.46(3). I find that there was an irregularity in the seizure stage of levying distress, in that exempted furniture was seized.

Having found this irregularity proved, I have to consider next whether the irregularity was rectified by Mrs Ambrose having entered into a walking possession agreement. The law is unclear as to the precise effect of such an agreement. What is clear to me, however, is that such an agreement is concerned with the impounding stage of the distraint and is capable of completing that final stage of the process. The seizure has already taken place before a walking possession agreement is entered into. The walking possession agreement then regulates what is to happen to the goods after seizure. A debtor such as Mrs Ambrose is faced with the stark choice of either entering into such an agreement- and thereby retaining the use of the seized goods for the time being- or refusing to enter into such an agreement and thereby facing the prospect of them being removed or, at the very least, held in close possession. I do not think it right to interpret such an agreement as acquiescing to a seizure that has been irregular. The essence of the agreement is concerned with what happens after seizure. I do not accept that Mrs Ambrose waived the irregular seizure of her furniture by signing a walking possession agreement and I think that it is right to regard her as aggrieved by the levy for the purposes of reg.46(1) of the 1992 Regulations.

The bailiff also seized a television and video recorder that did not belong to Mrs Ambrose, but were hired. I have found that she mentioned this to the bailiff at the time of the seizure, although she clearly did not provide further proof until a later date. Regulation 45(1) provides the power to levy the appropriate amount by "distress and sale of the goods of the debtor." The television and video recorder that the bailiff distrained upon were not sold; the levy on them was abandoned. I am only concerned in this case with the distress. The meaning of the words "goods of the debtor" is open to interpretation, as it is not further defined in the regulations and I have been referred to no decision of any court on the point. Does it mean that the debtor must own the goods outright or is an interest short of that sufficient? In practice it is very easy for the debtor to claim that articles in his house do not belong to him and I can see that an interpretation of these words in the regulations that would require a bailiff to ascertain the ownership of goods before distraining on them would be likely to frustrate the whole process of distraint. I cannot accept that this is what was intended when the Regulations were made. I am satisfied that regulation 45(1) of the 1992 Regulations is wide enough to authorise distraint on goods that are the goods of the debtor in the sense that the debtor has physical possession and control of them.

I now turn to the issues concerning the final words of the notice of distress. Those words evidence the fact that the bailiff in this case distrained upon "all other goods on the premises unless exempt or specially exempt by statute" without inspecting the premises to ascertain the extent of the seizure or listing exempt articles. It seems to me that this is a dangerous practice and deserves the criticism that a similar levy of distress attracted in *Wakeman v Lindsey.* The bailiff is risking levying an excessive distress and is entirely reliant upon an assessment made from what he sees in one room of the premises and what he may be told by a debtor who may have every reason to conceal the truth from him. In the present case, there was no excessive levy, as it turned out. The facts of the present case also illustrate the danger of seizing exempted goods.

The issue here is whether proceeding in this way gives rise to any irregularity. Parliament, for many years, has required a notice of distress and an inventory in distress for rent cases, but it is clear from *Wakeman v Lindsey* and *Davies v Property & Reversionary Co Ltd* that, even where such documents are required, the law does not compel the bailiff to search the premises and complete an item by item inventory where, on the facts, the value of all of the property is less than the debt owed. On the other hand, where the total value of the goods in the house is, or may be, higher than the debt and charges owed, it is clearly necessary to identify which goods have been seized in order (a) to avoid an excessive levy and (b) so that the debtor knows which articles have been distrained upon and which have not. That issue is different from ascertaining which items may be necessaries and, as a result, exempt from the levy, but it is argued that there is a similar need for certainty.

I have in mind the practical implications. What items are necessary for the debtor's work or domestic needs surely cannot be ascertained by a bailiff without some input from the debtor. A bailiff can only guess at what tools and equipment a debtor might need for his work, or what clothing, equipment, provisions etc a debtor might need for the family. All kinds of scenarios could arise concerning family members with special needs etc. Account also has to be taken of the fact that the debtor might not always be present when the bailiff arrives to distrain.

Having said all of that, however, I return to reg.45(1A) itself, which prohibits seizure of necessaries in very clear terms. Where a bailiff is said to have seized all goods except those exempted, without identifying the items that are exempted, has there been a seizure that contravenes the Regulations? On the bare wording of it there has not, but in reality it is left to the van bailiffs to decide which articles are exempt from seizure after the seizure has taken place.

In this case there was a walking possession agreement, whereby Mrs Ambrose agreed to the bailiff taking possession of "those goods." How can "those goods" be identified? The words clearly relate to the goods mentioned on the notice of distress, but this does not help in identifying precisely which items in the house are exempt. If Mrs Ambrose wanted to exchange some of her personal belongings that could come under the heading of exempt goods, she would not know what was included in the agreement and what was not. The same would apply if her daughter left home and wanted to take some of the necessaries with her.

None of the authorities that I have been referred to deal with the question of identifying exempt goods when carrying out a global seizure. In *Davies v Property & Reversionary Co Ltd* the notice of distress included an inventory, setting out various articles of household furniture, followed by the words "and all other goods upon the premises (unless specially exempt) sufficient to satisfy the amount of this distress and expenses." That case, as I have already said, did not turn on the effect of the words "unless specially exempt" in parenthesis and there appears to have been no discussion or argument relating to those words. I am not impressed with the argument to the effect that this form of words is acceptable because no point was taken on it in the *Davies* case and it has been widely used in practice. In my judgment, a global seizure that is said to exclude exempt goods can be a regular seizure only if the exempted goods are identified so that it is possible to ascertain exactly what has been seized at the time seizure took place.

I have to interpret the law within the framework of the 1992 Regulations. The walking possession agreement is part of that framework. In the present case, it is impossible to ascertain what is meant by the words "those goods" in the walking possession agreement, because of the uncertainty as to precisely what articles are exempted. It follows that I find that the levy was irregular for this reason in addition to my other findings. I recognise that, if I am right in my judgment, there would have to be a fundamental change of practice to avoid irregularities. I do not accept the submission that the availability of legal advice on what may or may not amount to necessaries is an answer to this problem. Neither do I accept the argument that Mrs Ambrose has waived her right to complain by entering into the agreement. The 1992 Regulations clearly prohibit any seizure of proscribed articles and it must, in my judgment, be possible to ascertain at the time of seizure what has been seized and what has not.

I reject the argument advanced on behalf of Mrs Ambrose that the levy was also irregular because it is unreasonable and disproportionate to levy on all of a debtor's goods. I see no justification for placing this gloss on the clear terms of the 1992 Regulations, which permit a levy of the "appropriate amount."

I do not think it is necessary for me to consider, for the purposes of this appeal, whether the walking possession agreement was, or was not, a valid contract. So far as the complainant's submissions about the ECHR are concerned, I do not find it necessary to deal with this point because of my findings on domestic law.

Order distress irregular and seized goods to be released to Mrs Ambrose."

Commentary

I shall begin by making a few observations on the judgment:

- *The meaning of irregular* in regulation 46. It is surprising that neither party was able to direct the district judge to authority on the meaning of the term in the context of local tax distraint. It was held in *Steel Linings v Bibby* [1993] (see chapter 7) that 'irregular' denoted *any* wrongful act by a bailiff. The *Ambrose* case proceeded on the basis that the levy was not unlawful, but it appears that aspects of it in fact were:
    - *Levy on exempt goods-* by seizing items exempted from distraint by the Regulations, this aspect of the levy was

illegal and invalidated as a result. That said, it did not prejudice the entire levy;[28]

- *Levy on third party goods* - as in the paragraph above, seizure of third party property was a trespass to the extent that such property was distrained (but see later discussion).

On the key issue of the form of the inventory, this probably was an irregularity in the strict sense of the term.[29]

- *Nature of walking possession*- the district judge did not feel that he needed to explore the question of whether the walking possession agreement constituted a valid contract, but he did find that its signature, under duress, did not bar Mrs Ambrose from later bringing proceedings to challenge its validity. On this point it is worth observing that it is a common misconception to treat walking possession as some form of contract freely entered into between equal parties. This view arises naturally from the use of the term 'agreement' but it loses sight of the nature and purpose of walking possession. In the last decade of the nineteenth century walking possession was devised as a substitute for close possession, whereby a bailiff was left guarding goods on the premises. Understandably, close possession had become inconvenient and costly and an alternative more acceptable to both parties was developed.[30] Effectively, the debtor (or another person on the premises) is appointed as possession man to guard the distrained goods. This being so, the signatory is merely assenting to the duties of the role. If s/he does not agree to these responsibilities, or the bailiff does not consider that the person is suitable, another form of impounding may be chosen (see also the discussion of walking possession in chapter 3).
- *Seizure of hired goods*- in the absence of case law guidance, the district judge reached the conclusion that third party goods might lawfully be levied as it was in the "order and disposition" of the debtor. Very possibly he was influenced in this by the law of distress for rent.[31] If this speculation is correct, it would have been a false analogy as statutory distraint, such as for local taxes, is far more analogous to executions than to distress for rent.[32] There is good authority to the effect that rented goods are not distrainable in statutory distraint.[33]

---

[28] *Canadian Pacific Wine Co v Tuley* [1921] 2 AC 417; *Elias v Pasmore* [1934] 2 KB 164; *Owen & Smith v Reo* (1934) 151 LT 274.

[29] See *Law of seizure of goods,* 2nd edition, 10.8.

[30] See *A lawful trespass,* chapter 8.

[31] Law of Distress Amendment Act 1888 s.4(1); see *Law of seizure of goods* 9.24.

[32] *Hutchins v Chambers* (1758) 1 Burr 579; *Potts v Hickman* [1941] AC 212; *Steel Linings v Bibby* & *Quinlan v Hammersmith & Fulham* in chapter 7.

[33] *Prudential Mortgage Co v St Marylebone (Mayor)* (1910) 8 LGR 901; *Carter v Vestry of St Mary* (1900) 64 JP 548; *Law of Seizure of Goods* 9.16 & 9.17.

The main part of the judgment is that concerned with the form of the inventory. In this regard the *Ambrose* case significantly develops the decision in *Davies* (see earlier). This was necessary and important for a couple of reasons:

- The law has changed appreciably since 1929. When the inventory used in *Davies* excluded any goods "specially exempt" it referred, in part, to the statutory exemptions of wearing apparel and bedding and tools of the trade to the value of £5. This is, of course, very different from the extensive and subjective exceptions set out in reg.45(1A) of the 1992 Regulations; and,
- *Davies* was a distress for rent case, a situation markedly different in some respects to statutory distraint for local taxes and the like. The district judge was at pains several times to point out that distress for rent expressly requires a notice of seizure and inventory. This is not the case in council tax; rather, reg.45(5) requires various documents including any walking possession agreement made to be left at the premises. Of course, as the judgment itself suggests, a possession agreement is substantially meaningless without some related inventory of the goods impounded, so that in practice all enforcement agencies will deliver a combined notice of seizure, inventory and walking possession agreement when levying.

What the *Ambrose* judgment does is to develop the law on the treatment of exempt property. The risk of a global seizure without a proper search of the premises is that it may be excessive and may include exempted items. There has been a longstanding duty on bailiffs to conduct a thorough and diligent levy;[34] the *Ambrose* case extends this by demonstrating that under the present law, some form of dialogue with the debtor is required to determine what items should be treated as basic necessities. If 'all goods except exempt goods' are to be seized, which goods are to be treated as excepted must be ascertained and identified. Just as the court in *Davies* felt that the inventory used was too vague because it claimed 'all goods sufficient', the inventory in *Ambrose* was too vague because it failed to clarify what was regarded as exempt. Some firms have tried in recent years to get around the judgment by supplying (or at least claiming that they supply) a leaflet outlining the statutory exemptions. It should be apparent that this is an inadequate response as the bailiff's job is to apply these exemptions in each individual case.

---

[34] *Mullett v Challis* (1851) 16 QBD 239; *Doe d Haverson v Franks* (1847) 2 C&K 678.

Lastly, arguments about the disproportionate nature of the levy were rejected in the case of Mrs Ambrose. It was accepted that she had insufficient goods to cover the sum due under the liability order, so from that point of view a levy against her could never be disproportionate. There will still be cases where particular levies are disproportionate in the sense in which the district judge used it- excessive amounts are seized to cover the debt and costs. This is the traditional interpretation of an 'excessive distress.' However, as suggested earlier in chapter 1, excessive should perhaps be understood as 'unreasonable' and should also comprehend levies on valueless or negligible quantities of goods. Indeed , in such cases, the proper response of the bailiff may be to accept that there are 'no goods' and to abandon the levy. See for example the case of *Dennis v Whetham* from 1874. Archbald J stated in his judgment that if it is found that the rent that is due exceeds the value of the goods available, an officer levying execution is excused from levying and can make a return of *nulla bona.* He continued by saying that, if the fees and expenses of the levy absorb the proceeds of sale, the officer might also return *nulla bona.* Presumably, if the officer judged that the value of the goods was too low, he might be excused from levying and might simply make a return of no goods without the need for a seizure and sale.[35]

One startlingly thing about the decision in *Ambrose,* and that in *Davies* before it, is that it has been substantially ignored by the enforcement sector. Several large national firms continued to use identical forms of inventory for another 6 years at least after the judgment. Equally common is the continued appearance of levies substantially comprising basic, exempt furniture such as (just as in Ambrose) all forms of seating. It is often said that these have been listed on the inventory, but with no intention ever of removing them. The judgment in *Ambrose* deals with this spurious response: what counts is seizure is on the inventory and impounding by walking possession- as happened in this case- and which was found to be 'irregular' and wrongful. As the District Judge said, "The prohibition ... applies at the point of seizure and if proscribed articles have been identified and seized the bailiff has exceeded his authority."

In this connection, the reader is referred to the judgment in *Culligan* in chapter 5 in which the district judge warned that, whilst he would not countenance a certification complaint at that time, continued use of practices held to be unlawful could be good grounds for considering revocation of a certificate in the future. The practice of the two stage levy, which motivated the adoption of the 'global seizure' also persists. It may be worth concluding by reviewing its lawfulness more broadly.

[35] *Dennis v Whetham* [1874] 9 QB 345.

As District Judge Cooper observed, Mrs Ambrose's appeal was "clearly intended to mount a legal challenge to the so-called 'two tier' procedure..." The decision on the form of the inventory obviously undermined a key element of this procedure. Other case authorities suggest that there are fundamental problems with other aspects of it too. Two separate but related principles of the laws of distress are involved. The first was seen earlier in the judgment in *Bishop v Bryant*: "once an inventory has been taken, the bailiff cannot add to it later." If, for whatever reason, more, better or more valuable goods are found at a later occasion, they may *not* be levied and tacked onto the seizure. The bailiff's duty is to do a thorough search of the property at the time of taking the inventory. If goods are overlooked but found later, they cannot be seized. If such items are seized, the debtor would be able to claim for damages.[36] It seems that this will be the case even if the seizure of the extra items was unintentional.[37]

That the bailiff should be penalised for his own negligence is quite predictable. This first principle is very clear cut; the second principle is a little more nuanced. This is the important rule is that bailiffs only get *one* chance to levy; second levies are prohibited. This is because, as Baron Parke explained in *Bagge v Mawby* (1853), a landlord "must not vex his tenant by the exercise on two occasions of this summary remedy ... It is vexatious to levy twice unless there is some legal ground for doing so."[38]

As a general statement, then, second levies are oppressive and excessive and should be avoided. If a second levy is made without good reason, the debtor would be able to claim damages.[39] There is a number of ways in which wrongful second levies can come about:

- The debt may be split between two separate levies;[40]
- A perfectly lawful levy may have been made, but possession is then abandoned without good cause;[41] or,
- Most relevant to our present discussion, the bailiff had a fair opportunity to levy but, through his own "folly" or negligence, he failed to seize sufficient when it was available.[42]

---

[36] See *Bishop v Bryant* earlier.
[37] *Smith v Torr* (1862) 3 F&F 505.
[38] (1853) 8 Exch 64.
[39] *Lear v Caldecott* (1843) 4 QB 123.
[40] *Wallis v Savill* (1701) 2 Lutw 1532.
[41] *Smith v Gordon* (1833) 4 B&A 413; *Dawson v Cropp* (1845) 1 CB 961; *Bagge v Mawby* (1853) 8 Exch 64. Note, however, that the debtor will have to show that the value of the goods distrained on the first occasion was sufficient to cover the debt and costs- *Lear v Edmonds* (1817) 1 B&A 157, *Lingham v Warren* (1820) 2 B&B 37 & *Hudd v Ravenor* (1821) 2 B&B 662.
[42] *Anon* (1550) Moore KB p.7 pl.26; *Anon* (1583) Cro Eliz p.13 pl.8.

Despite what has just been said, and as has already been suggested, in certain situations a second levy *may* be permissible and lawful:

- After a replevy or where one party dies;[43]
- If there is a genuine mistake about the valuation of the goods, or if the value of the items is uncertain and the bailiff wishes to avoid an excessive levy, as a result of which he acts with "tenderness and moderation" towards the debtor by taking a number of small inventories;[44]
- If insufficient goods were found on the premises at the time of first levy;[45] or,
- If the bailiff agrees to withdraw or postpone the levy at the behest of the debtor.[46]

To summarise, if there is a lawful or legal reason why the first levy was not carried through to its logical conclusion (payment or sale), the bailiff is entitled to return and try again. This can include acting at the instigation of the debtor.[47]

It does not seem that either of these principles apply to 'two stage levies' as they are normally conducted. If it is accepted that 'catch-all' inventories are not lawful, then the subsequent addition of any items is also unlawful. Next, none of the reasons which would validate a second levy seem to apply. The cursory inventories taken do not allow the bailiff fully to assess the value and quantity of goods available (and, of course, the whole point of the procedure is to avoid spending time in this way). Likewise, the summary nature of the first inventory is the bailiff's initiative, not the debtor's, although it may be presented as being for the debtor's benefit in terms of upset and disturbance minimised. In summary, two stage levies are a short cut procedure which (like many short cuts in the law of distress) are seriously flawed.

Conclusions

Subjective categories of exempt goods benefit debtors, but they are demanding of enforcement agents in terms of time and diligence. In a pressured industry attempts are likely always to be made to save staff resources at this most intensive phase of the process. This is unwise, as the lawfulness and validity of levies depends upon accurate procedure.

---

[43] *Lingham v Warren* (1820) 2 B&B 37.
[44] *Hutchins v Chambers* (1758) 1 Burr 579; *Bagge v Mawby* (1853) 8 Exch 64.
[45] *Anon* (1583) Cro Eliz p.13 pl.8.
[46] *Bagge v Mawby* (1853) 8 Exch 64.
[47] See *Quinlan* in chapter 7.

Chapter 5

REMOVAL AND SALE

Introduction

Most judicial attention has focused on the conduct of sale, ensuring there is no negligence in the handling of the goods or of the proceeds,[1] but more recently the focus has shifted earlier in the process. Both the cases featured in this section are interesting because the courts, when asked to look closely at stages in the levy process which had previously been considered uncontroversial and routine, concluded that the accepted practice was not actually lawful. In the first instance this was for the benefit of debtors, in the second, it was not.[2]

Khazanchi & another v Faircharm Investments Ltd & another; McLeod v Butterwick [1998] 1 WLR 1603

Facts Both these cases concerned the rights of enforcement agents with valid pre-existing levies to force re-entry to premises for the purposes of removal. In the case of *Khazanchi* a bailiff enforcing rent arrears forced re-entry when both of the tenants were absent from their trade premises on business purposes; in the case of *McLeod* a sheriff's officer enforcing a judgment debt called to remove whilst Mrs McLeod was absent from her home at work. Fuller details of both situations are laid out in the judgment.

Judgment of Morritt LJ: "1) These appeals raise a common question of some general importance as to the powers of a bailiff distraining for rent or a sheriff executing a writ of *fieri facias* forcibly to re-enter the premises in which the relevant goods are kept for the purpose of removing them. It is not in dispute that entry for the purpose of effecting the initial seizure may only be made with the consent of the occupant or other person in possession of the premises. The question is whether in any and, if so, what circumstances the bailiff or the sheriff in walking possession of the goods is entitled forcibly

[1] *Forrester v Caswell* (1906) 14 PMR 497; *Mills v Langford* (1911) 99 Property Owner's Journal 12.

[2] See *Law of Seizure of Goods* c.10 or *Powers of distress* c.4.

and without the consent of the occupant or other person in possession of the premises to re-enter in order to remove the goods for the purposes of sale...
4) Though there are similarities between the position of a bailiff and a sheriff their respective legal rights and obligations are not the same. Thus, it is necessary to consider the two cases separately. Equally it is helpful to test the apparent position of the one against that of the other. For that reason I propose to consider the position of the bailiff and the sheriff separately, but in respect of the common question I have identified, before considering the other questions which arise in and the outcome of each appeal.

Distress for rent
5) Though the remedy of distress is available for liabilities other than rent I confine my comments to the remedy as incident to a demise of land for the recovery of rent. The process consists of three stages, namely, entry into the premises, seizure of the goods and securing or impounding the goods. Originally goods so seized might only be impounded in the local pound to which the distrainor was obliged to take them. Further, the goods there impounded might only be detained until the outstanding rent was paid.
6) Section 1 of the Distress for Rent Act 1689 amended the law so as to entitle the distrainor to sell the goods so impounded and to recoup the arrears of rent out of the proceeds of sale. Originally the goods had to be appraised before sale but this requirement was abolished by Law of Distress Amendment Act 1888 s.5.
7) Section 10 of the Distress for Rent Act 1737 amended the law by enabling goods to be impounded and, indeed, sold on the premises where they were at the time of seizure ...[3]
8) The section contains no express provision as to the right of the distrainor to return to those premises for the purpose of removing the goods for sale elsewhere but provides, in a later passage, that:

> "it shall and may be lawful to and for any person or persons whatsoever, to come and go to and from such place or part of the said premises, where any distress for rent shall be impounded and secured as aforesaid, in order to view, appraise, and buy, and also in order to carry off or remove the same, on account of the purchaser thereof ..."

That section may be contrasted with section 7 which authorises a landlord seeking to levy a distress and those authorised by him in the daytime to break open and enter a house or other building in which he suspects that there are goods on which he is entitled to distrain but which have been fraudulently concealed from him. In the case of a dwelling house the power

[3] For text see chapter 1.

might only be exercised after the landlord had sworn before a justice as to the reasonable ground for his suspicion.

9) It is also necessary to notice section 19 of the Act of 1737. The purpose of the section was to prevent an irregularity during the course of the distress giving rise to a trespass *ab initio* with the consequence that the distrainor was liable for the value of the goods without a set-off on account of the arrears of rent...[4]

11) At some time following the enactment of the Law of Distress Act 1737 a practice grew up of an agreement, commonly called a walking possession agreement, being entered into between the landlord or bailiff on the one hand and the tenant on the other to regulate their relations after the initial entry and impounding of the goods. It is apparent from the decision in *Lavell v O'Leary* [1933] that at that period the form of agreement authorised the bailiff to "re-enter the premises peaceably or by force, if required, at any time."[5] Likewise in *Watson v Murray* the walking possession agreement in use in January 1952 by the sheriff executing a writ of *fi fa* authorised the sheriff to "re-enter my house and premises ... at any time you may think proper ... and if necessary to use force for that purpose."[6] In January 1954 the Distress for Rent Rules 1953 made by the Lord Chancellor under Law of Distress Amendment Act 1888 s.8 prescribed, for the first time, a form of walking possession agreement which might be "used with such variations as circumstances may require."[7] The form so prescribed provided simply that "you [the bailiff and the man in walking possession] may re-enter the premises at any time while the distraint is in force." Though the rules and other parts of the walking possession agreement have been amended from time to time no change has been made to the provision entitling the bailiff to re-enter...

13) It is in these circumstances that the tenants contend that the bailiff had no right to re-enter their premises without their consent. They submit that the walking possession agreement gave no such authority and no right to act as he did was conferred on the bailiff by the common law. Judge Roger Cox disagreed. He said:

> "Was the bailiff entitled to break in on 17th February 1992? If it was illegal, he was not. I have resolved that point and it was not an illegal distress. Granted that the original distress was not itself illegal, it is well settled that a bailiff may enter and, having levied distress, subsequently return and remove the goods and on the second occasion can in certain circumstances force entry, particularly if the premises have been barred

---

[4] For text see chapter 1.
[5] 2 KB 200.
[6] [1955] 2 QB 1.
[7] Rule 1(2).

against him. That goes back a long way. The problem is where the premises are simply locked, can they be said to be barred against the bailiff when he returns? There is a problem in that the occupiers may have gone out and locked the doors. I accept that times have changed since the 19th century when these rules were first laid down and it is now usual for people to lock the doors when they leave premises unattended. This is a matter that was considered at some length by Judge Roger Cooke sitting in Chancery Division in *McLeod v Butterwick.*[8] That decision, if it is a decision which I should follow, resolves the point against the plaintiffs. It is persuasive upon me but not binding. Mr. Hamer says it is plainly wrong and pointed me to an analogy against forced entry in aid of an Anton Piller order. It seems to me that an Anton Piller order is a very different situation indeed, just as other forms of distress are different. In *McLeod v Butterwick* the court was dealing with a writ of *fi fa*, and there was no need for form 7 (the notice of seizure). I have read Judge Roger Cooke's judgment with great care. Whilst he feels driven to the conclusion he reaches that where the door is locked the bailiff is entitled to assume that it is locked against him I find these reasons compelling: but I do note that it may be thought to produce an anomalous position in this day and age. I share Judge Roger Cooke's reservations but I feel compelled to come to the same conclusion. The bailiff was entitled to force entry"

14) The tenants have renewed their submissions to this court. They submit that the judge was wrong because on its true construction the walking possession agreement did not authorise the bailiff to use force at any time and the common law did not entitle him to do so in the circumstances of this case. In my view, it is convenient to consider the position at common law before seeking to construe the walking possession agreement. As I have already indicated, it is not disputed that in the case of distress for rent, whatever the nature of the premises, the initial entry must be peaceable and with the consent of the tenant. Once the initial entry has been achieved and the goods impounded, then, they are in what is called "the custody of the law."[9] If thereafter the distrainor were forcibly ejected or having left the premises for a temporary purpose his return is deliberately barred by the tenant then he may re-enter by force. This proposition is amply established by a number of cases to which we were referred. In view of the submissions made to us it is convenient at this stage to refer to them shortly in chronological order.

---

[8] [1996] 1 WLR 995.

[9] *Abingdon RDC v O'Gorman* [1968] 2 QB 811.

15) The first is *Francombe v Pinche.*[10] In that case the bailiff distraining the goods of a tenant was forcibly ejected when preparing the inventory. After about an hour the bailiff, having obtained reinforcements, returned and, having been refused admittance, broke open the door. Wilmot J. held that he was entitled to do so because "this was a recontinuance of the first taking and so was lawful"
16) In *Russell v. Rider* (1834) the landlord put in a bailiff on December 27th.[11] He left in an agitated state on December 29th because, as the landlord supposed, his liquor had been drugged. On January 4th agents of the landlords broke into the premises under the same authority as previously held by the bailiff and removed goods. Bosanquet J decided that they were not entitled to do so because "possession had been left so far back"
17) In *Eagleton v Gutteridge* (1843) the defendant bailiff had entered the dwelling house of the plaintiff under a warrant for distress for rent and was forcibly ejected by the plaintiff. The defendant thereupon forcibly re-entered and was sued for trespass. Parke B held that the forcible re-entry was justifiable at common law.[12]
18) In *Brown v Glenn* (1851) the defendant bailiff distrained horses of the plaintiff in the stable by breaking open the locked door. Lord Campbell CJ, distinguishing the case of the bailiff from that of the sheriff, held that the forcible entry was not justified "for the fact of the stable door being locked does of itself render this distress unlawful."[13]
19) In *Bannister v Hyde* (1860) a bailiff in close possession of a shop and dwelling house by way of distraint for rent left for a short time to get himself some beer.[14] During his absence the plaintiff locked him out and refused his requests to be let in again. Thereupon the bailiff broke down the back door and re-entered. It was held, by Crompton J, following *Eagleton v Gutteridge*, that the bailiff was entitled to use force to effect his re-entry for "being forcibly kept out ... amounted to the same thing as ... being forcibly turned out"
20) In *Eldridge v Stacey* (1863) a bailiff distraining goods in a dwelling house for unpaid rent was forcibly evicted. Three weeks later he re-entered by force. Erle CJ, considered that as he "was put out by force, he was justified in resorting to force in order to regain possession ..."[15]
21) Finally in *American Concentrated Must Co v Hendry* (1893) a landlord, by a bailiff, had sought to distrain goods in a warehouse. The bailiff had

[10] (1766) *Espinasse's Digest*, 3rd ed., p.382.
[11] (1834) 6 C&P 416.
[12] 11 M & W 465.
[13] 16 QBD 254.
[14] 2 E&E 627.
[15] 15 CB(NS) 458.

entered by breaking down the door. This was held by Bowen LJ to be unlawful. The bailiff's appeal was dismissed.[16]

22) The legal position is summarised in *Halsbury's Laws of England* in the following terms:

> "*Forcible re-entry.* After an entry has been made and not abandoned, but the distrainor has been forcibly expelled or driven away by the tenant's violence, he may obtain the assistance of a peace officer and break open the outer door, even after a considerable interval. On the same principle a forcible re-entry may be made where the man in possession voluntarily goes away for a short period, and not with the intention of abandoning the distress, and on his return finds the door locked. In such a case he may break open the door. It is a question of fact in each case whether there has been an abandonment."[17]

To the like effect are the passages in *Eddy on the Law of Distress*, *Hill & Redman's Law of Landlord and Tenant* and *Woodfall's Law of Landlord and Tenant.*[18]

23) The tenants relied on all these cases and textbook references for the proposition that except in the limited circumstances of forcible ejection or exclusion which would justify the use of force on the part of the bailiff in retaking the goods he had already impounded there was no right of forcible entry. They relied particularly on *Brown v Glenn* and *American Concentrated Must Co v Hendry.* This was disputed by counsel in his excellent argument on behalf of the bailiff. He contended that once the goods had been impounded following the initial entry, so that they were in the custody of the law, then, so long as the distress had not been abandoned, the bailiff on his return finding the door to be locked was entitled, without more, to force an entry. He submitted that the authorities dealing with forcible expulsion or exclusion, when properly understood, are only considering the impact of those circumstances on the question of abandonment. He took us through the authorities relied on by counsel for the tenants to indicate the way in which, in his submission, they should be read as supporting his proposition as opposed to that of the tenants. Both counsel accepted that, ultimately, this point depended on how one should read the judgments in *Bannister v Hyde.*

24) As I have already indicated the facts in that case were that a bailiff in close possession of a shop and dwelling house by way of distraint for rent left for a short time to get himself some beer. During his absence the plaintiff

[16] 68 LT 742.

[17] 4th ed., vol.13 (1975), p.155, para.306.

[18] Respectively 4th ed., vol.13 (1975), p.155, para.306; 18th ed., vol.1, at A [1874] & loose-leaf ed., vol.1, para.9.128.

locked him out and refused the bailiff's requests to let him in again. Thereupon the bailiff broke down the back door and re-entered. At trial the judge had considered that the forcible re-entry was justified. During the course of the argument counsel seeking to uphold the judge's order conceded that the distress had not been abandoned. He relied on the fact that the bailiff had not been forcibly ejected but had gone of his own accord and for his own purposes. The report indicates that during the course of argument Crompton J intervened when shown the report of *Russell v Rider* to the effect that, if there had been no abandonment, there would have been a right to re-enter. It is true that this intervention suggests that Crompton J considered that in *Russell v Rider* if the distress had not been abandoned then the bailiff would have been entitled to re-enter by force but it is not apparent whether that view depended on treating the drugging of the bailiff's liquor as equivalent to a forcible exclusion or indeed remained his view at the conclusion of the argument.

25) In his judgment Wightman J said:

> "In the present case there was no evidence of an abandonment, but the contrary. The man quitted, for a short time, the house in which the goods were, but clearly had no intention of abandoning them. On his return, he found the door locked against him; that placed him in the same position as if he had been forcibly ejected from the house, and therefore, as was held in *Eagleton v Gutteridge*, gave him the right to break open the outer door, if necessary, to regain possession"

The use of the word "therefore" in the last sentence is inconsistent with the submission for the bailiff. The other members of the court agreed with Wightman J. Thus Crompton J said:

> "when it was once admitted that there was no evidence of abandonment, the plaintiff's case was at an end. During the temporary absence of the man in possession, the goods remained in the custody of the law; and, on his being forcibly kept out, which amounted to the same thing as his being forcibly turned out, he was justified, as was laid down in *Eagleton v. Gutteridge*, in breaking open the door in the exercise of his right, not to retake (for he had not abandoned), but to retain possession of the goods distrained."

Blackburn J., who had been the trial judge, added:

> "I directed the jury, first, that, if he went out with the intention of returning, the distress had not been abandoned in point of law; and I directed them, secondly, that, in such case, he was justified in using force, if necessary, for the purpose of re-entering. The counsel for the

> plaintiff, upon this, elected to be nonsuited. *Eagleton v Gutteridge*, is a conclusive authority that the person in possession, if kept by force from the actual possession of goods distrained and in his constructive possession, has a right to use force for the purpose of re-entering upon such actual possession"

26) In my view, that case does not support the proposition for which counsel for the bailiff contends. As counsel for the tenants submitted, if there was a right to re-enter by force in any circumstances so long only as the distress had not been abandoned, then the passages from the judgments I have quoted referring to the justification for the use of force were wholly irrelevant. The same is true of *Francombe v Pinche, Eagleton v Gutteridge* and *Eldridge v Stacey*. In each case the references to the forcible ejection of the bailiff would have been otiose if there were an unconditional right to re-enter by force. In particular, the direction of Lord Denman CJ to the jury in *Eagleton v Gutteridge*, that if the jury were satisfied that the bailiff was forcibly turned out the subsequent re-entry by force was justified would have been wrong. Likewise the conclusion of Erle CJ in *Eldridge v Stacey*, that if the bailiff were put out by force he was justified in resorting to force to regain possession would have been unnecessary. It would have been sufficient for him to have said "unless indeed he had abandoned the original distress" without the reference to the circumstances of being put out by force.

27) Accordingly, I reject the principal submission for the bailiff to the effect that after impounding he has at common law an unconditional right to re-enter by force the premises where the goods are impounded. There is, in my view, no authority to support it. Such a right would be inconsistent with the view that those premises constitute the pound for there has never been any suggestion that a landlord or his bailiff was entitled to break into the pound. Moreover to recognise a right of forcible re-entry in all circumstances would be inconsistent with the provisions of the Law of Distress Act 1737. As I have already indicated, s.7 conferred a right of forcible entry in the case of goods fraudulently concealed but s.10 made no similar provision when providing for the first time that goods might be impounded on the tenant's premises. If it had been clearly established before that Act was passed that there was a right of forcible re-entry in all cases the omission might have been explicable, but it was not, and, indeed, could not have been, for previously the goods could not be impounded on private property. I do not doubt that, subject to any question of duress, a tenant might lawfully agree that the bailiff might re-enter by force. *Lavell v O'Leary* is such a case. But in my view it is not a right conferred by the common law in the absence of such an agreement.

28) In *McLeod v Butterwick* Judge Roger Cooke was dealing with the case of a sheriff executing a writ of *fi. fa.* not a bailiff levying a distress. But his decision and the reasoning behind it was adopted by Judge Roger Cox and applied to

the case of the bailiff levying a distress. Thus it is appropriate to consider in this context what Judge Roger Cooke held. He, too, considered *Bannister v Hyde* and the conclusions which might be drawn from it. He said:

> "it seems to me that the authorities, particularly when one looks at *Bannister v Hyde*, go a good deal further than actual expulsion (that is, removing from the premises the person who is already there). They must, I think, extend to any forcible prevention of the continuing of the execution. There is an indication in some of the books that notice ought to be given first, and, as a matter of practice, I am bound to think it ought to; but there is also an indication on other authority that there is no point in giving notice if there is nobody there to give it to. The real question is: does the principle extend (and there is no clear authority on this) to cases where, in fact, the premises are locked, not because the house owner is deliberately trying to exclude the bailiff or the sheriff, but simply where, put neutrally, the householder has locked the house, and in this particular case, as Mrs. McLeod tells me and I have no reason to doubt her, she had locked it because she had gone to work. The difficulty with qualifying the principle in such a case is this. From the point of view of the sheriff's officer, who is coming to execute his writ and to take, physically, possession of that which he already has by operation of law, he does not know why he is being kept out. All he knows, and can know, and possibly can ever know (unless the circumstances are such as they were in *Bannister v Hyde*) is that he *is* being kept out. It seems to me to follow, as a matter of strict reasoning, that, whatever is the case, if he comes back to continue the possession which started as walking possession by taking possession, and the door is barred against him, he can break through it. That being so, he was right to do it in this case too. It seems to me that the intellectual purity of the argument is convincing and I think I am bound to go down that road. I observe that it represents on evidence what has been the accepted practice of sheriffs, at least in Greater London, for a long period. I view it in modern conditions, however, with some degree of disquiet. It is all very well in an earlier world where, perhaps in the class of society where people had enough money for anybody to bother with an execution, it was most unusual to find a house to be locked, bolted and barred, unless that exclusion was the intention. Not so today. People are frequently out and about their lawful business, both sexes working, mothers out with their children, in circumstances that in the 19th century would have seemed odd and unusual; today we take for granted. I cannot help feeling that this practice is due for review, and I hope it will be by somebody. But there it is."

29) In my view, this conclusion involves an extension of the principle and of the existing authorities on the circumstances in which a bailiff may re-enter by force which I am unable to accept. If no notice has been given by the

bailiff of his intention to re-enter and the only circumstance is that the outer door is locked that is, in my view, insufficient to justify a forcible re-entry. The justification for permitting force in response to cases of forcible expulsion or forcible exclusion is that given by the Privy Council in *Aga Kurboolie Mahomed v The Queen* (1843).[19] In that case, a sheriff executing a writ in Calcutta sought to arrest the appellant in his house. He entered through an open door but was then expelled by force and the door shut and locked behind him. Having obtained reinforcements the sheriff then, though under fire from within, re-entered by force. On appeal to the Privy Council, Lord Campbell giving their advice, held that the original entry through the open door was lawful, that the appellant was guilty of trespass in expelling the sheriff and could not rely on his own wrong to object to the subsequent forcible re-entry. The Privy Council also concluded that in the circumstances a demand for re-entry was not required as the appellant knew the purpose of the sheriff's call. Lord Campbell said:

> "their lordships think that as they had once been lawfully in the house, and he knew they were lawfully about to arrest him, and he unlawfully caused them to be expelled for the purpose of preventing them from so doing, he cannot be permitted to take advantage of his own wrong, by thus defeating the process of the law; and that they had a right to place themselves in the position which they occupied when his unlawful act began. Without an actual arrest, there was no rescous or escape; but the proposition, that till an actual arrest had taken place, the prosecutor might forcibly expel the officer and those acting in his aid, and lock the outer door, so as to entitle himself to the protection of his castle, cannot be supported. The outer door being open, they were entitled to enter the house under civil process; and then being lawfully in the house, to arrest him, he was guilty of a trespass by expelling them. The act of locking the outer door was unlawful, and he could confer no privilege upon himself by that unlawful act. Again, there is no doubt that, generally speaking, before an outer door can be broken open, even to execute criminal process, there must be a demand of entry, and a refusal. But to what extent? To inform the owners of the house of the purpose for which entry is to be made, and to afford him the opportunity of opening the door and personally admitting the parties who are to execute the process of the law. Here the prosecutor, who had just expelled the defendants from his house, that they might not arrest him, full well knew the purpose for which they returned, and he showed a determined resolution to oppose their admission."

[19] 4 Moo PC 239

30) If that case truly expresses the rationale for the circumstances in which a forcible re-entry is justified then the mere fact that the door is locked cannot suffice. It is not wrong for a tenant, without more, to lock the door to the demised premises whether they be domestic or commercial. If he knows that the bailiff is seeking to re-enter but locks or leaves the door locked to exclude him then the tenant commits a wrong for he is wilfully obstructing the right of the bailiff to possession of the goods. But if he does not know of the bailiff's intended re-entry at any particular time then to leave his door locked and to absent himself about his normal affairs is his right. As the Privy Council indicated if the person in possession knows the purpose of the bailiff's visit then there is no need to give further notice of it. But that is no reason for concluding that where the tenant does not know of the bailiff's intention to re-enter at a particular time and leaves his door locked the bailiff may break in.

31) It is objected that if notice is required then by giving it the bailiff will provide the opportunity to the tenant to conceal his goods, thereby frustrating the object of the re-entry. This is true but insufficient reason to reach a different conclusion. It is common ground that the initial entry must be effected peaceably, usually by consent. The tenant then has five days to pay off the arrears. If the tenant has not used that opportunity to conceal his goods then I see no compelling reason on that ground why the bailiff should not be required to give notice of his re-entry.

32) Then it is suggested by reference to *Semayne's Case* (1604) and *Lee v Gansel* (1774),[20] to which I shall refer in more detail in connection with the execution of a writ of *fi fa*, that the reason for not permitting forcible re-entry is the risk of civil disturbance and the possibility of letting in robbers. It is suggested that the latter reason is not a good one because of the practice of the bailiffs to secure the premises with a new lock on leaving. Whilst this may remove much of the force from the second reason it does not affect the first, nor in my view can it provide a justification for a forcible entry on the premises of another.

33) For all these reasons, I would conclude that a bailiff is not entitled to re-enter by force except where, having gained entry peaceably, he was expelled by force or he has been deliberately excluded by the tenant. What amounts to deliberate exclusion must be recognised on a case by case basis. It will include cases where the tenant knowing of the intended visit deliberately locks the door and goes away or when invited to admit the bailiff refuses to do so. But, in my view, it does not include the case of a tenant who has no knowledge of an intended visit by the bailiff at any particular time and locks his premises in the ordinary way and goes about his business as normal.

---

[20] See, respectively, chapter 2 & (1774) 1 Cowp 1.

34) It is necessary to construe the walking possession agreement against that background of the common law. It is in the prescribed form and embodies an agreement between the bailiff and the tenant that the former "may re-enter the premises at any time while the distress is in force." The bailiff relies on the use of the unqualified words "at any time." He submits that they mean just that, so that the right is not dependent on the consent of the tenant or the presence of other circumstances sufficient to justify a forcible re-entry. I do not accept that submission. It cannot have been intended by the parties that the bailiff should be entitled, without notice, to break in at any time of day or night. If such a power were intended then it would require to be expressed in plain terms. That is certainly the case if the power were conferred by a statute.[21] In my view, it would not be right to attribute an intention on the part of the tenant to confer such wide-ranging rights on the bailiff without clear expression. I do not think that the use of the words "at any time" is sufficient, for they deal with time not method and must be read against the background of being a prescribed form which superseded the form previously in common use which expressly referred to the use of force.

Execution of a writ of fieri facias
35) A writ of *fi fa* is a command to the sheriff "that of the goods and chattels and other property of [the judgment debtor] in your county authorised by law to be seized in execution you cause to be made the sum of [the amount of the judgment] ... and that immediately after execution of this writ you pay [the judgment creditor] in pursuance of [the judgment] the amount levied in respect of the said sum." The statutory authority of the sheriff to perform the command is now contained in section 138 of the Supreme Court Act, as amended.
36) It is not disputed that the sheriff in execution of a writ of *fi fa* may not make a forcible entry into a dwelling house unless and until he has completed his seizure of the goods in consequence of the first entry: *Halsbury's Laws of England*.[22] The rule is otherwise in the case of commercial or business premises.[23] The, origin of the rule may be traced at least as far back as *Semayne's Case*. The report is in the form of a number of resolutions which, so far as material, are sufficiently recorded in the side note in these terms:

> "1. The house of every one is his castle, and if thieves come to a man's house to rob or murder, and the owner or his servants kill any of the thieves in defence of himself and his house, it is no felony and he shall

[21] *Grove v Eastern Gas* [1952] 1 KB 77.
[22] See loose-leaf ed., vol.1, para.9.128.
[23] *Hodder v Williams* [1895] 2 QB 663- in execution an officer may force entry to a workshop or other premises where are neither a dwelling house nor connected to one. Only a debtor's home is protected by law.

> lose nothing ... 4. Where the door is open the sheriff may enter, and do execution at the suit of a subject, and so also in such case may the lord, and distrain for his rent or service. It is not lawful for the sheriff, on request made and denial, at the suit of a common person, to break the defendant's house, that is, to execute any process at the suit of a subject ... 6. If the sheriff might break open the door to execute civil process, yet it must be after request made."[24]

37) Following the initial entry and seizure the rights of the sheriff are very similar to those of the bailiff. He may remain in possession of them without any physical presence. This is normally, but not necessarily, evidenced by a walking possession agreement. Thus, unless he has abandoned the goods, which is a question of fact, he may re-enter in order to remove the goods for the purposes of sale.[25] As in the case of the bailiff distraining for rent the question is whether the sheriff may forcibly re-enter and, if so, in what circumstances.

38) We were referred to a number of cases on this issue too. It is convenient to refer to them shortly and in chronological order before turning to the submissions of the parties. The first after *Semayne's Case*, was *Lee v Gansel.* In that case an officer seeking to arrest General Gansel peacefully entered the house from the street but then broke through an inner door. It was held that he was entitled so to do. Lord Mansfield CJ explained that the special position or privilege of a dwelling house, not to be extended by any equitable analogous interpretation, rested on policy for the protection of a man and his family for:

> "otherwise the consequences would be fatal: for it would leave the family within, naked and exposed to thieves and robbers. It is much better therefore, says the law, that you should wait for another opportunity, than do an act of violence, which may probably be attended with such dangerous consequences."

Lord Mansfield CJ reiterated a passage in *Semayne's Case*, that "the same strict doctrine ... 'that breaking open the *outer* door was a trespass, but that taking away the goods was lawful.'"

39) In *Pugh v Griffith* (1838) the sheriff seeking to execute a writ of *fi. fa.* entered lawfully into a room occupied by a tenant from year to year and thence obtained access to the part of the house occupied by the plaintiff.[26] There he seized certain goods. On seeking to remove the goods he found that the only exit available for that purpose was locked. He thereupon broke the

---

[24] See chapter 1.

[25] *Halsbury's Laws of England*, 4th ed., vol.17, pp.297-298, para.491.

[26] 7 A&E 827

lock and left. Lord Denman CJ held that he was entitled to do so for there was "nothing else to be done but to open it [the door] himself ..."

40) I have already referred to *Aga Kurboolie Mahomed v The Queen*. In *Hodder v Williams* the sheriff sought to execute a writ of *fi fa* over goods in a workshop. He requested entry and was refused. He then entered by force and was sued for trespass by the judgment debtor. The Court of Appeal considered that the forcible entry was justified. Kay LJ drew a distinction between that case and one of distress for rent over goods in a dwelling house.

41) In her very cogent submissions Mrs. McLeod pointed out that she had refused to sign a walking possession agreement. She asked where is the authority entitling the sheriff forcibly to re-enter her home? The response of the sheriff was to refer to *Mather on Sheriff and Execution Law*.[27] The passage relied on states:

> "If after having obtained peaceable possession of a dwelling house the sheriff's officers be forcibly ejected, or be obliged to fly under threat of bodily injury, they may forcibly re-enter, and in such cases the sheriff can send as many additional officers as he may deem necessary ... Again, where the sheriff, having obtained peaceable possession, cannot carry away the seized effects or execute the writ without breaking the lock, etc. of the outer door because of its being locked, etc., and neither the execution debtor nor anyone on his behalf are on the premises to enable the sheriff to request them to open such door, he is justified in breaking it open."

The authorities cited as support for the statement in the last sentence are *Pugh v Griffith, Eagleton v Gutteridge, Aga Kurboolie Mahomed v The Queen*, and *Bannister v Hyde*. The sheriff did not submit that any of those authorities directly justified the proposition stated in the text. The most he felt able to submit was that if a sheriff might use force to get the goods out, as indicated in *Pugh v Griffith*, why should he not do so for the purpose of getting in.

42) I am unable to accept that submission. In *Pugh v Griffith* the decision of Lord Denman CJ is all dependent on the facts that the sheriff had achieved a lawful entry and seizure. Lord Denman said:

> "The sheriff shows a lawful entry into the house, and a lawful seizure of the goods; and ... it cannot be said that there were any other doors, or any other mode of getting the goods out. Then what was the sheriff to do? The goods could not be kept forever in the house; and neither the plaintiff, nor anybody else, was there so that he could request them to open the door, and there was nothing else to be done but to open it

[27] 3rd ed. (1935) p.88.

himself ... he appears to be justified as a matter of necessity in order to get the goods out to execute the writ."

There is no authority to the effect that as a matter of necessity the sheriff is entitled forcibly to re-enter. He may be justified in doing so where he has been forcibly ejected or excluded, as indicated by the other cases cited in the footnote, but that is not what is suggested.
43) The statutory power conferred by s.138 authorises the sheriff to seize the goods. It contains no express power to make a forcible entry for that purpose and I see no grounds for implying one. Nor does the common law recognise such a power in respect of a dwelling house. Accordingly, in my view, and for substantially the same reasons a sheriff is entitled forcibly to re-enter a dwelling house in the same circumstances as a bailiff, disregarding the statutory restrictions I referred to earlier, but not otherwise. I should reiterate, in case it is not clear already, that this conclusion is confined to re-entry to a dwelling house. If and in so far as a sheriff may forcibly enter premises other than a dwelling house I see no reason why he may not re-enter such premises in a similar fashion.
44) It follows that in both appeals, because that concerning the sheriff also concerns a dwelling house and there is no question in either of them of the bailiff or sheriff being expelled by force, the question is whether the bailiff or sheriff on seeking to re-enter had been deliberately excluded by the tenants or Mrs. McLeod respectively. In each case that is a question of fact to be considered in the light of the individual circumstances. But in neither case if they had no knowledge of an intended visit by the bailiff at any particular time will it be enough that they had locked their premises in the ordinary way and gone about their business as normal. I turn then to the facts of each appeal and the other points which arise in respect of each of them.

Khazanchi v. Faircharm Investments Ltd
[paras. 45-50) In 1990 Faircharm Investments Ltd let premises to the plaintiffs, Mr. Khazanchi and Mr. Rattu, for use as a recording studio. By January 1992 the tenants owed the landlord £8,914.54. A bailiff was instructed and, on 17th January, the bailiff attended, levied on "all recording equipment" and entered into walking possession. The tenants had until 22nd January 1992 to pay. As the rent arrears were paid, the bailiff returned on 12th February 1992 at about 4.45 p.m. He had tried unsuccessfully to contact the tenants beforehand and came accompanied by a police officer and a locksmith. The door was locked and the premises were unoccupied as the tenants were each away on business. The bailiff forced entry, removed the goods, changed the lock and left new key with the caretaker. On 26th February 1992 the goods removed were sold at auction for the total sum (net of VAT) of £12,315. On September 3rd 1992 the tenants started the proceedings in Uxbridge County Court. They claimed that the distress was

unlawful because the walking possession agreement was not in accordance with the regulations and because the bailiff was not entitled forcibly to re-enter the premises. In addition they alleged that there had been an agreement with the landlord over instalment payment and that their goods had been sold at a gross undervalue, for which they claimed damages based on their true value, which they put at not less than £65,498.

50) The claim was heard by Judge Roger Cox who concluded that the walking possession agreement was valid, that the bailiff had been entitled to force re-entry, that no payment agreement had been made and that there had been no sale at undervalue.]

51) On this appeal the tenants claimed that the judge was wrong in three respects. First, it was contended that the judge was wrong in law to have concluded that the bailiff was entitled to make a forcible entry to the premises on February 12th 1992. Second, the tenants submitted that the judge was wrong not to find that the agreement they alleged had been concluded between the tenants and the landlord on February 25th 1992. Third, they suggest that the judge was wrong to conclude that the value of the goods was that realised at auction or, in the absence of any second-hand market, other than the price as new discounted for any element of betterment.

52) I have already quoted the judge's conclusion in respect of the first issue and decided that as a matter of law where the premises are merely locked and unattended that is insufficient to justify a forcible re-entry. But counsel for the bailiff pointed out that at the trial it was never suggested that the bailiff should have given notice of his proposed re-entry so that the question of whether the bailiff had been deliberately kept out was never examined. He relied on the facts that the bailiff had telephoned the premises and left a message on the answering machine on 29th January and 7, 10 and 12th February. But there was no evidence what those messages were nor whether any of them was received by either tenant. Counsel for the bailiff did not ask for a new trial or for leave to adduce fresh evidence. In those circumstances, in my view, the proper decision for this court to arrive at is that the forcible re-entry was unjustified as a matter of law. The tenants clearly alleged that the original entry was forcible and wrongful. By the various defences the defendants relied on the fact that the bailiff was executing a warrant for distress. As a matter of law that defence was insufficient. In my view, it was for the bailiff to plead and prove sufficient justification in law. Accordingly, the absence of any investigation at the trial of what the messages were, whether either tenant received any of them or why the premises were wholly unoccupied when the bailiff called is no reason for refusing to conclude that the re-entry was unjustified and so a trespass at law.

53) The tenants did not, in my view sensibly, pursue their contention that the judge should have found that there was on 25th February an agreement between them and the landlord during the course of the hearing. Accordingly, the only remaining issue is that of damage. In view of the

judge's findings this was not an issue which arose before him. But he dealt with it in conjunction with an allegation that the distress had been excessive in that the bailiff had seized goods to a value substantially greater than that which was required to pay the rent in arrears. In this connection he had to consider the allegations of the tenants that the auction sale had not realised the true value of the goods.

54) The evidence for the tenants on this issue was that of Mr. Khazanchi to the effect that he had used the recording equipment for about five to six years. He said that some of the equipment could not be bought second-hand and that he had not intended to replace any of it in the near future. Originally he had valued the equipment at £65,000. After he heard the evidence of Mr. Jackson, the expert witness for the tenants, as to value he dropped his original estimate to £50,000. The evidence of Mr. Jackson was to the effect that there was little or no second-hand market for goods of this sort and that his estimate of value was the product of his inquiries of others concerned in the business of sound recording. The values he used were for similar goods when new as shown in catalogues issued in 1992. He himself had not seen the goods, did not know their age or condition and had made no allowance for depreciation. The judge's conclusion was:

"I can place little or no reliance on the valuation evidence. However when the goods were sold at auction they reached a price of £12,315. This is the only hard evidence I have so far as the value of the goods is concerned. This is evidence on which I can do no other than rely. Of course, it was a forced sale. However it was still a sale at which persons were in competition with each other, and therefore a realistic value was achieved and I must accept that that was the value. That sum, as a matter of fact either only just covered the distress or fell a little short of it. Therefore it would be wholly wrong to suggest that the distress was excessive regarding the value of the goods, and further any claim which the plaintiffs might have based on the distress being unlawful rather than illegal fails on the basis that they have not showed they suffered any loss. Any claim for damages by the plaintiffs fails."

55) For the tenants it is claimed that the judge was wrong to accept the price realised at auction as the best evidence of the value of the goods. They also contend that the judge was wrong to have determined that the tenants had failed to prove that they had suffered any loss. I would reject both those submissions. The price realised at auction is not necessarily the best evidence of value at any particular date but if there is no evidence, and there was none in this case, to the effect that the auction had not been properly advertised or conducted it is evidence a judge is entitled to accept. But as the judge had rejected the evidence of value given by Mr. Khazanchi and Mr. Jackson for good reason in this case it was the only evidence of value before the court. In those circumstances not only was the judge entitled to accept the evidence of the prices realised at auction but, as he indicated, in practice bound to do so

for it was both credible and unchallenged. I propose to consider the question of loss on the basis of the prices for the goods realised at auction.

56) The total realised was £12,315 to which was added VAT on the hammer price of £2,155.19. The auctioneer's commission and charges for advertising and porterage, before VAT, were £1,847.25 (VAT £323.27), £325 (VAT £56.88) and porterage £1,000. The cheque sent by the auctioneers to the bailiff was for £10,917.79. The cost of the new locks fitted on 12th February, inclusive of VAT, was £94.31 and was paid by the bailiff on 3rd March. The bailiff deducted from the amount he had received from the auctioneer his charges of £916.74, which included VAT, and sent a cheque to the landlord for £10,001.05. The rent for which the distress had been levied amounted in all to £8,914.54.

57) It was contended by counsel for the tenants that on these figures it was shown that the tenants had sustained a loss because it was not shown that the landlord would account for the VAT on the hammer price. If that were so then the gross proceeds, including VAT on the goods distrained, would have been £14,470.19 and the total charges of the auctioneer and the bailiff including VAT to be deducted therefrom was £4,469.14. It is not clear whether the price of the new lock was included in the charges of the bailiff or was extra, but it does not matter. The surplus on this basis was £10,001.05 or £9,906.74. This exceeds the amount of £8,914.54 for which the distress had been levied. I do not accept this submission. There was no investigation at the trial of how the VAT element on the sums realised and the charges paid was or should have been dealt with. The onus was on the tenants to establish their loss. If the landlord was not registered for VAT then the auctioneer and the bailiff should not have accounted to it for the VAT on the hammer price; if it was I see no reason to infer that the VAT would not have been properly accounted for. In my view, it is clear that VAT should be left out of account in respect of both the receipts and payments. On this footing the amounts realised by the sale of the goods distrained was £12,315, the charges and expenses of the auctioneer were £3,172.25 and those of the bailiff were about £750. Thus the net realisation was £8,392.75 or some £521.79 1ess than the outstanding rent for which the distress had been levied. Accordingly, in my view, the judge was right to conclude that the tenants had not established any loss arising from the sale of the goods removed on 12th February.

58) The tenants claim that, nevertheless, they are entitled to damages under a variety of heads and descriptions, namely, nominal damages for trespass, damages for breach of the covenant for quiet enjoyment and/or wrongful exclusion from the demised premises and damages for breach of the walking possession agreement. These claims and that for damages for wrongful interference with the goods were disputed by the bailiff on the grounds that recovery under any of the suggested heads would be contrary to the requirements of the Distress for Rent Act 1737 s.19.

59) That section applies: "where any distress shall be made ... and any irregularity or unlawful act shall be afterwards done by the party ... distraining ..." In my view, it is plain that the section applies, at least, to the stages of the overall process of distress which follow the initial seizure and impounding. Thus the section is applicable at the stage of re-entry with which this appeal is concerned. In cases to which the section applies the consequences are stated to be that:
"the distress itself shall not be therefore deemed to be unlawful, nor the party ... making it be deemed a trespasser or trespassers *ab initio*; but the party ... aggrieved by such unlawful act or irregularity shall or may recover full satisfaction for the special damage he ... shall have sustained thereby, and no more, in an action of trespass or on the case ..."
60) Thus the bailiff may not be treated as a trespasser *ab initio* because of some intervening irregularity. And the claimant may only recover satisfaction for the special damage sustained because of that irregularity. The only special damage must be that arising from the wrongful re-entry. But on the facts of this case the only damage which can be suggested, and it was not in fact claimed, is the damage (if any) to the door. But the cost of the new lock, £94.31, was not charged to the tenants because the proceeds of sale of the goods, after deduction of the other costs and expenses for which the tenants were liable, were insufficient to cover it. Nor was there any suggestion of any damage to the door for which the tenants were liable or charged.
61) Further it is clear that even if it had not failed on the facts the claim for unlawful interference with the tenants' goods would have been barred by this section. There is no doubt that the bailiff was entitled to possession of the goods for he had impounded them and had the benefit of the walking possession agreement. As pointed out in *Lee v Gansel*, in relation to the execution of a writ, though the entry may have been wrongful the removal of the goods was not. It is only possible to avoid this consequence if the bailiff is treated as a trespasser *ab initio* by virtue of the unlawful re-entry. But that is precisely what the section prohibits.
62) In any event, in my view, the claim would have failed on the grounds of causation. Even if, as I have held, the bailiff was not entitled to re-enter on 12th February in the way he did he was entitled to re-enter by force if he was wrongly excluded. Had he given proper notice of his intention to re-enter I have no doubt he would have been entitled to obtain the goods for the purpose of the auction on 26th February. In that event, he would have sold them in precisely the same circumstances as those in which in fact he did. There is no suggestion that the goods were damaged or depreciated by the manner or timing of their removal. In my judgment, no claim under this head is made out.
63) I would also reject the claim for damages for breach of the walking possession agreement. The wrong for which damages is sought is the bailiff's forcible re-entry of the demised premises without the consent of the tenants

or justification in law. The fact that the walking possession agreement did not give the requisite consent does not mean that the wrong of which complaint is made is for a breach of that contract rather than for the trespass. In my view, the tenants cannot avoid the restriction in the section by pleading their claim as a breach of contract.
64) For similar reasons I would reject the claim for breach of the covenant for quiet enjoyment. This covenant ... was in the normal form whereby the landlord covenanted:

> "that the tenants paying the rents hereby reserved and performing and observing the covenants on their part herein contained shall peaceably hold and enjoy the demised premises during the said term without any interruption by the landlords or any person rightfully claiming under or in trust for them."

It was established in *Dawson v Dyer* (1833) that the payment of the rent is not a condition precedent to the performance of the covenant.[28] But the unlawful act or interruption complained of is still the forcible re-entry. The tenants are entitled to full satisfaction but no more for that wrong. They cannot avoid the prohibition by pleading the wrong in an alternative form.
65) In these circumstances, in my view, the tenants have failed to make out any special damage for the purposes of Distress for Rent Act 1737 s.19. It is established that in those circumstances the bailiff cannot be liable for nominal damages either.[29]
66) The overall result is that, though the judge was wrong in respect of the lawfulness of the re-entry, on the facts of the case and applying the provisions of Distress for Rent Act 1737 s.19 no recoverable damage has been made out so that the action fails. In those circumstances, in my view, the appeal should be dismissed because there is no reason to vary the order of the judge.

McLeod v. Butterwick
[paras. 67-72) In 1992 the plaintiff, Mrs McLeod, brought and lost proceedings in the county court against various parties. One issued a writ against her for £7,295.43, which was directed to the Sheriff of Greater London, the defendant Mr. Butterwick. On January 24th 1995 a sheriff's officer attended Mrs McLeod's home in Greenford and claimed formally to have seized the goods then in the premises, although Mrs McLeod refused to enter into a walking possession agreement. She brought unsuccessful interpleader proceedings, after which the sheriff was instructed to continue

[28] 5 B&A 584.
[29] *Rodgers v Parker* (1856) 18 CB 112; *Lucas v. Tarleton* (1858) 3 H & N 116.

with the execution no earlier than December 18th 1995. On 19th December 1995 an officer attended at the house to execute the writ. Mrs McLeod was out at work. Finding the door locked the officer called a locksmith, forced entry and new locks fitted so that the premises would be secure after he left. Having been alerted by a neighbour, Mrs McLeod returned home but, despite her protests, the officer removed the goods to which, in accordance with the order in the interpleader proceedings, he considered that he was entitled. Mrs McLeod started some further unsuccessful court proceedings and then on December 27th issued a writ in Chancery Division of the High Court seeking damages for trespass arising from the illegal entry combined with an injunction against sale of her goods or re-entry into her home. The injunction application was heard by Roger Cooke J on February 13th 1996 and was dismissed. He concluded there had been a valid seizure followed by a lawful re-entry by force and that the sheriff was lawfully entitled to sell. Mrs McLeod appealed to the Court of Appeal.]

73) By her appeal Mrs. McLeod seeks from this court the interlocutory relief she sought from Judge Roger Cooke, namely an injunction restraining the sheriff from selling the goods removed from her home on 19th December 1995 and an injunction restraining him from entering her home save pursuant to an order of a court of competent jurisdiction made after hearing both parties. There has been no trial and we are not concerned with whether she is entitled to any damages, including the aggravated and exemplary damages she has claimed. In passing I observe that we were not referred to any statutory provision applicable to a sheriff comparable to Distress for Rent Act 1737 s.19...

75) Mrs. McLeod criticised the judge's uncritical acceptance of the sheriff's allegations of seizure and impounding on the occasion of his first visit on 24 January 1995. In her affidavit sworn on 11th January 1996 she had stated in unambiguous terms that there had been no indication of seizure, merely a demand for payment of the judgment debt. She was not cross-examined on that affidavit at the hearing of the interpleader proceedings before Mr. Baker. The oral evidence which Mr. Baker accepted was the one-sided version of the sheriff's officer. She submits with some force that the so-called finding of Mr. Baker was not made after hearing oral evidence on both sides and is open to challenge by her. But the judge only found that on the application before him he should be slow to regard this issue as a serious one to be tried. He proceeded on the basis that the issue was likely to be decided in all probability in the sheriff's favour. For my part I think that the judge was in the circumstances entitled to take that approach. He was not deciding the issue, merely weighing it for the purpose of exercising his discretion.

76) I pass then to the question whether the sheriff's re-entry on 19th December 1995 was lawful or not. I have already quoted the passage from the judge's judgment in which he concluded that point against Mrs. McLeod. He did so on the footing that the door was locked and that was sufficient

justification for the forcible re-entry, notwithstanding that no notice had been given to Mrs. McLeod of his intention to re-enter. For the reasons I have already given I disagree with the judge's conclusion. In my judgment, the sheriff's forcible re-entry on 19th December 1995 was unlawful and a trespass. It may be that it will be held at the trial that Mrs. McLeod is entitled to damages on account of that trespass but it does not follow at this stage that she is entitled to either of the injunctions she seeks.

77) The judge held that in the absence of a walking possession agreement the sheriff does not have to remain in close possession to avoid abandoning possession of the goods seized. He concluded that notwithstanding the interval of 11 months between the first entry and the second there had been no abandonment because of the prosecution of the interpleader proceedings. In my view he was right in respect of both matters. Thus at the time of the forcible re-entry the sheriff was in possession of the goods which, by virtue of s.138 of the 1981 Act, he had been entitled to seize and was entitled to sell. In these circumstances, I do not see how an injunction to restrain the sale of the goods so seized and now stored in a warehouse off Mrs McLeod's premises could be justified. Mrs. McLeod has not paid the judgment debt and, apparently, has no intention of doing so. As pointed out in *Lee v Gansel*, though the re-entry may have been wrongful the removal of the goods was not. The statutory right to sell continues to subsist and I see no reason to inhibit its exercise.

78) The same point may be made with regard to the injunction sought to restrain entry except pursuant to an order of the court. The sheriff does have a right to re-enter otherwise than pursuant to an order of the court, namely if removed or excluded by force. But I have no reason to think that he threatens and intends to re-enter the home of Mrs. McLeod otherwise than as permitted by law as established by the decision of this court on these appeals. Though his re-entry on 19th December 1995 was unlawful and a trespass, there is no reason to think that it will be repeated unless an interlocutory injunction is granted. It may well be that at the trial it will be appropriate, if the judge thinks fit, to make a declaration as to the unlawfulness of the re-entry as well as giving judgment for such damages as Mrs. McLeod may establish. But, in my judgment, there is no good reason for granting the injunction sought at this stage.

79) It follows that, as in *Khazanchi v Faircharm Investments Ltd*, though for different reasons, I see no reason to interfere with the order the judge actually made. Accordingly, though I disagree with the judge's conclusion on the lawfulness of the re-entry, I would dismiss this appeal.

Conclusion

80) In the event, I would dismiss both appeals though, in each case, I have concluded that the judge was wrong on the important point of principle. This may appear to be an unsatisfactory result for in one sense it means that

an illegal act has been inflicted on the plaintiffs without any immediate means of redress being afforded to them by the law. But this is the consequence of the application to the facts of the provisions of Distress for Rent Act 1737 s.19 in the one case and the circumstances including the fact that there has not yet been a trial in the other. However, it should be noted that in cases such as these there may be a sanction pursuant to either Criminal Damage Act 1971 s.1 or Criminal Law Act 1977 s.6."

Commentary

This judgment is chiefly notable for the fact that it challenged accepted practice in the enforcement sector. It had been widely accepted that re-entry to premises could be forced so as to remove goods previously levied - a further example of the common practice in the enforcement sector of practices becoming established which are not actually sanctioned by law. The Court of Appeal decided that this was incorrect, after reviewing the case law. The right to force re-entry arises only where the bailiff is being deliberately excluded and, accordingly, in these two cases, the re-entry had been illegal.[30] It may be added that, whilst the re-entry may be forced, the minimum of force should be used and the bailiff should avoid acting in a manner that could constitute a breach of the peace.[31]

The curious fact was that, in both cases, the dissatisfied debtors lost their appeals despite the fact that the entries were deemed unlawful. They were the victims of wrongful acts but this did not effect the overall outcome of the decisions. There were separate reasons for this:

- *Khazanchi* - the wrongful re-entry was treated as an irregularity under Distress for Rent Act 1737 s.19. As a result, only the special damages proved could be recovered and none were shown;
- *McLeod* - the appeal related to a refusal to grant Mrs McLeod two injunctions against the High Sheriff. These applications failed, but her claim for damages for trespass against the sheriff had yet to be heard. As the Court observed, nothing in sheriff's law equates to Distress for Rent Act 1737 s.19, and as a result a wrongful re-entry could render a levy trespass *ab initio.*

The judgment otherwise is valuable because:

---

[30] See also *Stubbings v Stokes* (1840) 6 LT 123 - a tenant's appeal against a failed claim in trespass was dismissed because the landlord forced re-entry only after ejection.
[31] *R v Lockwood* (1856) *The Times,* April 23rd, 10f, QBD.

- It provides a useful summary of the principles and case law relating to rights of entry generally in distress and execution;
- It gives a working analysis of a claim for irregular distress; and,
- It examines how a claim for excessive distress, and/or sale at an undervalue, might be assessed on the evidence of the auction proceeds.

Wilson v South Kesteven District Council [2001] 1 WLR 387

Facts The case concerned a levy of distraint for business rates against hotel premises in Stamford. Removal of the distrained goods was arranged by the bailiffs and a dispute then arose over how much was payable to stop this process. The detailed facts of the case are given in the judgment.

Judgment of Simon Brown LJ: "If ever clarity were needed in the law it is surely with regard to the seizure and sale of a debtor's goods. What are the powers and obligations of the bailiff? What rights has the debtor? The answers to such questions should be simple and readily accessible. Yet the process of levying distress is an arcane one and the present law, as noted in the Law Commission's Working Paper on *Distress for Rent*, "is riddled with inconsistencies, uncertainties, anomalies and archaisms."[32]

The present appeal centres upon regulation 14 of the Non-Domestic Rating Collection & Enforcement) (Local Lists) Regulations and Schedule 3 (the fee scale) to those regulations, and raises a number of issues of obvious importance. It is convenient at once to set out the relevant provisions and this I shall do by reference to their terms following minor amendment in 1990; the particular distraint with which this appeal is concerned occurred in September 1992 before certain further amendments were made in 1993.

> "14(1) Where a liability order has been made, the authority which applied for the order may levy the appropriate amount by distress and sale of the goods of the debtor against whom the order was made.
> (2) The appropriate amount for the purposes of paragraph (1) is the aggregate of -
> (a) an amount equal to any outstanding sum which is or forms part of the amount in respect of which the liability order was made; and,
> (b) a sum determined in accordance with Schedule 3 in respect of charges connected with the distress.
> (3) If, before any goods are seized, the appropriate amount (including charges arising up to the time of the payment or tender) is paid or

[32] Law Commission no.97 (1986), p.145, para.5.1(1).

tendered to the authority, the authority shall accept the amount and the levy shall not be proceeded with.
(4) Where an authority has seized goods of the debtor in pursuance of the distress, but before sale of those goods the appropriate amount (including charges arising up to the time of the payment or tender) is paid or tendered to the authority, the authority shall accept the amount, the sale shall not be proceeded with and the goods shall be made available for collection by the debtor.
(5) The person levying distress on behalf of an authority shall carry with him the written authorisation of the authority, which he shall show to the debtor if so requested; and he shall hand to the debtor or leave at the premises where the distress is levied a copy of this regulation and Schedule 3 and a memorandum setting out the appropriate amount, and shall hand to the debtor a copy of any close or walking possession agreement entered into ...
(7) A distress shall not be deemed unlawful on account of any defect or want of form in the liability order, and no person making a distress shall be deemed a trespasser on that account; and no person making a distress shall be deemed a trespasser from the beginning on account of any subsequent irregularity in making the distress, but a person sustaining special damage by reason of the subsequent irregularity may recover full satisfaction for the special damage (and no more) by proceedings in trespass or otherwise."

The appeal is brought by the defendant rating authority against the order of Judge Julian Hall made in the Peterborough County Court on 18 March 1999, entering judgment on the issue of liability in favour of the plaintiff debtor for damages to be assessed for "unlawful distress starting on 22 September 1992". Ordinarily at this stage of the judgment I would set out at least the basic facts of the case and the trial judge's main conclusions. However, for reasons which will eventually become clear this would, I believe, tend to cloud rather than illuminate the real issues arising. Instead, therefore, I turn at once to these, different though they are from those regarded as determinative below. As I see it, the critical issues are these:

1. Is a debtor entitled to halt the distraint process by payment or tender at any time or only at either of two specific stages during the process, respectively before seizure and before sale?
2. What should be stated in the memorandum required by reg.14(5) and when should it be handed over to the debtor or left at the premises? and,
3. What is the consequence of completing the distraint process without having complied properly with the requirements of reg.14(5)?

Issue 1- when may the process be halted? This dispute hitherto has been litigated on the basis that the debtor is entitled to halt the distraint process by an appropriate payment or tender at any time. The bailiffs advanced no contrary contention and, indeed, no one questioned the correctness of that assumption until we ourselves questioned it in the course of the plaintiff's submissions. Nor, surprisingly, did the local authority appear avid to encourage the court in its doubts. And yet I have come to the clear conclusion that the assumption was wrong and that, so far from the debtor having a continuous opportunity to end the process, that opportunity arises only (a) before any goods are seized (reg.14(3)), and (b) after seizure and before sale (reg.14(4)). There is, in short, no opportunity to redeem the goods afforded during the period of seizure itself.

We are, as it seems to me, driven to that conclusion both by the scheme and language of the regulation and by consideration of the practicalities. As to the former, it is evident that paragraphs 3 and 4 of the regulation are directed at two distinct stages. Paragraph 3 in terms applies only to the period "before any goods are seized" whilst para.4 postulates that the relevant goods have been seized and in terms applies to the next stage, "before sale". Had it been intended to provide for payment or tender to halt the actual process of seizure, there would have been no need for two separate paragraphs framed as they are; rather a continuum of opportunity would have been reflected in a single paragraph allowing for payment or tender at any time before sale. And consider the practicalities. The payment or tender has to include the accrued charges. These are readily calculable before the process of seizure is begun. And after seizure and before sale comes an interval of time sufficient to consider the charges and in the event of dispute have them taxed, if necessary obtaining meantime a county court injunction to restrain sale: see *Steel Linings v Bibby*.[33] During seizure, however, the determination of the accrued charges will almost inevitably be difficult. They are likely to be accruing minute by minute. They may well depend upon the charges of others such as transport and removal contractors. And, depending upon the precise point at which the tender is made, they may also be affected by the debtor's own ability to undo the seizure process, for example by unloading or collecting goods already seized. All that, as will appear, is well illustrated by the facts of this very case.

Issue 2 what memorandum is required by regulation 14(5)? The only explicit requirements of para.5 of the memorandum are that it shall set out "the appropriate amount", and that "the person levying distress" shall hand it to the debtor or leave it at the premises. What, let us first consider, is "the

[33] See chapter 7.

appropriate amount"? Were reg.14 better drafted the answer would be a good deal clearer than it is. The phrase, of course, appears in each of the first five paragraphs of the regulation (and again, indeed, in regs 16 & 17). Paragraph 2 defines it as (a) the sum due under the liability order (including the court costs: see reg.12(6)(b) and (b) the Sch.3 charges). Ostensibly, however, it defines it only "for the purposes of para.(1)". Paragraphs (3) and (4) each refer to "the appropriate amount (including charges arising up to the time of the payment or tender)". Why, one wonders, was it thought necessary in these paragraphs to specify that the appropriate amount includes accrued charges? Would not the same result have been more simply achieved by extending the paragraph (2) definition to paragraphs (3) and (4) as well? But more importantly, what is the suggested meaning in paragraph (5) of the bare phrase "the appropriate amount", there being in this paragraph (in contrast to paragraphs (3) and (4)) no express inclusion of accrued charges?

For my part I would construe paragraph (5) purposively so as to ensure that the memorandum achieves its maximum benefit. That must surely be to inform the debtor as fully as possible of the nature and extent of his liability. To that end "the appropriate amount" should, I think, include the basic scale charge for the distress, i.e. that appropriate to head B "for levying distress" which will by then have accrued. It might also with advantage specify the stipulated head D daily charge, at all events in cases where the debtor has been prepared to enter into a close or walking possession agreement.

To the same end it seems to me plainly desirable that the memorandum should be handed over to the debtor at the earliest opportunity, ideally when the person levying distress first enters the premises and thereby embarks upon the distraint process. I suggested in *Evans v South Ribble BC* when seeking to distill the relevant law into a number of basic principles, that the first principle was this: "The process of distress consists of three stages: the entry into the premises, the seizure there of goods, and the subsequent securing of the goods (generally called impounding)".[34]

I would hold therefore that anyone entering the premises with a view to the immediate seizure of some or all of the occupier's goods is a "person levying distress" within the meaning of regulation 14(5). He must carry for the purpose (and if requested show to the debtor) his written authorisation. He does not need actually to seize (let alone remove) any goods before he comes under this obligation. True, as Mrs Wilson points out, head A of the fee scale clearly contemplates that premises may be visited without any levying of

[34] See chapter 3.

distress. I would construe this, however, to refer only to a preliminary visit to premises, perhaps to see whether they have been vacated or are otherwise worth distraining upon, and not to a visit upon which, for example, the bailiff proposes to invite the debtor to sign a walking possession agreement. I do not think any of this conflicts with what Donaldson J said in *Brintons v Wyre Forest DC.*[35] If, however, it does, then I would overrule that decision.

The advantages of handing over the memorandum (and, of course, copies of reg.14 and Schedule 3, as para.5 specifies must also be done) as soon as possible are surely obvious. The debtor will then be given the maximum opportunity to pay off his liability before the process gets fully under way and charges begin to escalate. Unless the debtor is shown regulation 14(3) before seizure of goods begins, his chance of buying off the bailiffs at that initial stage will obviously have gone before he even learns of his rights. I would accordingly construe regulation 14(5) to require the bailiff on or shortly after entry onto the premises to hand over to the debtor (if present) a memorandum setting out the sum owing including the Sch.3 scale charge for the levying of distress under head B.

If the debtor is not present so that the memorandum (and copies of reg.14 and Sch.3) will instead have to be left at the premises, then the memorandum ought properly to alert the debtor to the fact that further Sch.3 charges under head C have already accrued (if goods have already been removed) and/or are likely to accrue unless the appropriate sum is now paid. I may perhaps note that the 1993 amending regulations introduced a new head C into Schedule 3, namely "For one attendance with a vehicle with a view to the removal of goods (where, following the levy, goods are not removed): Reasonable costs and fees incurred". Clearly, if that particular expense were nowadays to be incurred, the memorandum should make express reference to it.

Issue 3 what is the consequence of non-compliance with regulation 14(5)? I can deal with this issue altogether more shortly. A failure to provide the required memorandum and/or copies of regulation 14 and Sch.3 would clearly constitute a "subsequent irregularity" within the meaning of reg.14(7) and would thus entitle the debtor to recover any special damage proved to have resulted from it. Special damage has a wide meaning and covers all loss occasioned by the irregularity: see *Steel Linings v Bibby.* The important point to note, however, is that causation must be established; the distraint process itself is not rendered unlawful by such an irregularity: see *Quinlan v LB Hammersmith & Fulham.*[36]

---

[35] See chapter 3.
[36] See chapter 7.

With that approach to the regulations in mind let me at last come to the facts of the present case which, since it will be seen to have been litigated below on a misconceived basis, I can take comparatively shortly.
The plaintiff, Mrs Wilson, was the proprietor of the Stamford Post Hotel in Stamford (the premises). She fell into debt. On July 29th 1992 a liability order was made against her by the Stamford Magistrates in respect of unpaid non-domestic rates due to the defendant authority in respect of the premises for the year 1992-1993. The liability order was in the sum of £3,266.25 for arrears plus £16 for court costs.

On September 11th 1992 bailiffs, Jefferies & Pennicott (Northern) Ltd, paid the first of three visits to the premises. The bailiffs, I should note, were brought in by the defendant authority as third party to the action but thereafter joined with the authority in presenting a united front to Mrs Wilson's claim and, indeed, became jointly represented below.

The bailiff's representative on September 11th 1992 was a Mr Goodwin who is said to have made an inventory of the premise's contents and who certainly handed over to Mrs Wilson a completed pro forma document purporting to be the required regulation 14(5) memorandum. The document is headed "Notice of seizure of goods and inventory" and makes reference to the relevant 1989 Regulations. It then identifies the debtor and the premises and continues:

"Amount for which this distress is made:

Arrears due to authority:	£3,266.25
Court costs awarded by the court	16.00
Levy fee to scale schedule:	78.66
Statutory walking possession fee (15 days @ 45 p per day)	7.93
Amount now due:	£3,368.84 "

Having then stated that all payments must be made to the bailiffs and not to the authority, the form continues:

> "Take notice that by virtue of an authority given to me by the above council I have this day seized and distrained on the premises situated at the address shown above the goods specified in the following inventory for the sum due for the arrears and costs under the liability order issued to the council in the magistrate's court as shown above. And further take notice that unless the amounts be paid inclusive of all the costs and charges of

> this distress, within six days from the date hereof, the goods listed below will be removed from the premises and sold according to the law."

There then follows an inventory (which, on the copy produced, is unclear as to the details), and, at the foot of the document, Mr Goodwin's signature and the date. Schedule 3 (although not regulation 14) is printed on the reverse side of the form. I shall postpone until later my criticisms of that form. In the week following Mr Goodwin's visit, Mrs Wilson paid off £200 towards her outstanding liability but that, perhaps unsurprisingly, did not halt the process of distraint.

On September 22nd 1992 the bailiffs made their second visit to the premises, intent this time on seizing (assuming seizure had not already constructively taken place on September 11th), and more particularly upon removing (and thereby impounding), the goods. On this occasion their representative was a Mr Harris and he attended with two lorries and two men hired from a firm in Louth to assist him. The men seem to have been there at least intermittently from about 4 pm to about 9 pm and, during this time, a number of crates of beers and minerals were loaded onto the vehicles. The visit ended, however, when, as the judgment below records:

> "[Mr Harris] made the mistake, as [Mrs Wilson] saw it, of popping outside to talk to his fellow bailiff or fellow helper, driver, and she took the opportunity to slam the door behind him, locked all the other doors and kept him out. One way or another, his file stayed in the hotel while he did not."

The file was never recovered and thus it is that the only copy of the memorandum of September 11th available is the one with the unclear inventory produced on discovery by Mrs Wilson herself.

The bailiffs made their third and final visit the next day, September 23rd, when again Mr Harris attended with two drivers and two men hired from Louth. They were accompanied by the police and were permitted entry and on this occasion, over a period of many hours, the seizure and loading up of the contents of the hotel onto the lorries was completed. At about 6 o'clock, however, whilst the work was still under way, Mrs Wilson tendered £3,500 in cash in discharge of her liability. £1,000 of this was produced by a friend and backer, a Mr Brennan, whom the previous day she had asked for help and who had brought the money down overnight from Darlington. The remaining £2,500 was cash which she had been keeping against her quarterly VAT return and which she went to fetch that afternoon from a safe deposit box in her bank at Corby. Mr Harris rejected the tender, however, on the grounds that it was by then insufficient to meet Mrs Wilson's liability. He is said to have demanded an additional £1,300 or perhaps £1,800 by way of charges. The removal process therefore continued. Finally, by now late in the evening, when all the contents of the hotel had been loaded onto the lorries, Mr Harris handed to Mrs Wilson a further memorandum in similar form to that which Mr Goodwin had previously left with her save that this second form (a) put the "amount now due" at £3,360.91 (i.e. it omitted the suggested walking possession fee of £7.93) and (b) had attached to it by way of inventory a number of sheets which listed every single item removed from the premises and stated:

> "Re outstanding non-domestic rates- balance outstanding £3,271 plus removal costs and storage fees and waiting time and auction fees-pursuant to the above order, the items listed below have today been seized and will be sold by public auction without reserve unless full payment including all costs are paid into our office by 29th September 1992."

By the time the loading process was completed on 23rd September it was too late to deliver the goods to the auctioneer's sale room at Alford. They therefore had to be taken that night to Louth and delivered to Alford the next day. In due course they were all sold at auction in the course of three successive sales, the sum realised being sufficient to meet the whole of Mrs Wilson's liability including the full charges of the distress and sale, leaving her a small credit balance of some £73. Precisely how much the charges were at any particular stage, it has proved impossible to discover. The action was not brought until 1996 and the hearing in March 1999 took place over six years after the events in question. But realistically these details do not matter. The approach taken by the judge below, as he himself put it, "side-stepped the question of what was owing". My own approach, different though it is, likewise makes the details of the charges immaterial.

As already indicated, the case below was contested on the mistaken footing that regulation 14(4) allowed the debtor to tender payment at any time, including therefore in the middle of the removal process which was when finally Mrs Wilson came to make her offer of £3,500. The evidence at the hearing stretched over three days, the fourth day being devoted to legal submissions and an extempore judgment. The first main factual issue at trial was whether Mrs Wilson had ever in fact made any offer. Mr Harris denied this. That issue, however, was resolved in Mrs Wilson's favour and the finding is, of course, unassailable. The critical next issue arising was whether the offer had been made in a sufficient sum given that charges had obviously been accruing up to the point when it was made. The judge expressed his conclusions upon that issue (the issue he plainly regarded as determinative) as follows:

(1) As to the memorandum which was handed over when the bailiffs finally left the premises on September 23rd 1992 (the defendants were not, apparently, relying on the earlier memorandum of September 11th):
(a) that memorandum "was, by that time"- that is, by the time when the first seizure was held to have been made on 22nd September-"not written. There was therefore no memorandum, no copy of Sch.3, no copy of regulation 14 provided at the time of seizure, and all those mean that there had been what I regard as a gross breach of regulation 14."
(b) "The form of this memorandum, in my judgment, conceals the true position, and is inadequate to alert the plaintiff to what the true position was. It is positively misleading, I find".
(2) "In my judgment, regulation 14(4) implies an obligation on the bailiffs to know the up-to-date figure, and to be prepared to put it in writing. It seems to me, and in my judgment I rule, that at the time when a document is served or relied on, it must be as up to date as possible. In regulation 14(4) the appropriate figure, on the face of the document, 'amount now due', must reflect the instant position. It is not enough to say that, 'Oh, by the way, everything else is covered by, 'inclusive of all the costs and charges of the distress'."
(3) "Either this document does not conform with regulation 14(4), or in my judgment, by their conduct and lack of knowledge, the bailiffs have precluded the plaintiff from relying on a remedy by the regulations ... I find that £3,500 was offered which was, in my judgment, more than enough to satisfy what was then lawfully claimed, £3,360.91. As I say, in my judgment, by producing a memorandum that is so misleading, the defendants have precluded the plaintiff from relying on the remedy provided by the regulations and are precluded from relying on it. Either way, in my judgment, it was an unlawful distress thereafter."

In short, the judge appears to have concluded that a tender of no more than £3,360.91 was required to terminate this distraint under regulation 14(4) unless and until a regulation 14(5) memorandum was handed over specifying some larger sum to be due as a result of accrued charges, and that, of course, never happened. In the result, Mrs Wilson's goods should never have been removed so that she has become entitled to damages, apparently on the footing that, but for this unlawful distress, she would have continued trading as the proprietor of the Stamford Post Hotel.

That conclusion is, no doubt, understandable given the way the case was conducted below. But it is not to my mind a conclusion which is sustainable in the light of what I would hold to be the correct approach to regulation 14. In my judgment, Mrs Wilson had no legal right to buy off this distraint process on September 23rd 1992. The whole of that day was devoted to the seizure and removal of her goods and it fell, therefore, between the two opportunities for tender afforded respectively by regulation 14(3) (before seizure began) and by regulation 14(4) (after seizure ended and before sale). Of course debtors can always hope to persuade bailiffs to call off a distraint by making a sufficient offer during the seizure process. But they cannot compel this and can hardly complain if the bailiffs demand as the price of co-operation the full payment of all their charges (which is likely to be put at a round figure broadly calculated to meet all expenses incurred). Take this very case. It seems to me entirely unsurprising that by 6pm or thereabouts on September 23rd the bailiffs were demanding accrued charges substantially exceeding the £340 representing the difference between (a) the amount due under the liability order, £3,360.91, and (b) the £200 already paid together with the £3,500 tendered.

As for the memoranda dated respectively September 11th and 23rd, it seems to me that the former (handed over as it was before the seizure process began) was altogether a better candidate than the latter for satisfying the requirements of regulation 14(5). The former gave the debtor a six day opportunity (which continued in fact for 11 days) to buy off the distraint process for £3,368.84. The latter notice really was of very little value to the debtor, telling her no more than that various unspecified further charges would accrue and have to be paid within six days if the sale of the goods thereafter was to be prevented. Why then should the defendants not rely on the earlier memorandum? True, its inclusion of a statutory walking possession fee of £7.93 was incorrect (a) because the figure itself is a plain miscalculation and, (b) more fundamentally, because no walking possession agreement was in fact entered into. True, too, the form by its first recital states that the bailiff's representative has "this day seized and distrained ... the goods specified in the ... inventory" whereas, certainly on the judge's finding, no such seizure took place that day. That first recital, of course, contrasts with the second recital which threatens removal and sale after a further six days, apparently inferring that once the goods have been removed there will be no further opportunity to redeem them. Better, surely, that the memorandum should specify the sum to be paid to halt the process before seizure (in the sense of removal) begins, and should then indicate that, if the goods have to be removed for sale, further charges will accrue and have to be paid if such a sale is thereafter to be prevented. But none of these criticisms were apparently advanced by the debtor; rather her case appears to have been that the tender which she made on September 23rd could only lawfully be refused if a memorandum specifying charges which took the outstanding total to above £3,500 had already been (or perhaps was then and there) served upon her, to my mind an impossible argument.

Let it be assumed, however, that neither of the memoranda served in this case strictly satisfied the requirements of regulation 14(5). That failure, just as the bailiff's failure (as the judge also found) to serve on the debtor a copy of regulation 14, would clearly constitute an irregularity in the process. But would such irregularities of themselves entitle the debtor to succeed in her claim for damages for unlawful distress? In my judgment they would not and nor, indeed, do I understand the judge to have concluded otherwise. His judgment, as already indicated, was squarely based upon his conclusion that the bailiffs were legally bound to accept the debtor's tender. Assume, as I would hold, that they were not so bound. The debtor would then need to establish that, because of the non-service upon her of (a) a memorandum in different form or at an earlier time than those served and/or (b) a copy of regulation 14, she failed by payment or tender to halt this distress and sale which otherwise she would have done. On no view of the evidence, as it seems to me, could such a conclusion be reached.

From all this it follows that I for my part, whilst naturally accepting all the judge's findings of fact, would hold his conclusions to be unsustainable. I would allow this appeal."

Commentary

The judgment is an illuminating discussion of a previously little examined aspect of distress and, rather like *Khazanchi*, it gives new perspectives on a subject which may have been considered uncontentious before. The Court of Appeal's judgment, briefly stated, is that the debtor may make payment *before* removal or *after* removal, but not during the process because the charges are accruing second by second and cannot be ascertained with certainty.

Unfortunately, this clear decision is bedevilled by an imprecision in language at a vital point. This was forced upon Simon Brown LJ by the Regulations, a statutory instrument which has never been noted for its lack of ambiguity as the judge himself observed. When discussing issue 1 Simon Brown LJ speaks repeatedly of 'seizure' when given, the context of the case, one might more properly expect him to discuss 'removal.' Indeed, near the end of the judgment he clearly states that he is discussing "seizure (in the sense of removal)"- acknowledging, it would seem, the shortcomings of the wording of the Regulations. This has generated further regrettable confusion since.

It could well be that costs cannot be fixed during seizure (in the sense of levying) but in *Wilson* we are indisputably concerned with a later removal (though again this could occur immediately after an initial entry and seizure): Simon Brown LJ mentions "transport and removal contractors" and "unloading and collecting goods" for example. It is of course likely that removal will be an extended process during which considerable charges will be accruing, unlike most seizures. The looseness of the Regulations and the terms the judgment was therefore obliged to use have given rise to other disputes about local tax distraint, most particularly the correct interpretation of the Head H 'redemption fee' in the fee scale.

The court criticises the documents supplied by the bailiffs to Mrs Wilson. However, these errors are treated as irregularities only. They were not such profound mistakes as to undermine the entire levy and render it illegal. It seems clear that bailiffs should be prepared to provide several sets of documents to debtors (for example, after seizure and again immediately before physical removal commences) or to ensure that the first notice of seizure is detailed in setting out the subsequent charges which may be added to an account. We may note that two separate such documents are mandatory in distress for rent and execution for road traffic penalties, as discussed in the case of *Culligan* in the next chapter.

Conclusions

Fortunately for most debtors, removals and sales are rare occurrences. The expense and inconvenience militates against them in many cases. Certainly, the result is unlikely to be the discharge of the debt if domestic chattels are being sold and the case of *Wilson* has shown how charges can mount whilst sale prices will be low. The next chapter considers bailiffs' fees specifically.

Chapter 6

FEES FOR ENFORCEMENT

Introduction

Inevitably, because enforcement agents are commercial enterprises rather than state employees, the need to make a profit in a competitive market from levying distress and execution has always been a source of friction between debtors and bailiffs. Indeed, it can also be a source of friction between bailiffs and their client creditors. This was as true in Victorian times as now. In 1849 a solicitor with 50 years' experience wrote to the *Legal Observer* to complain that "the exactions of sheriff's officers are proverbial. Not content with the poundage allowed by law, out of which the expenses of sale ought to be liquidated, they use every device to extort a larger sum." Differences over this kind of practice could lead to enforcement agents suing their dissatisfied principals. Similar complaints may still be heard today from judgment creditors and legal action still takes place between the parties. A modern example is the recent decision in *JBW Group Ltd v Westminster City Council* [2010].[1] In this case JBW unsuccessfully appealed a judgment of the High Court rejecting a claim issued by them against the city council. The company had been contracted by Westminster to collect road traffic penalties. When the contract was terminated, the company was still holding 9,400 warrants upon which work to the value of £500,000 had been done. Having returned the warrants to the authority as required, JBW sued to recover these unpaid fees. In his decision Pill LJ highlighted the risk taken by enforcement agencies in such cases, observing that the company had to take "the rough with the smooth" - that is, if a contract is not extended or continued, uncollected fees may be lost. This is because fees are only recoverable from debtors and local authorities have no liability to pay them. There was no express term on this matter in the contract, but the judge did not accept that there should be any implied term either. As a result, JBW had no right to recover their fees either from the council or from any other firm chosen subsequently to deal with the same cases. The next firm of bailiffs

---

[1] *Legal Observer* (1849) vol.45, p.279; *Smith v Broadbent* (1892) 66 LT 260; (2010) EWCA Civ. 413; see too [2009] EWHC 2697 QB.

appointed was under no obligation to collect fees earned by JBW or to account for them to the company. Indeed, there was no exclusivity in the contract. Westminster could issue warrants to JBW, or it could issue them to another firm, or it was quite within its rights to choose to issue them to none. Lastly, there was no assignment by Westminster to JBW of any right to the fees (or to the debt).

Fee scales have regulated the relationship between bailiffs and debtors for the last two hundred years, with the courts given a power to settle disputes. Each different form of seizure of goods has a subtly different fee scale and, of course, the scales in operation in earlier decades had their own unique features too. What is emphasised in this chapter is the broad principles to be applied to the interpretation of scales. For example, fees are only permissible if they are for work that was verifiably and justifiably undertaken. Where a sheriff's officer first justified an extra amount as auctioneer's fees - and later said that it represented the extra costs of conducting the levy- the sum was disallowed and had to be refunded.[2] Likewise fees charged for being in possession when no such work was done have been repeatedly struck out by the courts.[3] Fees that are far higher than the sums permitted, or which are simply not allowed by the fee scale, should not be charged.[4] If they are, the courts may take a very serious view, treating them as 'excessive and extortionate' and ordering their repayment along with costs and interest.[5] Under the Distress (Costs) Act 1817 a treble penalty for wrongful charging could be imposed and it may be instructive to note that bailiffs were often penalised by magistrates for making charges higher than those allowed for in the fee scale, for adding on fees simply not permitted by the scale and for charging for work not actually undertaken.[6]

Just as the detail of fee scales may have changed, the name of the principal remedy for resolving disputes has altered. Before 1998 it was termed 'taxation' but since has been called 'detailed assessment.' Nonetheless, the approach of the judges is still very much the same. Detailed assessment continues to provide the main forum for examining bailiff charges, although

---

[2] *Haydon v Barton* (1849) 5 Ir LR 410 Ex.

[3] *Warden v Richardson* (1888) 33 EG 143; *Mutter v Spearing* (1905) 119 LT 134/ 13 PMR 392; *Edwards v Morey* (1905) 13 PMR 460; *Scott v Denton* (1906) 121 LT 95; *Baldry v Cane* (1906) 14 PMR 808.

[4] *Stokes v British Mutual Banking Co Ltd* (1886) *The Times* July 13th 6c.

[5] *Masters v Lowther* (1852) 11 CB 948. There are many cases on this subject, for example: *Smith v Mall* (1623) 2 Rolle 263, *Nash v Allen* (1843) 4 QB 784, *Wrightup v Greenacre* (1847) 10 QB 1, *Pilkington v Cooke* (1847) 16 M&W 615, *Ellison v Fazakerley* (1848), *The Times* April 11th 7c, *King v Milne* 1 LJKB 108; *R v Villers* 11 Price 579.

[6] See for example, *The Times* August 18th 1825 3d, May 31st 1836 6g, September 21st 1852 7e & March 20th 1882 12a, November 13th 1888 4a.

it was recently held in the case of *Omega Logic v Clive Oddy, Mrs Susan Oddy interpleader claimant* (2010) that, once fees have been cancelled by order of the court, there is no scope for their retrospective endorsement.[7]

In addition to detailed assessment of disputed (and generally unpaid fees) there is also an option to recover fees paid under protest by means of civil court claim.[8] Lastly it should be recalled that linked to, and in addition to, assessment, there is a sanction against improper and excessive fees through the certification complaints process in the county court (see chapter 1). As Lord Tenterden expressed it in a case in 1829, bailiffs have a duty "to take care not to make unreasonable or improper charges."[9]

Whilst the courts may excuse an incorrect charge made in error, they certainly will not forgive deliberate overcharging. Arguing that the statutory scale rates are too low- and that only disreputable firms would work for the set fees alone- was a defence attempted in one case. The court rejected this as an indirect admission that the illegal charges had been imposed intentionally. The suggestion that extra charges were the "universal custom of the trade" was equally of no assistance to the defendants.[10]

Much of the case law on fees was developed in the context of execution by sheriff's officers. Curiously, the modern fee scale currently applicable to High Court enforcement officers under Schedule 3 of the High Court Enforcement Regulations 2004 allows the greatest leeway in charging in this area compared to other forms of seizure of goods. This was confirmed recently in *Bernard Loynes v Beswicks Solicitors* that: "Any business is entitled to seek to reduce the transaction cost (if I can describe it in that way) of calculating charges and to standardise them, not in an unreasonable way, but in a reasonable fashion. As I understand it, that is what the respondents [the HCEO] have done ... although these charges are at least in some degree standardised, it is because that is the cheaper and more economical way of approaching the fixing of such fees." [11] Accordingly, a calculation of the average cost of (say) running a call centre, which is then spread across every warrant executed, would not necessarily be regarded as improper by the Court.[12] Nonetheless, as Irwin J stated in his judgment, any "charges that go

---

[7] County court claim 9BQ00071, Queens Bench claim WF001820/99.
[8] *Veale v Atwood* (1833) *The Times* February 2nd, 5g, CP.
[9] *In Re: Longstaffe ex. p. Robinson* (1896) 49 LT 60; *Duncombe v Hicks* (1898) 42 Sol Jo 343; 47 EG 171; *Streek v Gill* (1829) *The Times* July 13th 3e, KBD.
[10] *Black v Standage & Price* (1831) *The Times*, June 27th, 6e.
[11] (2010) Queens Bench Division.
[12] See further in *Powers of distress* 4.6. *Law of seizure of goods* c.11 and *Persons of no value? cc.5 & 10.*

beyond [standardised charges] require an order from [the Court]." *Loynes v Beswicks* is a clearly valuable decision for HCEOs. However, specific fees and figures are not identified in the judgment we have, which was not a decision in a detailed assessment but on an application for permission to appeal. Different charges calculated by the firm on the same basis of an 'average' charge would probably still need the Court's sanction. Other firms could clearly adopt the same approach, but it would seem safest to argue that they would need their own specific Court orders to be certain that their fees were lawful.

Ex parte Arnison & others (1868) 3 Exch 56

Facts The case concerned a levy of distress for tithe rent charge on growing crops. The only matter to concern us now was the calculation of the distrainor's fees. The bailiff levied on growing grass and charged 2/6 daily for a man in possession (a total of £5 5/-). The debtors disputed that any such charge was necessary or could be justified.

Judgment of Kelly CB: "... Then, as to the charge for retaining possession: in my opinion the distrainor under the circumstances of this case is not entitled to make any charge whatever, unless it be some trifling sum, such as for putting up a notice board, for example, to notify that the land was in the custody of the law, or for taking any other step whereby he might reasonably assert his possession of the land. It is unnecessary to enter into a general argument as to the manner in which possession of growing crops may be taken. The manner in one case may vary from the manner in another. But where we are dealing with a piece of land of the sort described in this case, it is contrary to common sense to say that a person is to take possession for nearly two months, charging all that time at the rate of 2s. 6d a day. After possession had once been taken, the only expense of retaining it which we could reasonably allow, would be that of putting up a public notice, or the adoption of some similar precaution. And I think the few shillings left undisposed of out of the £3 would amply suffice to meet that expense."

Martin B: "As to the charge of 2s. 6d. a day for a man in possession, I do not think that in such a case as this it can be made. The Distress (Costs) Act 1817 does not, in my judgment, apply under the circumstances we are dealing with here, and that being so, we have to consider whether the charge is "reasonable." Now I do not think we could possibly hold expenses sixteen times as great as the amount distrained for to be reasonable. Yet, adopting the claim made for a "man in possession," that is what the expenses in this case amount to. I, therefore, think that the rule should be made absolute."

Commentary

Although the Distress (Costs) Act 1817 may have allowed a sum for a man in possession, it could not be charged regardless of circumstances. This is a constant theme in debates over bailiffs' fees. The inclusion of a fee on a fee scale does not automatically permit its inclusion on the bill unless the work charged for can be shown to have been carried out- and also was actually and necessarily required. However, if a person in possession is made necessary by the circumstances- for example, the debtor's refusal to pay or a refusal to allow goods to be removed forthwith- then a possession fee may be regarded as a proper and legal expense incidental to a levy.[13] Needless to say, perhaps, any fee that is included must be justified by the work which has, in reality, been undertaken. It should not only be reasonable in itself but should be proportionate to the debt being recovered.

Lumsden v Burnett [1898] 2 QB 177

Facts The collector of taxes distrained for a tax debt of under £20. A walking possession agreement was made with the debtor's daughter without his consent. The outstanding tax was then settled, but a demand was made for a fee of 15 shillings for the man in possession which paid under protest. The debtor then sued in the county court to recover this amount.

Judgment of A L Smith LJ: "The amount in dispute in this appeal is insignificant, but the point raised is of some practical importance, and the case has acquired the name of 'The Walking Possession Case.' It raises the question, whether a collector of income tax when he distrains upon the goods of a taxpayer for unpaid income tax which does not exceed £20 (in this case amounting to the sum of 13s. 4d.) is entitled to levy upon the taxpayer, in addition to the tax due, 2/6 a day for a man in possession (amounting in this case to 15/-, that is, six days at 2/6 per day), when in truth and in fact the man had not been really in possession, but at the most has been in constructive possession of the goods distrained.

The inventory of goods seized was thus filled in, "shop, eight pair trousers." The other printed document which the collector then took with him to the plaintiff's house was the following:

> "To Mr. H. E. Burnett, 24, Queen's Road, S.E., or whom it may concern." (This is the defendant's, the collector's, name) "I hereby authorize you to re-enter at any time upon the premises, by force or as you may think fit, and to break open doors or windows for the purpose

[13] *Ex parte Sims, in re: Grubb* (1877) 4 Ch D 521.

> of taking possession under your warrant of distress, and I also undertake not to move away, or allow to be moved away from the said premises any of the goods and chattels which are now therein, until the amount levied for, together with all costs and charges of maintaining the levy, are duly paid and settled. And in the event of the man now in possession quitting the said premises temporarily, or from any cause whatever previous to the removal, by you, of the said goods from the above-mentioned premises, or the distraint being otherwise satisfied, it shall not be considered in any way an abandonment of the levy.
>
> I also undertake not to replevy the said goods and chattels and not to bring any action or actions at law against you or either of you, or prefer any indictment for any of your proceedings in this matter.
>
> Dated this 29th day of April, 1897."

The only person the tax-collector and his man found upon the plaintiff's premises upon April 29th, 1897, was the taxpayer's daughter, a child of about thirteen and a half years of age, whose signature the tax-collector then obtained to the printed document above mentioned, having first demanded the tax of 13/4 from her. This child had no authority whatever from her father, the plaintiff, to sign this document, then for the first time produced by the tax-collector, and, indeed, the father never knew of this document, nor that his child had signed it, till long afterwards, when the tax-collector was insisting that the taxpayer should pay him 2/6 per day for the man having been, as he alleged, in possession for six days, amounting to the 15/- then claimed by him... The collector and his man then left the plaintiff's premises taking with them the document signed by the plaintiff's child, neither the collector nor the man remaining in possession of the goods distrained, though it appears that during the six days the man daily returned to the neighbourhood to keep, as he said, "watch on the premises and to see that nothing was removed," and this man also stated that sometimes he was in possession of two houses in one day...

The county court judge states that the defendant levied a distress which was in the first instance improper; and he afterwards abandoned it by not having a man in possession in such a way as to make it continuous possession.

We held in this Court not long since, in the case of *Bagshawes v Deacon*,[14] after full argument and discussing, amongst other authorities, *Ackland v*

[14] [1898] 2 QB 173.

Paynter, *Swann v Earl of Falmouth* and *Eldridge v Stacey*,[15] that where a sheriff goes out of possession and the point arises as to whether he has abandoned possession or not, the question always is one of fact, and is whether the sheriff by going out of possession, as he did here, abandoned the possession. A sheriff in some circumstances may go out of possession and again re-enter without having abandoned possession, and the question always is whether what he has done amounts to an abandonment of possession. Although the document signed by the child in this case clearly does not bind the plaintiff and is no evidence against him, yet it is strong evidence to show that the collector did not abandon possession, and his employing and paying a man to go and see that the goods distrained were not removed affords corroborating evidence that he went out with the intention of returning, and not of abandoning possession. But these findings of the county court judge are immaterial to the real question he had to try, which is the right of the collector apart from agreement to levy upon the plaintiff for the 15/- for the man said to have been in possession when the distress was for an amount not exceeding £20. This question has to be decided upon the statute regulating distresses for income tax not exceeding £20, which appears to have been altogether overlooked by the county court judge, and is not alluded to in the Divisional Court, which decided the case upon the question of whether there had been an agreement by the taxpayer to pay the 2/6 per day whether the man was in real possession or not, of which in my opinion, with submission to the Divisional Court, there was not a tittle of evidence.

There is an Act of Parliament which regulates what is to be charged by a collector for distress for income tax when such unpaid tax does not exceed 20l., and this is the Act of 1827. The question arises- What are these costs and charges? This brings me to the Distress (Costs) Acts of 1817 and 1827. By the Act of 1817, after reciting that divers persons acting as brokers, and distraining on the goods and chattels of others ... have of late made excessive charges to the great oppression of poor tenants and others, it is enacted that "from and after the passing of this Act no person whatsoever making any distress for rent, where the sum demanded and due shall not exceed the sum of £20 for and in respect of such rent .... shall have, take, or receive out of the produce of the goods or chattels distrained upon and sold, or from the tenant distrained on .... any other or more costs and charges for and in respect of such distress, or any matter or thing done therein, than such as are fixed and set forth in the schedule and hereunto annexed, and appropriated to each act which shall have been done in the course of such distress; and no person or persons whatsoever shall make any charge whatsoever for any act, matter, or

[15] Respectively 8 Price 95, 8 B&C 456 & 15 CB (NS) 458.

thing mentioned in the said schedule, unless such act shall have been really done." In this schedule, which is headed "Schedule of the limitation of costs and charges on distresses for small rents," is set forth as follows:

> "Levying distress, 3/-; man in possession, per day, 2/6."

Ten years afterwards, in the year 1827, all the provisions of the 1817 Act which related to distraining for rent not exceeding £20 were extended to any "distress or levy made for ... assessed taxes or other rates and taxes ... whatever where the sum demanded and due for such taxes ... should not exceed the sum of £20."

What, then, are the charges which can be made for a distress for income tax when an amount not exceeding £20 is due? It is clear that in such a case by the statute the charge for a man in possession may be made of 2/6 per day, but only if the act for which the charge is made has been really done, i.e., if the man charged for has really been in possession.

In the present case, at the most the man charged for at 2/6 per day has but been in constructive possession, and it is impossible to hold that constructive possession is the same thing as real possession, for the one is a reality and the other is not. For instance, how can there be real possession by one man of two, six, eight, or ten houses upon the same day? The thing is impossible. As, however, the statute of 1827 is a statute in favour of a taxpayer owing income tax not exceeding £20, I do not see why such a taxpayer may not agree with a collector, if the former desires neither to pay the tax due nor to suffer the inconvenience of having a man in real possession, to pay the 2/6 per day to the collector, even though the man does not remain in real possession; but unless such an agreement is made, I am clear that the collector cannot claim the 2/6 per day if the man does not remain in real possession. It is for these reasons I think, there being no agreement to the contrary, that the tax collector cannot charge 2/6 per day for the man who has not been really in possession of the goods distrained when the income tax due amounts, as in this case, to less than £20. I think, therefore, that this appeal must be allowed with costs to the appellant (who is the taxpayer) here and below."

Chitty LJ read the following judgment: "I am of the same opinion. Upon the undisputed facts there was, first, a valid demand for the tax; secondly, a refusal to pay; thirdly, a right to distrain for the tax; and, fourthly, a valid distress actually levied for the amount of the tax - 13/4- and the levy fee 3/-. The question of abandonment of the possession of the goods seized is one of fact. The document signed by the plaintiff's daughter does not bind him as an agreement: the daughter's signature was without any authority express or implied on his part. But the document is of importance on the question of abandonment. It shows an intention on the part of the defendant not to abandon the possession, but to retain it. Taking into consideration the document, but merely for the limited purpose above stated, and the other undisputed facts relating to the watching of the shop by the defendant's man, and his occasional entrances to see that the goods had not been removed, I say unhesitatingly that possession was not abandoned. As to the law on the subject, it is sufficient to refer to *Swann v Earl of Falmouth*, a case of distress, and to the recent case in this Court - *Bagshawes v Deacon* - relating to the analogous case of the sheriff.

The real and important question on this appeal is whether the defendant was entitled to the charge of 2/6 a day for the man in possession. By virtue of the statutes already referred to, the statute of the 1817 is made applicable to a distress for income tax, and inasmuch as the sum due for income tax did not exceed £20, that statute applies to this case. As appears from the preamble, the mischief against which the Act was directed was the oppression of poor tenants and others by excessive charges enacted in levying distresses. The enactments of the first section are clear, direct, and stringent. Where the sum demanded does not exceed £20, the section prohibits the having, taking, or receiving any other or more costs and charges for and in respect of the distress or any matter or thing done therein than such as are fixed by the schedule and appropriated to each act which shall have been done in the course of such distress, and the section concludes by declaring emphatically that "no person or persons whatsoever shall make any charge whatever for any act, matter, or thing mentioned in the said schedule unless such act shall have been really done." Clearly the charge for 2/6 for "man in possession per day" cannot be lawfully made where the possession is merely constructive or notional: to render the charge lawful within the Act the possession must be real or actual. In this case the possession of the defendant's man was constructive merely, and not real.

Had the document signed by the plaintiff's daughter, and taken away by the defendant, been signed by the plaintiff or by his authority, the case would have stood differently. The statute does not preclude the tenants and persons for whose benefit it was made from contracting themselves out of those benefits. It would often be to the advantage of the person upon whose goods the distress is levied for a sum which he is not prepared to pay at once to get rid of the inconvenience of having the bailiff's man in actual possession; and I can see no valid reason why he should not be at liberty to contract to pay the 2/6 a day for the man in constructive possession. To hold that he cannot so contract would inflict upon him an unnecessary inconvenience."

Commentary

Three principal findings were made by the court in this case:

- Walking possession is a valid means of impounding goods so that it was not necessary for the bailiff to remain physically in possession. The evidence of the walking possession agreement will contradict any argument that possession had been abandoned. The earlier cases cited in this judgment (*Ackland v Paynter, Bagshawes v Deacon)* show that any abandonment of possession, however urgent and necessary, must be sufficiently justified. A signed possession agreement with the debtor addresses these issues;
- The fees allowed by the fee scale are only chargeable if the conditions of the fee are complied with. It followed that if a fee was allowed for a man in possession, a man should actually have been in real possession. The Distress (Costs) Act 1817 stipulated that charges were only recoverable for acts that "have been really done." The Distress for Rent Rules 1988 still make a similar stipulation, which is applicable also to road traffic cases (see *Culligan* later).
- The debtor may agree to pay extra charges if they are for his/her benefit. In this case the agreement was made by a child without her father's knowledge and could not bind him. However, an agreement made by the debtor in order to avoid a man in possession was accepted as being lawful. Any such charges must, however, be for the convenience of the debtor and with that person's express agreement. Charges for payment by credit or debit card might fall into this category if properly evidenced, but other non-statutory charges more for the benefit and profit of the bailiff, such as for clamping or interference with clamps, might not be lawful.

Glasbrook v David & Vaux [1905] 1 KB 615

Facts The sheriff of Glamorgan sued the defendants for £22 13/-, the charges he had incurred levying execution on a writ issued by the defendants as judgment creditor, a writ later withdrawn at the request of the defendants because of the judgment debtors' bankruptcy. The amount of the plaintiff's charges had been settled by taxation (detailed assessment) at the sum claimed. The defendants nonetheless continued to dispute £19 which had been allowed for possession money (at 5/- for each day). They contended that this was a sum which plaintiff had no right to charge as one man had been left in possession under several writs issued by several creditors.

Judgment of Farwell J: "The question, to my mind, turns simply upon the construction of the rules under the Sheriff's Act 1887. The last clause of the rule provides that, "In every case where an execution is withdrawn, satisfied, or stopped, the fees under this order shall be paid by the person issuing the execution": that is this case. The sheriff seized, and for the purpose of my decision I assume that he seized all the goods once for all. I think that is the fair meaning of the admissions, and I think that is the point the parties have come here to try. There were seven levies altogether, and, the goods having been once seized, there could be no subsequent seizure. The intention of the Act of 1887 was no doubt to enable the sheriff to recover the poundage and his expenses. Although the Act of Parliament uses the word "fees," and, of course, the rule follows it, when you come to look at the details they are the actual expenses: first, of making inquiries; secondly, of seizure; thirdly, of mileage; fourthly, of the man in possession.

The sheriff claims to have payment for the same man in possession from each of the judgment creditors. The result would be that the sheriff would get a very large sum (I am told £120) as possession money. I do not think that can be the true meaning of these rules. I think the proper view is that the sheriff was entitled to have his poundage, and, in addition to that, these fees, which are actual out of pocket expenses, and all of which stand on the same footing.

It has been held that there can be only one fee for seizure and one for mileage. If there can be only one seizure, and one journey to make a seizure, the possession also, so long as there is only one man in possession, must, it seems to me, be treated as a single possession. And I come to that conclusion the more readily because the rule provides that the man is in every case to provide his own board. That looks as if this 5/- a day is meant to keep the sheriff from being out of pocket. In *Ex parte Sims* James LJ treats possession as being one of the incidental expenses that the Act intended to provide for; and I think this case is indistinguishable in principle from the decision of Vaughan Williams J in *In re Wells, ex parte Sheriff of Kent.*[16]

I am unable to see any ground for distinguishing between seizure, mileage, and possession. The three really hold together, and I think Wright J. in *In re: Morgan* took that same view. The result is that, whatever may be the liability of the various judgment creditors to the sheriff so long as he remains unpaid- and as to that liability I say nothing- when he has been paid in respect of seizure and mileage and possession by one creditor he cannot recover the same sum from any of the others."

Commentary

This case is a simple confirmation of the fees principle that undertaking only one task, regardless of the number of warrants involved, should attract only one fee. The judgment may be compared it to the recent decision in *Throssell*

[16] 5 Ch. D. 375; (1893) 68 LT (NS.) 231.

(see later) and contrasted to other cases of the time. In *Re: Wells ex parte the Sheriff of Kent* (1893) it was ruled that, if a sheriff has made a seizure under one writ, and then has a second writ delivered to him, he cannot charge a further levy fee or mileage unless there is a second levy at a different location.[17]

In *Re: Morgan* [1904] the High Court considered the charges permissible in a situation where a county court bailiff levied under two warrants of execution issued by separate creditors against the goods of the debtor. A couple of days later, while still in possession under the previous two warrants, the bailiff levied a third execution on the goods of the debtor on the same premises. In each case the bailiff seized and impounded different chattels to satisfy each warrant. Possession under all three executions was held by the same person and was retained until the debtor was made bankrupt shortly afterwards, at which time the goods were handed over to the Official Receiver. The court bailiff claimed his costs in the bankruptcy, asserting that he was entitled to possession money under each execution, notwithstanding the fact that possession under the second and third warrants was held simultaneously with that under the first warrant and by the same person. The Official Receiver disputed this claim. At taxation the court found for the bailiff. The Receiver appealed to the High Court. Based on the wording of the fee scale then applicable, the court found that separate levies on different groups of goods should attract separate fees. Although the goods were kept in possession in one place on the same premises, there were still three separate possessions under each of the warrants. Wright J inclined to the view that, as a general principle, separate seizures with separate inventories deserved separate fees. Similarly, in *In Re: Broster ex. p. Pruddall* (1897) a county court bailiff who had levied execution on a warrant was required to levy for rent arrears as well under the provision now to be found as section 102 of the County Courts Act 1984. This was treated as a separate seizure and on taxation was held to entitle the bailiff to a separate fee. Although once again the decision is founded on the form of the applicable section of the relevant statute, it is indicative of the courts' attitude.[18]

Day v Davies [1938] 2 KB 74

Facts Davies, a bailiff, distrained on the goods and chattels of the plaintiff for arrears of rent due in respect of certain premises and entered into a walking possession agreement with Day that included an undertaking that Day would pay all costs. Davies visited the premises for a few minutes on each of five days and charged the plaintiff 6/- for each of those days. On the last day on which Davies came, the plaintiff paid him a total sum which included £1 6/- for

[17] (1893) 68 LT 231.
[18] [1904] 1 KB 68; (1897) 103 LT 133.

possession fees. Day then applied to his local county court for an order for the return of the sum paid to for possession fees. Judgment was given in his favour. The county court judge on an appeal by Davies dismissed the appeal, whereupon Davies appealed to the Court of Appeal.

Judgment of Slesser LJ: "This case is of considerable importance to bailiffs and those who are reluctantly compelled to entertain them. The case first came before the registrar in the county court, who held that the bailiff had no right to charge 6/- a day during the time in which he held only walking possession. There was an appeal to the county court judge, who upheld the decision of the registrar. From this decision the defendant, the bailiff, now appeals to this Court.

In the county court, the question whether on any view the plaintiff could recover the money so paid by him to the bailiff, even if he were right in his contention that the bailiff in law was not entitled to payment, was not argued; nor does that consideration form any part of the learned county court judge's judgment. Counsel for the defendant does not take the point, saying that he desires rather to have the case decided upon the footing that, if he is wrong in his contentions, the plaintiff would be entitled to the recovery of his money. I come therefore at once to the issues litigated in this case before the learned county court judge.

In the case of there being a man lawfully in possession, the right to charge has been made the subject of legislation and of rules. By Distress for Rent Act 1737 s.10 it was provided that distress may be secured and sold on the premises. Before that time, distress generally could not be impounded on the premises unless the tenant otherwise agreed, and as a consequence of this legislation it became usual to put a man into possession. The costs of distress levied for payment of small rents was first regulated by the Distress (Costs) Act 1817, which, by section 1, provided, so far as here material, that:

> "no person whatsoever making any distress for rent, where the sum demanded and due shall not exceed the sum of twenty pounds for and in respect of such rent, nor any person whatsoever employed in any manner in making such distress, or doing any act whatsoever in the course of such distress, or for carrying the same into effect, shall have, take, or receive out of the produce of the goods or chattels distrained upon and sold, or from the tenant distrained on, or from the landlord, or from any other person whatsoever, any other or more costs and charges for and in respect of such distress, or any other matter or thing done therein, than such as are fixed and set forth in the schedule ...; and no person ... shall make any charge whatsoever for any act, matter, or thing mentioned in the said schedule, unless such act shall have been really done."

The material words in the schedule are "man in possession, per day, 2/6."

By the Distress (Costs) Act 1827, these provisions were extended to distress for taxes, rates, tithe, etc., where the sum did not exceed £20 and finally by Law of Distress Amendment Act 1888 s.8, it was provided that the Lord Chancellor might from time to time make, alter and revoke rules "(2) for regulating the fees, charges and expenses in and incidental to distresses." Such rules as concerned rent were made under the Distress for Rent Rules1920 and provided by r.22 that no person shall be "entitled to any fees, charges, or expenses for levying a distress, or for doing any act or thing in relation thereto, other than those specified in and authorised by the table in Appendix II to these Rules." The material one now is Scale II(2) "for man in possession, 6/- per day; to provide his own board in every case."

In *Walker v Retter* it was held by the Divisional Court that these rules (or rather those then extant in similar terms) were not *ultra vires* and no suggestion is now made that that case was wrongly decided.[19] The critical words here are those contained in r.22 that "no person shall be entitled to any fees, charges or expenses for levying a distress, or for doing any act or thing in relation thereto, other than those specified in" the Appendix which I have already quoted.

The legal effect of walking possession was discussed in the case of *Lumsden v Burnett* in this Court.[20] In that case, the walking possession, as it was there called, was described by A L Smith LJ to be a condition "when in truth and in fact the man had not been really in possession, but at the most has been in constructive possession of the goods distrained." As the learned judge points out:

> "where a sheriff goes out of possession and the point arises as to whether he has abandoned possession or not, the question always is one of fact. ... A sheriff in some circumstances may go out of possession and again re-enter without having abandoned possession and the question always is whether what he has done amounts to an abandonment of possession."

Dealing with the document there signed, which though ampler in terms as to the right to re-enter at any time upon the premises (here the matter is compendiously dealt with in the phrase "holding walking possession"), Chitty LJ said:

---

[19] [1911] 1 KB 1103.
[20] [1898] 2 QB 182- see earlier.

> "Taking into consideration the document [on the question of abandonment], but merely for the limited purpose above stated, and the other undisputed facts relating to the watching of the shop by the defendant's man, and his occasional entrances to see that the goods had not been removed, I say unhesitatingly that the possession was not abandoned."

The same view has been taken on the facts of the present case by the learned county court judge when he refers to this constructive possession as "a method of taking possession." Whether the matter be founded upon r.22 of the 1920 Rules, which I have cited, that all the acts of the bailiff were done in relation to levying distress, or whether it be founded upon the language of the Distress (Costs) Act 1817 s.1, that he was doing acts "in the course of such distress, or for carrying the same into effect," in either case I am of opinion that he cannot be entitled to any charges other than those specified in and authorized by the table of Appendix II, Scale II(2), of the 1920 Rules which has superseded the Schedule to the 1817 Act. Now that Schedule only provides, so far as regards matters here material, for a fee for a man in possession; and as in this case no man was in possession, no provision is made entitling him to any fee. This view, apart from any question of special agreement, has already been held by this Court in *Lumsden v Burnett*, where it was held that where goods and chattels are distrained for taxes less in amount than £20, the collector who distrains has no right to the statutory charge for a man in possession unless he has remained in real possession. In that case, the agreement purporting to give a right to walking possession had been signed by the plaintiff's daughter and it was held by the Court that consequently the plaintiff did not agree to the walking possession or to the charges which the alleged agreement purported to authorise; and, it being held that there was no real possession, he succeeded in his action to recover the charges of 2/6 per day which was then the authorized charge under the Act of 1817. In that case undoubtedly there are obiter dicta by both the judges that it would have been competent for the plaintiff to have made a special arrangement to pay the 2/6 per day even though the bailiff did not remain in real possession. A. L. Smith LJ says:

> "I do not see why such a taxpayer may not agree with a collector, if the former desires neither to pay the tax due nor to suffer the inconvenience of having a man in real possession, to pay the 2/6 daily to the collector, even though the man does not remain in real possession; but unless such an agreement is made, I am clear that the collector cannot claim the 2/6 per day if the man does not remain in real possession."

And Chitty LJ says:

> "The statute does not preclude the tenants and persons for whose benefit it was made from contracting themselves out of those benefits. It would often be to the advantage of the person upon whose goods the distress is levied for a sum which he is not prepared to pay at once to get rid of the inconvenience of having the bailiff's man in actual possession; and I can see no valid reason why he should not be at liberty to contract to pay the 2/6 a day for the man in constructive possession. To hold that he cannot so contract would inflict upon him unnecessary inconvenience."

These *dicta* have seriously to be considered here where such an agreement is relied upon.

In *Robson v Biggar*, the appellant, who was the landlord, had agreed on a printed form as follows:

> "I also consent to your deducting 5% as commission over and above the statutory costs allowed on the amount recovered."[21]

This she declined to pay on the ground that under the Act of 1817 and the Act of 1888, no person should be entitled to any fees for levying distress other than those specified in the Act or rules. Lord Alverstone CJ and Ridley J came to the conclusion- Darling J dissenting- that the statute was not concerned with special bargains made between the parties. And the learned judge in the present case felt himself bound by that authority. The particular case to which I have referred of *Lumsden v Burnett* was not cited. This decision is of course not binding upon us, and the observations of the two members of the Court of Appeal in *Lumsden*'s were made *obiter*; but now that the matter has been expressly raised in this Court I feel that it must be directly dealt with, giving due consideration to the weighty judgments of the learned judges in *Lumsden's* case.

In my view once it is determined that all the acts in the constructive walking possession are acts in the course of the distress or the carrying of it into effect or acts done in relation to levying distress, it follows that no charges may be made other than those provided in the Schedule; and there being in fact no man in possession within the meaning of that provision, there is no power to charge, but on the contrary, a direct prohibition. Section 2 of the 1817 Act supports this view: that section provides:

---

[21] [1907] 1 KB 690- fee scales in legislation aim to avoid oppression by excessive charges. Oppression is demanding sums that neither the creditor nor the debtor can decline to pay. In this case, though, there was express consent to pay the extra.

> "if any person ....shall ... take ... from any person or persons whatsoever, ... any other or greater costs and charges than are mentioned and set down in the said schedule or make any charge whatsoever for any act, ... mentioned in the said schedule, and not really done ..."

they may apply to the justices of the peace, who may order and adjudge treble the amount of monies so unlawfully taken to be paid by the person so having acted to the complainant.

In the present case it would appear that the charge which is made is, if based upon an act mentioned in the Schedule, namely for a man in possession, a charge for "an act not really done" and the charge is therefore unlawful. The combined effect of ss.1 and 2 of the 1817 Act and the Rules under the Act of 1888 appear to me to amount to a prohibition - to charge only for acts mentioned in the sections really done - and there is no power to charge at all for any other act done in making the distress. As to reliance upon any special agreement, where a prohibition under a statute is absolute, it (the statute) cannot be waived by the party for whose benefit it is made.[22] If an act be prohibited, it cannot be the subject of a valid contract: according to Bramwell B in *Cowan v Milbourn*.[23] No special agreement as to charges for an act of distress otherwise than those permitted by the Legislature or rules can be made, and the agreement relied upon to justify a charge for walking possession cannot be enforced.

The learned county court judge, who was of opinion, which I hold to be erroneous, that the parties might make a special agreement to deal with constructive possession, has nevertheless come to the conclusion that the document actually signed by the plaintiff is of no effect because no amount of charge is mentioned. He adds:

> "If I have to consider what is a reasonable fee for a few minutes in a day, I certainly do not think that 6/- per day would be a reasonable figure."

In my new of the case that question does not arise, because for the reasons I have endeavoured to state, there was no power in the circumstances for the bailiff to make any agreement to charge at all, either under the statute of 1817 or under the Rules of 1920 or by any special agreement. For reasons different from those of the learned judge, I nevertheless agree with his conclusion and this appeal will therefore be dismissed with costs."

---

[22] *Bisgood v Henderson's Transvaal Estates Ltd* [1908] 1 Ch 743.
[23] [1867] 2 Ex 230.

Commentary

The main relevance of this judgment is to levies of distress for rent or of execution for road traffic penalties. Both are subject to the Distress for Rent Rules 1988 which are the successor provisions to the 1920 Rules discussed in the judgment. The prohibition against extra charges survives in rule 10 of the current Rules, so that we may assume that the court's findings are still directly applicable to modern levies. Particularly significant is Slesser LJ's conclusion that the prohibition *cannot* be overridden by any agreement or waiver on the part of the debtor. In this case a charge for walking possession was disallowed as it was merely a constructive form of possession as opposed to a man in actual possession of goods, for which a fee was provided in the scale. This principle was already very well established in the courts- for example *Duncombe v Hicks* (1898).[24] It follows that no extra charges of any description may be made. Scales that do not include such an explicit prohibition may not prevent certain additional charges being made, but it would have to be clear that these were for the debtor's benefit and paid with his/her express consent.[25]

Flanagan v John Crilley & Sons (1987) Birmingham county court[26]

Facts Mrs Flanagan fell into arrears with general rates due to Birmingham City Council. A summons was issued, on the basis of which she paid the rates arrears outstanding. She did not, however, pay the court costs of £11 so that a distress warrant was passed to Crilleys for enforcement. Distress was levied at her home on a colour television. As she still failed to pay the set was later removed and sold at public auction for £10. The account produced after the sale was as follows:

• Sum due on warrant	£11
• Levy fee	£2.50
• Walking possession fees	£14.25
• Van hire	£46
• Total due	£73.75
• less net proceeds of sale	£8.27
• still due	*£65.48*

The total fees charged represented 570% of the debt. Mrs Flanagan sought legal advice and was advised to challenge the bailiff's fees by way of 'taxation' in Birmingham county court.

---

[24] (1898) 42 Sol Jo 393.

[25] See *Lumsden v Burnett* earlier.

[26] This case report has been adapted from an article written in the *Adviser magazine*- 'Taxing the bailiffs', by T Rust & K Demian, in *Adviser* no.7 p.29.

Judgment The bailiffs were entitled to make charges on the basis of the Distress for Rates Order 1979 article 3. It was accepted by Mrs Flanagan that the charges made for levying and walking possession were in line with the Order and were correct. Her dispute related to the van hire charge, which was being recovered under article 3(2) of the 1979 Order- "for the removal and storage of goods, the reasonable expenses thereof." Mrs Flanagan contended that the charge made under this heading had not been reasonable and the county court registrar accepted that he had the power to assess these costs and that the test of reasonableness in doing this should be what an ordinary person would consider to be just and sensible.

The defendants presented evidence as to their calculation of the fees for removal and the district judge found that:

- a flat fee was currently charged to all debtors; but,
- properly, this charge should relate to the work actually done on an hourly basis.

Mrs Flanagan presented evidence about the cost of renting a van on a private hire basis for a half day. On the basis of these figures, and making allowance for profit and VAT, the registrar decided to allow Crilleys £19.50 per hour. As only one hour's work had been done (inclusive of travel) in removing Mrs Flanagan's television set, this figure represented the maximum sum fairly chargeable to her. Accordingly, the bill produced by Crilleys was 'taxed down' from £46 for van hire to £19.50 and the balance still payable was adjusted accordingly.

Commentary

Detailed assessment in particular focuses upon the question of whether the sums charged are reasonable. This is assessed in light of several factors: the amount of the work done, the cost of that work and the degree of proportionality between the fee and the debt. The *Flanagan* decision is worth reporting to a wider audience because:

- It is a neat demonstration of the working of a detailed assessment in a county court;
- It indicates the sort of evidence that might be presented to the court in the course of such a challenge. Mrs Flanagan's solicitor simply contacted van hire firms in the city to establish what would be the most expensive and least cost-effective means of supplying a van- a half day hire. This was contrasted to the sum charged by the bailiffs, which was a flat rate fee unrelated to their actual costs; and,
- It concerns that issue of perennial disagreement- the cost of a van.

Throssell v Leeds City Council (1993) Leeds county court, case no.9350977

The facts The brief facts are that on the evening of November 12th 1992, which was after sunset, a bailiff attended to levy distress under three liability orders to levy a total sum of £610.10 council tax arrears. He was not admitted to the applicant's address and subsequently arrangements were made to discharge the sums due to the council. The council then sought to recover the sum of £49.90 as the costs of the attempted distress. As a result Mr Throssell challenged the right of the Leeds City Council (the respondent) to make a charge for an attempt to levy distress at his home. There was a subsidiary application that the court tax the costs if it was found that there was indeed a valid attempt at distress.

Judgment "The relevant statutory instrument is the Community Charge (Administration & Enforcement) Regulations 1989 under the Local Government Finance Act 1988. Reg.39 sets out in nine paragraphs the right of the authority to levy distress. It is argued by the applicant that the common law rules touching distress and the conduct of bailiffs must be considered alongside the regulation- including the common law rule that distress should not be levied after sunset. There is no authority which the applicant can produce to support this contention. The respondent on the other hand contends that the regulations are solely the creature of statute and all the rights and powers of the authority are exhaustively to be found therein. They cite as authority for that *Abingdon DC v O'Gorman* [1968] and the comments of the learned authors of *Hill and Redmond.*[27] I find that reg.39 does not preclude this distress being *prima facie* lawful and one for which the authority may charge a reasonable amount as provided for in the schedule to the regulations.

There is a further point made by the respondent that any person aggrieved by the levy should appeal to the justices. The applicant however says that if he goes there, there is a danger he may be condemned in costs if the justices find as a fact that no distress had been attempted. On the facts as I have found them I am satisfied that the applicant is entitled to have the charges taxed by this Court.

Turning to the taxation it seems to me that notwithstanding the fact that there were three liability orders but one visit was made by one bailiff and the maximum that the council's reasonable charges can be is the result of

[27] See chapter 7 for case report.

applying the formula contained in Sch.5 para.2(1) b) of the regulations. This I now do:

Amount of total due under liability order and costs	£610.10
12.5% on the first £100	£12.50
4% on the next £400	£16.00
2.5% on the next £110.10	£2.75
Total costs	£31.25

It is further argued that this is a maximum and not necessarily reasonable *per se*. I have considered that a bailiff would need to consider the matter and to make a trip across the city and to be engaged at the applicant's house for some time, thereafter to return to the respondent's offices and make his report. Taking those circumstances into account I am satisfied that £31.25 is a reasonable charge and I tax and allow it accordingly. No order for costs."

Commentary

In a detailed assessment of bailiff's fees the court will particularly consider whether the sum charged to the debtor's account was a reasonable allowance for work actually and necessarily undertaken. In the case of local taxes this situation is further reinforced by the statement in the relevant fee scale that a 'reasonable' sum may be charged for levying which is less than that achieved merely by multiplying the fees allowable by the number of liability orders.

In this case, three liability orders were held by the bailiff but only one levy was conducted. In such situations it is obviously arguable that less than three levy fees ought to be allowed and this was exactly the approach of the district judge. The additional paperwork which will be involved might suggest that slightly more than one fee should be allowed but the district judge did not take such a course, although in light of the bailiff's workload he resisted an argument that *less* than the scale fee should be allowed.

We may also note that the debtor failed in an argument that the levy was illegal because it took place after sunset. This is solely a distress for rent rule. Statutory forms of distraint, such as for local taxes, should properly be compared to execution rather than rent distress. A HCEO may levy at any time and so may a council tax bailiff.[28] Note also that the district judge rejected the argument that the only remedy was through the magistrates' court (see *Steel Linings v Bibby* in chapter 7).

[28] See *Quinlan* in chapter 7.

Culligan v Simkin & Marston Group Ltd (2008) DJ Avent, Central London county court, September 24th 2008

Background This was an application for 'detailed assessment' of the fees charged by Marston Group and their employee, Mr Simkin, in respect of the enforcement of a road traffic penalty due to LB Camden. The defendants levied execution upon the claimant's motor car by clamping it on his drive and leaving him with a copy of the 'Notice of seizure of goods and inventory' (Form 7) prescribed by the Distress for Rent Rules 1988 (which are applied to this form of execution). This form set out the penalty which was being enforced and demanded payment of the outstanding penalty charge notice plus their costs- a total of £417.97 including VAT. The disputed fees were those for levying (£38.14), for immobilisation (£100) and for attendance to remove (£100). In the event Mr Culligan was absent on business at the time of the levy and his wife paid the entire sum demanded in order to have the car released.

Bailiffs levying these warrants of execution operate under a fee scale laid down in Schedule 1 of the Enforcement of Road Traffic Debts ((Certificated Bailiffs) Regulations 1993. In paragraph 2 this scale allows for a charge to be made for levying on goods, which is calculated as a percentage of the sum due (as was the case here). At paragraph 6 the scale allows a reasonable charge for "removing goods, or attending to remove where no goods are removed." It was these two fees on his bill which Mr Culligan disputed. He did not feel that an immobilisation fee could be charged if a levy fee had already been added to the account; secondly, he did not agree that £100 was a reasonable sum. Mr Culligan also did not feel that the 'attendance to remove' fee could properly be charged as the prescribed form (Form 9) required by the Rules had not been issued. Mr Culligan also sought to challenge the bailiff's fitness to retain his certificate on the basis that he had behaved improperly and dishonestly. The judge did not accept this allegation and did not pursue the matter as Mr Simkin was merely following his employer's normal practices.

Judgment Having outlined the facts of the case the district judge stated "it seems to me that there are five issues, the first of which is a subsidiary point but nonetheless needs to be dealt with, as follows:

a) Does failure by the bailiff to deliver a memorandum in the prescribed form 9 setting out the expenses of removal mean that an essential precondition has not been complied with such as to make the removal expenses irrecoverable?

b) In any event, does the application of an immobilisation device (i.e. a wheel clamp) fall within that part of the enforcement process relating to levying distress or as part of the removal process?
c) If it relates to levying distress, is the bailiff restricted in what he can charge by the effect of paragraph 2 of Schedule 1?
d) If it relates to the removal process, is the charge of £100 made with respect to the immobilisation device reasonable?
e) In any event, is the charge of £100 for the attendance to remove goods, even though they were not removed, reasonable?

The answer to the final issue lies in a consideration of the Rules and relevant case law. Rule 12(2) and (3) specify that:

> "(2) A bailiff levying distress shall deliver to the tenant, or leave at the premises where distress is levied, a memorandum in Form 7 identifying the bailiff and specifying in an inventory the goods distrained and setting out the amounts for which the distress is levied and the fees, charges and expenses authorised by these Rules and being actually and necessarily incurred under them.
>
> (3) A bailiff or his agent attending to remove goods from the premises or withdrawing from possession prior to sale of the distrained goods shall deliver to the tenant or leave on the premises where distress is levied a memorandum in Form 9 setting out the expenses of removal authorised by and incurred under these Rules."

Accordingly, there is a clear distinction made by the Rules as to the type of prescribed form to be used between levying distress and attending to remove goods. Indeed, whilst the actual forms, Forms 7 and 9, are different to each other, they contain a considerable amount of detail which is common to them both. Mr Culligan's point is that Form 9 was never served, delivered or given to him. The defendants accept this.

To deal with this submission the defendants drew my attention to and relied upon a Court of Appeal decision in the case of *Quinlan v Hammersmith & Fulham London Borough Council* [1988].[29] The local authority in that case had obtained a distress warrant in respect of unpaid rates but failed to give the ratepayer, Mr Quinlan, a notice of distress and inventory in accordance with the provisions of the Distress for Rates Order 1979. The Court held that whilst thus was an irregularity in the execution of the warrant, it did not render the distress illegal and therefore Mr Quinlan could recover damages

[29] See chapter 7.

only if he sustained special damage as a result of the failure ... Mr Culligan accepted that the wrong form, being an irregularity, did not make either the levy or the proposed removal unlawful and that, accordingly, it did not preclude the charges being imposed or otherwise render them unlawful. Indeed, if he had not accepted this I would consider myself to have been bound by the *Quinlan* case and to have held that the absence of Form 9 was not fatal to the bailiff's case. Rule 12(3) requires the Form to set out the expenses of removal authorised by and incurred under the Rules and the Form 7 which was served in this case did just that. It enabled Mr Culligan to ascertain the amount that had to be paid.

The second issue, on its face, is considerably more problematical, not least because the law relating to distress treads a rather tortuous, inconsistent and complicated path. It also requires, in my view, an interpretation of Schedule 1 which I have found difficult because of the way in which the concept of distress is dealt with in the two sources to which I have referred. The first is *Halsbury's Laws of England* vol.13 relating to the law of distress and the second is the decision of Simon Brown J in the case of *Evans v South Ribble Borough Council* [1992].[30]

In the first instance *Halsbury's* at para.902 seeks to define distress in the following terms:

> "The term 'distress; primarily connotes a summary remedy by which a person is entitled without legal process to take into his possession the personal chattels of another person to be held as a pledge to compel the performance of a duty, or the satisfaction of a debt or demand. By almost universal sanction the term 'distress' is now used to designate both the process of taking and the chattels taken, though originally it applied only to the taking. By statute, remedies referred to as distress have been introduced for the recovery of rates and taxes and for the enforcement of certain fines imposed by or orders of magistrates' courts."

A footnote to that paragraph refers to the definition given in Bradby, *Law of distresses,* 2nd edition, which is:

> "A distress is the taking of a personal chattel, without legal process, from the possession of a wrongdoer, into the hands of the party grieved, for the redress of an injury, the performance of a duty or the satisfaction of a demand."

[30] See chapter 3.

So far so good. In this instance distress is being used, via statutory provisions, as a remedy to enforce non-payment of PCNs. However, at paragraph 992 and subsequently *Halsbury's* there is then a consideration of what might be considered to be the essential elements of a distress under the general heading of 'Levying the distress.' As well as the formal requirements necessary, it also deals with the issue of seizure which it notes:

> "To complete a distress a seizure of the chattels is necessary. A seizure may be either actual or constructive. It is actual by laying hands on the article, or on one of several articles, and claiming to detain them until the rent is satisfied. The most proper manner of making a distress is for the person distraining to go on any part of the premises out of which the rent issues and take hold of some personal chattel declaring that it is taken as a distress in the name of all the goods, or of so much as will be good seizure of all. No particular form of words is however necessary, provided the intention is manifest."

Para.1010 deals with the issue of constructive seizure as follows:

> "A constructive seizure may occur in various ways. It is enough that the landlord or his agent interferes to prevent the removal of the article from off the premises on the ground that rent is in arrear, and that he does this when he declares that the article is not to be removed until the rent is paid, and it is immaterial that the article is subsequently removed.
>
> Any acts indicative of an intention that antecedent steps should be treated as a distress, and assumed by the parties to amount to a distress, will be sufficient evidence of a seizure. Thus, if money is paid on the footing that there has been a distress, or if the bailiff after intimating his intention to distrain walks around the demised premises and, without touching anything, gives written notice that he has distrained, that will amount to a seizure."

This section of *Halsbury's* is then followed by a further general heading entitled 'Proceedings between seizure and sale.' This explains that:

> "When chattels have been seized, it is necessary to imprison and secure the chattels for safe custody until the cause of distress is satisfied or the statutory period has elapsed at the expiration of which the chattels can be lawfully sold by reason of the tenant failing to replevy them. This imprisonment, called impounding, places the goods in the custody of the law. If, before the chattels are impounded, the tenant tenders a sufficient amount for rent and costs, it is unlawful to proceed further with the

> distress. Chattels may be impounded on the premises unless the tenant otherwise requests or they may be removed to a pound off the premises."

It needs to be borne in mind that these sections of *Halsbury's* discuss the law of distress in the context of distress for rent and therefore should perhaps not readily be applied to the current situation without some consideration of the practical differences. The most obvious, of course, is that the bailiff in this instance did not have to effect an entry onto premises because Mr Culligan's vehicle was outside his house; entry, in such circumstances, would clearly have to be a prerequisite to a lawful distress.

It will also be appreciated, given the above observations and the fairly wide definition of 'a seizure', that the mere act of Mr Simkin placing a seizure notice (in form 7) on Mr Culligan's vehicle was sufficient in itself to amount to a seizure. Accordingly, in that sense, the defendant was correct to say that the fitting of an immobilisation device was not necessary to complete the seizure and was a distinct and separate act. Given that, there was clearly, in my judgment, on the facts of this case, an actual seizure. I do not therefore propose to consider any question of a constructive seizure, whatever that might or could have been in the context of this case.

Having therefore established that the immobilisation device was not a necessary and integral part of the seizure process, the next consideration is to look at what purpose it did serve. The defendant sought to persuade me that this was part and parcel of the removal process. They noted that unless there had been a seizure then there was no right to apply an immobilisation device (a submission with which I agree) and that because its application followed the seizure it could then form part of the removal process either directly or indirectly as preparation for removal. Indeed, they told me that this interpretation accords with the view of local authorities in London. Further, they suggest that as para.6 of Schedule 1 refers to "reasonable costs and charges" in the plural it envisaged that there may be more than one expense i.e. a cost of clamping and a cost of removal. With respect to them, it is no doubt correct that the plurality can cover several expenses, but, in my view, it does not validate a cost or charge that cannot be characterised as a removal expense in the first place.

I have considered and reflected on the defendant's viewpoint in some depth because in practical terms I understand why that submission is made. However as a matter of law I think, with respect to counsel and the London Boroughs, that it is wrong. In my judgment, the whole purpose of applying an immobilisation device to Mr Culligan's vehicle was to impound the vehicle and that is exactly what was achieved. I say this for three reasons. The first is that the bailiff's obligation will be to secure the vehicle so that, if need be, it can subsequently be sold in order to discharge the outstanding monies under the distress warrant and outstanding PCN. The simplest and cheapest way to do this is to immobilise the vehicle and to prevent it being driven away by the application of an immobilisation device or wheel clamp. This is effectively the equal of impounding the goods on the premises.

Again, it is necessary to remember that the bailiff was dealing with enforcement against a vehicle and was not distraining for rent. To gain access to a property to distrain will usually require the debtor to be present (because he will have to allow entry). The same will not usually be true in relation to a vehicle on a road where the owner/ debtor will not usually be present. The sheer reality of the latter situation would rather preclude the bailiff from, for example, seeking an agreement for walking possession as he might do if the goods were on the premises. An immobilisation device placed on a vehicle is nothing but the practical equivalent of a locked door within premises to secure goods.

Secondly, I note that r.12(2) and (3) of the 1988 Rules clearly envisage two stages. The first is the levying of the distress and the second is the removal of the goods. This gap between the two stages, and the requirement that forms 7 and 9 should be given, must be in order to allow the debtor to make payment of what is due at each stage.

Accordingly, in my judgment the bailiff should not, and as a matter of law cannot, take any steps to remove goods until he has given the debtor a reasonable opportunity to pay what is due at the time of seizure. This being so I cannot see that form 7 can or should include any costs of removal. Mr Simkin included on the form 7 he produced for Mr Culligan the sum of £100 in respect of the clamp. If, as the defendants now argue, that was part of the removal expenses, it should never have been included in the form 7. The fact that the immobilisation device was applied contemporaneously at the time of seizure is confirmation that this was an impounding and formed part of the levying distress.

Thirdly, by definition, an immobilisation device primarily does exactly that, it immobilises and prevents removal. On my interpretation of the wording of para. 6 of Sch.1, I cannot see that the application of an immobilisation device can fall within the definition of "removing." The *Oxford English Dictionary* states the verb 'remove' means to 'move or shift from or out of the place occupied, to lift or push aside, to lift up and take away, to take off, to take or convey from a place." That clearly is the exact opposite to what the immobilisation device is designed to do. Nor can I accept that its application forms part of the preparation for removal.

I turn now to the case of *Evans*. This case concerned the enforcement of a community charge liability where the bailiff simply posted a notice of distress through the debtor's letter box together with a draft walking possession agreement. On appeal by way of case stated Simon Brown J determined that the distress was effectively unlawful because no entry had been gained to the debtor's premises, which was an essential element of distress.

That, as I have already explained, is not in issue here but, in the course of his judgment Simon Brown J, having reviewed various matters, set out an exposition of the current position regarding distress, the relevant parts of which are as follows [District Judge Avent then cited the paragraph from the *Evans* judgment in which the stages of entry, seizure and impounding are identified and analysed- see chapter 3.] It is clear from the first and fifth principles set out by Simon Brown J in *Evans* that a distress does, and indeed according to his definition, *must* include the act of impounding.

Para.2 of Schedule 1 of the Regulations permits the bailiff to make a charge for 'levying distress.' The *Oxford English Dictionary* defines 'levy' as "the action of collecting debts or enforcing the payment of fines" and the action of levying as "the action of collecting an assessment, duty, tax etc." Accordingly, in answer to the second issue, I find that the application of an immobilisation device falls within the act of levying distress and does not form part of the removal process. The consequence of this, and the answer to the third issue, is that the bailiff cannot recover the £100 charge for the immobilisation device, regardless of what the contract with Camden may say, insofar as it exceeds the limits imposed by para.2 of Sch.1. In this case, as the levy fee of £38.14 plus VAT has already been demanded the bailiff cannot recover from Mr Culligan any more than that amount. I find therefore that in this instance the £100 charged for the immobilisation device cannot be recovered.

If I am wrong in relation to my analysis of the second issue and the act of immobilisation does, in fact, form part of the removal expenses, then to answer the fourth issue, I would still find that it cannot be recovered from Mr Culligan because the defendants have produced no evidence whatsoever that it is reasonable in amount. What they have done is simply reply upon the fact that their agreement with Camden stipulates a charge of £100 and suggested that this is enough. That is clearly not sufficient. Indeed, for myself, I would find very great difficulty in accepting that the cost of applying an immobilisation device to a vehicle, even allowing for the capital cost of the device (which could then, of course, be used many hundreds of times) was anywhere near the sum of £100. It seems to be a completely arbitrary figure which in realty should be substantially less. As regards the fifth issue, namely whether the charge of £100 was reasonable for the removal costs (although the vehicle was never actually removed), the same reasoning applies: namely, that the defendants have produced no evidence as to how the charge has been arrived at and therefore are unable to show that it is reasonable.

In passing I would mention that I take the view that even the removal of a vehicle to a pound appears to fall within the definition of levying distress. However, it seems that for the purpose of the bailiff's charges and costs both r.12 and Sch. 1 differentiate between the initial stages of the levy and the subsequent removal of goods (or effectively, impounding off the premises) allowing two charges to be made. As the Schedule specifically permits charges for removal this would, in my judgment, tend to stifle any argument to the effect that the removal charges were not recoverable except under para.2 of Sch.1.

In conclusion, therefore, I find that the immobilisation charge insofar as it exceeds the amount stipulated by para.2 of Sch.1 is not recoverable by the bailiff. Indeed, neither that charge nor that made in respect of the proposed removal of Mr Culligan's car is recoverable because there is no evidence by the receiving party of the reasonableness of those charges.

I realise that the non-payment of PCNs in London and other metropolitan areas is a huge problem. I am also conscious that my findings in this case (and I am clear in my conclusions on the arguments and authorities before me) may have wider consequences and may cause problems for bailiffs because they will not be able to charge for immobilising a vehicle as a separate charge but must include it within the cost of levying. To do otherwise would, in my judgment, be unlawful. I would also add that if the defendants or either of them, in the light of this judgment, now continue to apply such charges in the manner in which they have done up to now and, specifically, charge fees of £100 for applying an immobilisation device, then that would amount to conduct which may well then found a legitimate complaint because in my judgment it would be unlawful.

I will therefore order that the defendants pay Mr Culligan the sum of £235 being the sum due in respect of refunding the immobilisation and removal charges. I will also order that the defendants do pay Mr Culligan's costs of the detailed assessment, which as far as I can see, will only amount to the £40 issue fee."

Commentary

In analysing this judgment we should perhaps start with a couple of amendments to the judge's statements:

- Although often called 'distress', the enforcement of road traffic penalties is in fact a form of county court execution. The warrant issued by the Traffic Enforcement Centre is a warrant of execution for the enforcement of a county court order. It is because of this fact that county court execution is being placed in the hands of private rather than county court bailiffs that the elaborate regulations were devised. These borrow from the County Courts Act 1984 but also from the Distress for Rent Rules 1988, to which a link is made so that the county court has some jurisdiction and control over the bailiffs by means of the certification process. In this case, the judge declined to impose any sanction on the certificate held by the bailiff, but in the closing paragraphs he did warn explicitly that continued charging along the lines seen in this case *would* be the matter of a certification complaint.
- The district judge discussed the levy as if no entry had been made to premises. This is not strictly correct. Mr Culligan's house was not entered and household furniture and effects were not seized. However, the car was on his drive, not in the street. There was an entry onto his property under the bailiff's implied licence to enter land under a lawful warrant (see chapter 2).

The key points of the judgment are as follows:

- *Status of clamping* as impounding and not as removal. This seems hard to dispute, not least for the simple logical case that clamping is the physical opposite of removal. Of course, no argument about the legality of the act of clamping was raised and this was not therefore considered (see chapter 3).
- *Irregular seizure* - in concluding that the absence of the form 9 was only an irregularity, it would also be possible to use s.125 County Courts Act 1984 (which is applied to road traffic executions by the Enforcement of Road Traffic Debts Order 1993). Special damages could be claimed for any irregular act: this could be used to recover the removal fees charged without use of the proper notice.
- *Forms 7 & 9*- few enforcement companies seem to use form 9, despite its use being prescribed by the Distress for Rent Rules. In the *Culligan* case the form 7 was sufficiently detailed in its breakdown of the charges to make up for the absence of the form 9. However, some bailiffs merely include a total figure for charges of the notice of seizure. This is probably inadequate as a notice which complies with the requirements of either forms 7 or 9.
- *Delay between levy & removal*- most controversial amongst enforcement agents will be the decision that there *must* be a delay between seizure and removal. This is probably incorrect. There will plainly be cases, especially concerning cars, where removal follows immediately from

seizure. That said, where goods have been impounded by walking possession there is an implicit expectation that there will be a delay before removal, which may call into question the propriety of any removal charges added at the levy stage.

- *Assessment of fees-* lastly, this was an application for detailed assessment of the bailiff's charges and the district judge concluded his judgment by dealing with these issues. Detailed assessment involves consideration of a number of aspects of the fees added to the account. One involves the bailiff justifying the reasonability of a charge by demonstrating the basis upon which it is calculated (for example, the hourly rate of the bailiff, the costs of petrol etc). Neither for the clamping fee, nor for the attendance fee, could a breakdown of the fee be provided and, as a result, they were both disallowed. In this respect the case of *Culligan* echoes that of *Flanagan* (see earlier): a round figure was charged for an activity unrelated to the actual cost to the enforcement agency.

Conclusions

Reconciling a fair return for commercial enforcement agents whilst simultaneously protecting indebted individuals from an unfair burden of charges has been a constant concern for government for the last four centuries. The tension has yet to be resolved satisfactorily and all too often the result has been low statutory fees scales which have been circumvented or ignored. The courts continue to have a vital role as arbiters between the parties.

Chapter 7

OFFENCES AND GENERAL ISSUES

Introduction

We conclude with a consideration of some general issues, particularly what bailiffs and debtors may do wrong during a levy and what the consequences of these actions may be.[1]

Debtors' offences

Two interferences with levied goods by debtors (or others) are possible:

- *Rescue* - interference with seized goods; or,
- *Poundbreach* - interference with impounded goods.

The creditor has several remedies- to prosecute for the common law offence of poundbreach in the magistrates' court or to pursue one of the few statutory remedies which exist.[2] Landlords alone are entitled to compensation for the violation of the pound, as discussed in the first case that follows. It seems that a debtor's use of unwarranted and excessive force may justify an award of aggravated damages. If bailiffs are negligent in keeping possession of goods, leading to their loss by poundbreach, it will be possible for a creditor to make a claim for damages against them. In *White v Heywood* the High Court found that a broker had failed to take reasonable care to safeguard impounded goods, despite being warned to do so by the landlord who was distraining, with the result that an engine valued at £60 was removed. Damages of £50 were awarded.[3]

---

[1] For more discussion see *Law of Seizure of Goods* c.4 or *Powers of distress* c.5. See also chapter 4 of *Persons of no value?* for a discussion of poundbreach.

[2] See County Courts Act 1984 s.92, VAT Act 1994 s.68 & Distress for Rent Act 1689 s.3.

[3] *Featherstonehaugh v Steinway & Co* (1887) *The Times,* February 3rd, 3b, QBD; *White v Heywood* (1888) *The Times* December 5th, 11e, QBD.

Bailiffs' wrongful acts

Bailiffs' errors are classified in three ways, as follows.

- *Illegal levies* - An illegal levy is a trespass and as with any case of trespass, the remedy is a claim for 'general' damages for illegal distress, trespass or wrongful interference with goods. Alternatively the debtor may issue replevin in the county court or, in cases of local taxes or child support maintenance, an appeal in the magistrates' court;
- *Irregular levy* - An error made by a bailiff is only irregular if the legislation allows this (this is not the case for High Court or indirect or income taxes). In the absence of such a provision, every mistake may render the levy illegal. If the relevant statute allows for it, less serious errors may be treated as irregularities. The remedy for irregularity is a claim for 'special' damages. We have several times alluded to irregular seizures in earlier chapters.
- *Excessive levy* - Excessive levying is wrongful at common law. A debtor may issue either a claim for damages or a claim under Statute of Marlborough 1267 c.15 (see chapter 1).

Action against debtors for interference with impounded goods is exceedingly rare: the most recent reported case was in 1995. Claims of excessive seizure are rather more frequent- perhaps because of debtors' natural tendency to overvalue their own possessions.[4] It should be remembered, too, that any claim for wrongful distress may be made against the principal (the creditor) alone or as well as the bailiff who acted as enforcement agent.[5]

Abingdon Rural District Council v O'Gorman [1968] 2 QB 811

Facts In August 1966 the local authority, as landlords of a council house, issued a distress warrant for rent arrears of £23 17s. Under the warrant a bailiff seized various goods which included a coin-meter television set which was the property of the defendant. The tenant signed a walking possession agreement and the bailiff departed, leaving the goods on the premises, unsecured and without any indication that they had been impounded. During the following two weeks the bailiff called at the house on several occasions when the tenant was out. On August 19th he gained admittance but found that the television set had gone. It had been removed the day before by the owner, acting at the request of the tenant. The council brought an action

---

[4] See respectively *Cyril Morgan (Holdings) v Dyer* (1995) 11 CL 193 & *Bhatnagar & Elanrent v Whitehall Investments* (1996) 5 CL 166.

[5] *Preston v Peeke* (1858) EB&E 336.

against O'Gorman, claiming that he had breached the pound and that they had thereby lost the benefit of the distress and sustained £15 damages, the value of the set, and were entitled to treble damages, £45, for pound-breach. The owner denied liability. The county court judge awarded the landlords the sum claimed. O'Gorman appealed to the Court of Appeal.

Judgment of Lord Denning MR: "It is very rarely that we have a case about distress for rent. It is an archaic remedy which has largely fallen into disuse. Very few landlords have resort to it. But the Abingdon Rural District Council seem to find it a worthwhile remedy. So we are called upon to examine it. In particular, what acts are necessary to make an "impounding."

At common law the rent issued out of the land. The landlord was entitled to distrain on any goods or chattels that were on the premises, to whomsoever they belonged. As soon as he seized the goods, he had immediately to remove them from the premises and put them into a pound.[6] But he could not sell them. He could only keep them in the pound until the arrears were paid, or the goods were replevied. On the way to the pound, and whilst in the pound, the goods were in the custody of the law. If they were taken by the owner or anyone else, the taker was guilty of a misdemeanour called rescous (if taken on the way to the pound) and pound-breach (if taken after being put inside the pound).

Those strict rules of the common law were altered by statute. In 1689 the landlord was empowered to sell the goods if the arrears were not paid within five days. In 1738 he was authorised to impound them on the premises. If anyone broke the pound he was liable to treble damages. The material words for present purposes are contained in the Distress for Rent Act 1737 (see section 10 cited earlier in chapter 1).

In the years following that statute, the judges held that in order to "impound or otherwise secure" the distress on the premises the landlord had to move the goods into a fit and convenient place on the premises, such as one or two rooms, and lock them up. The goods had to be visibly secured on the premises against the danger of removal by the tenant or anyone else. If there was no fit and convenient place on the premises, the landlord had to remove the goods out of the house. It was so held in 1769 by Wilmot CJ in *Thornton v Cruther* and in 1774 by Lord Mansfield in *Washborn v Black* and accepted in 1846 by Parke B in *Woods v Durrant* and by Pollock CB in *Smith v.*

---

[6] see *Bullen on Distress*, 2nd ed. (1899), pp.170 & 176.

Ashforth.[7] So far as the tenant was concerned, however, it was open to him to agree to the goods being left as they were in the whole house, undisturbed, with his having the use of them. In that case the distraint was good as against him. They were to be regarded as impounded as far as the tenant was concerned, as in *Washborn v Black.* But, as against persons who were strangers to the tenancy, the goods had to be visibly secured. There had to be an open and manifest act, such as to show that the goods were "impounded or otherwise secured." That was the case in *Firth v Purvis* where the plaintiff had distrained four pipes of beer and had "put his mark upon them" and "had impounded them in a convenient part of the premises."[8] It was admitted that they had been validly impounded. That case was much considered in *Thomas v Harries* and I must say that I prefer the reasoning of Maule J to that of the other judges.[9] The doubts expressed by Bosanquet J were justified. In order to "impound or otherwise secure" the goods there must be some distinct act manifesting it. Words alone are not enough.

To prove the point, it is as well to remember the offence of pound-breach. As soon as the distress is impounded, whether on or off the premises, it is in the custody of the law: and anyone who breaks the pound (as by forcing the lock), or takes the goods out of the pound, is guilty of pound-breach. He is indictable for a misdemeanour for which he can be sent to prison, and is also liable to an action which carries penal consequences, namely, for treble damages. On principle, a man is not to be held guilty of this offence unless he has a guilty mind. He must know that the goods have been impounded or otherwise secured, on or off the premises. How can a stranger be expected to know this unless there is some open and manifest act to show it? I am prepared to hold, therefore, that, as against strangers, goods are not validly impounded unless they are locked up in a room or otherwise secured in such a way that it is manifest that they are not to be taken away. "Walking possession" may be sufficient as against the tenant who agrees to it, but not as against a stranger who knows nothing of it.

There are, however, two cases which need to be considered. In *Jones v Biernstein* the landlord had impounded the goods on the premises and put a man in possession.[10] The man went off for the Sunday. The true owner then retook his goods. It was held that he was guilty of pound-breach. But there it

---

[7] (1769) unreported; (1774) 11 East 405n; (1846) 16 M&W 158; (1860) LJ Ex 259. In *Woods v Durrant* (1846) the court said the landlord should select a room or remove; in *Smith v Ashforth* (1860) he either had to choose a fit place or remove.

[8] (1793) 5 TR 432.

[9] (1840) 1 M&G 695 - one cow in a field was touched by the bailiff, all were listed and notice of this was given to the debtor. This constituted valid seizure.

[10] See chapter 3.

was found as a fact that the goods had been impounded. The judges expressly declined to rule what acts will amount to impounding.

In *Lavell & Co Ltd v O'Leary* the members of the Court of Appeal expressed the view that "walking possession" was an impounding even as against strangers.[11] But their observations are not binding on us and I cannot agree with them. The tenant signed an agreement for "walking possession." He afterwards got removal contractors to carry the goods away. The removal contractors did not enter the house. They took the goods from the landing outside. It was held that they were not guilty of pound-breach because they had not entered the house. So it was not necessary to consider at all whether the goods had been validly impounded as against them. The court held that the trial judge ought not to have gone into the question. It follows that they ought not to have done so themselves, especially as they heard argument on one side only.

I think we should put those two cases on one side, and come back to the true rule, which is that goods are only "impounded or otherwise secured" when there is a distinct act (such as locking them up in a room) making it manifest that they are not to be taken away.

Applying this rule, I am of opinion that these goods were not validly impounded as against strangers to the tenancy. The "walking-possession" agreement prevented the tenant from saying they were not impounded. But it bound no one who did not know of it. It did not bind Mr. O'Gorman. He went and fetched his television set without knowing in the least that it had been distrained upon for rent. I do not think he was guilty of pound-breach.

I may say that this meets the justice of the case: because, if Mr. O'Gorman had known that the television set had been distrained upon for rent, he could have given a notice under the Law of Distress amendment Act 1908 and have immediately obtained the release of the set to him. He should not be in a worse position simply because he did not know that the television set had been distrained upon. In my opinion Mr. O'Gorman was not guilty of pound-breach: and is not liable for treble or any damages. I would allow the appeal and enter judgment for the defendant."

Davies LJ: "It is of cardinal importance to bear in mind, in considering this somewhat rare form of action under section 3 of the Distress for Rent Act 1689 for treble damages for pound-breach, that the action is a penal one. This was emphasised in *Jones v Jones*, where the plaintiff in such an action

[11] [1933] 2 KB 200.

sought, and indeed had obtained from the master, an order against the defendant for an affidavit of documents. That order was set aside by the Divisional Court, and in the course of his judgment Lord Coleridge CJ said:

> "He" (that is, the plaintiff) "claims the £120 as 'treble damages' under a statute which gives 'treble damages' to a 'person grieved' by pound breach and rescue against the 'offender.' 'Treble damages' cannot possibly be compensation to the person grieved, and are plainly inflicted on the offender as a punishment. In other words they are a penalty. The plaintiff is as much suing for a penalty as if he sued for a penalty *eo nomine* [12] and this application for an affidavit of documents is therefore made by the plaintiff in a penal action."[13]

It has also to be remembered that pound-breach was an indictable offence and that such a prosecution took place at any rate as late as 1893.[14]

On principle, therefore, one would not expect that a person could be held liable to such a penalty or could be convicted and imprisoned if he did not know and had no means of knowing that in fact he was breaking a pound, unless there is any provision in the statutes or some compelling authority which indicates that such a person is so liable.

At the time of the passing of the Act of 1689 and up to the passing of the Distress for Rent Act 1737 goods of the sort with which the present case is concerned, namely, articles of furniture, if seized by way of distress, could not be impounded on the premises but had to be taken to a pound, private or public. In that event, therefore, it would be plain and obvious to anyone, whether the tenant or the owner of the goods, or a third person, that the goods had been impounded and were in the custody of the law. But by section 10 of the later Act, so far as material,

> "it shall and may be lawful to and for any person or persons lawfully taking any distress for any kind of rent, to impound, or otherwise secure the distress so made, of what nature or kind so ever it may be, in such place, or on such part of the premises chargeable with the rent, as shall be most fit and convenient for the impounding and securing such distress; ..."

---

[12] "on that account."
[13] (1889) 22 QBD 425.
[14] See *R v Butterfield* (1893) 17 Cox CC 598.

Thereafter, then, it was lawful to impound and secure on the premises. But much argument and discussion has taken place in the authorities, many of which have been cited by my Lord, as to the meaning of the words "impound or otherwise secure."

The preponderance of opinion would appear to be, as stated by Lord Mansfield CJ, as long ago as 1774, in *Washborn v Black,* that in strict law the distrainor should place and secure the goods in one room or else remove them from the house. But this strict law has for many years been mitigated, for obvious reasons of convenience, as between the distrainor and the tenant, by the practice of entering into what is called a walking-possession agreement between the bailiff and the tenant. This is obviously convenient, since it permits the tenant to continue to have the use of the goods and avoids the expense of leaving a man in possession or of removing the goods from the house. But is such an agreement effective as against a third party? It seems very strange that it should be so. For in such a case, as in the present one, there is no indication upon the goods or in the house that there has been a seizure or impounding. The true analysis of the situation appears to be that there has not in fact been an actual impounding but that the effect of the walking-possession agreement prevents the tenant from saying that there has not been an impounding, actual or constructive. An innocent stranger, however, such as the owner of the goods, is in an entirely different position and it is to be observed that in the absence of any indication of the distraint or impounding or of notice to the third party, for which there is no provision in the Law of Distress Amendment Act 1908, the third party would be in no position to serve the statutory notice under section 1 of the Act.

In the light of these considerations I should have no hesitation in saying that the defendant in the present case was not guilty of pound-breach, but for the observations of this court in *Lavell & Co Ltd v O'Leary.*

That was an odd case. It is important to note that it was conceded by the defendants that the goods were validly impounded. It was also conceded "that if the offence of pound-breach is committed, the fact that it is committed unwittingly does not matter." Nevertheless, despite the first concession mentioned above, Macnaghten J. at first instance held that as against the defendants the goods had not been validly impounded. His decision was stated in the following words:

> "Now, in this case, these goods in an open restaurant are left just as they were. No step of any sort was taken to secure them against removal by anybody. Nobody was left in possession to guard against removal, and although as between Mr. Wong Gee and the plaintiffs Mr. Wong Gee could not be heard to say that the goods had not been impounded, as

> between the landlord and a stranger the landlords have failed to prove that they complied with the provisions of the statute of George II; they have failed to prove that they 'impounded, or otherwise secured' the goods, and having failed to prove that, they are not therefore entitled to their remedy given by the statute of William and Mary, and cannot maintain this action."

This court upheld the decision of the judge, but on an entirely different ground. They acquitted the defendants of pound-breach because they had removed the goods not from inside the premises but from outside, where they had previously been placed by the tenant, and therefore they could not themselves have been guilty of pound-breach. That, of course, was sufficient to dispose of the appeal.

But there is no doubt that each member of the court went on to express firm opinions upon and contrary to the views expressed by the trial judge. They held that the goods had been validly impounded (which, as I have said, was conceded) and against all the world. They also held that ignorance on the part of the alleged pound-breakers was no defence, as had also been conceded.

While acknowledging the weight of these observations, I cannot, with respect, regard them as anything but obiter. If the acts of the defendants could not in any event amount to pound-breach, which was the *ratio decidendi*, then it was unnecessary to consider whether there was a valid pound and whether the defendants' state of knowledge was relevant.

In the course of the judgment, Lawrence LJ said:

> "One of the examples given in the course of the argument seems to me to afford an apt analogy: supposing a pound-breaker were to hail a taxi-cab to the door of a house which had been made a pound, and were then to bring some of the goods out of the pound in a suitcase and ask the driver to place it in the taxi and order him to drive to a station or some other address, could it be said that the taxi-driver was guilty of pound-breaking? Assuredly not."

During the argument in the present case my brother Russell pointedly asked whether, if in Lawrence LJ's example the taxi-driver had been requested by the passenger to go into the house to assist in carrying out the suitcase and did so, the taxi-driver would be guilty of pound-breach. To that question I should answer, as did Lawrence LJ to his own question, "Assuredly not."

Freed therefore, as in my judgment we are, from the weight of the observations in *Lavell & Co. Ltd v O'Leary*, I am of the opinion that this case falls to be decided upon the basis of the principles which I have endeavoured to set out in the earlier part of this judgment. Accordingly, in my view, this appeal succeeds and there should be judgment for the defendant on the twin but overlapping grounds that as against him the goods were not impounded and that he had no knowledge of any impounding as against the tenant.

Russell LJ: "It seems to me that there are two questions for consideration in the present case. One is whether an impounding valid as such against the tenant is valid as such against all. The second is whether, if the answer to the first be Yes, pound-breach is committed by a person who removes goods that are impounded though he is wholly ignorant of the fact that the goods are impounded, bearing in mind that pound-breach not only attracts the penalty of treble damages in a civil action, but is also a criminal offence.

In considering the first question regard must be paid to the history of the matter. Originally distress for rent involved only the withholding from the tenant of the use of chattels found on the premises: there was no right to obtain the arrears of rent by sale: the withholding of the goods exerted pressure on the tenant to pay his rent. This was an inadequate remedy for the landlord, particularly so in so far as goods seized and impounded might not be the property of the tenant. The remedy of sale was introduced in 1689, and it no longer became essential to the effectiveness of the remedy that the nature of the impounding should prohibit the interim availability of the goods to the tenant. Nevertheless the ordinary form of impounding was still by removal from the premises. The reason for this was that a landlord had no right to use his tenant's premises as a pound unless statute gave him such a right as in the case of locking up crops. However, the tenant before 1737 was able to agree that his premises should be used for the purpose of impounding[15] and when he did so the goods were, I consider, in the custody of the law; nor so far as I am aware was any special step by way of securing required in cases of such agreement. Indeed a tenant might not agree to the use of his premises as a pound if the landlord wished, for instance, to lock the goods in one room or leave a man in possession, and the landlord might be satisfied with something far less drastic to avoid the need to remove the

---

[15] As is stated in the preface to the *Distress* section in *Halsbury's Statutes*, 2nd ed., vol.6 (1948), p.131 & also in *Halsbury's Laws* 3rd ed., vol.12 on *Distress* (1955), p.133. The case law evidence for these statements is very limited. *Browning v Dann,* heard in 1735 (Cas. T. Hard. 167) involved the impounding of 6 butts of beer in the cellar where they were kept. The court was concerned solely with the means of entry to the cellar and made no comment on the manner of impounding, which may be indicative of the fact that this practice had become widespread and unobjectionable by this date. That said, *Griffin v Scott* (1726) 2 Ld Raym 1424 and *Dod v Monger* (1704) 3 MR 215 both restated the rule against impounding on the premises, suggesting that any change of practice (and attitude) occurred not long before Parliament changed the law.

goods to another place. The Act of 1737 entitled the landlord against the wishes of the tenant to use the tenant's premises as a pound. Section 10, in extending this right, referred to the inconvenience to landlords in removing distrained goods off the premises "in cases where by law they may not be impounded and secured thereupon": this recognises that there were cases in which there could be lawful impounding upon the premises, and I take these to be cases such as the right by statute to lock up crops (already mentioned) and to cases where the tenant consented to the use of his premises as a pound. This section authorised not only the use of the premises without such consent as a pound, but also the use of them in a manner that would inconvenience the tenant. But I do not see that the section need be construed as limiting the ability of the tenant to agree to an impounding on the premises by a far less formal and inconvenient manner, and by such agreement to constitute an impounding of the goods so that they remain in *custodia legis* - for example, by leaving the goods *in situ* with a walking-possession agreement.

It is suggested that such an agreement may impound the goods and put them in the custody of the law as against the tenant only; there are in the cases some indications of this viewpoint, as has been pointed out. Indeed, to these may be added the case of *Swann v Earl of Falmouth*.[16] But I do not find this a very easy conception. Moreover, in so far as impounding is in law a necessary step towards ultimate sale, a sale of a stranger's goods after an "impounding" not valid as such against the stranger would, it seems to me, lead to liability to the stranger for the wrongful disposal of his goods, which would be a great stumbling-block in the way of distress carried out in a sensible, convenient and indeed humane manner. I would myself hold that "impounding" in this manner truly and in every respect puts the goods in the custody of the law as against the world. This was expressed to be the clear view of this court in *Lavell's* case, when considerable trouble was taken on the point, and the first part of the decision was devoted to reversing the views of Macnaghten J that the informal impounding was not such as against the defendants.

I turn to the second point. Can a person ignorant of the impounding be guilty of pound-breach whether in these civil or in criminal proceedings? An offence of absolute liability is odious, though it may sometimes be considered necessary to create one as a matter of expediency. But I do not see any matter of expediency that requires an innocent man to be guilty of pound-breach. It is true that this court *in Lavell*'s case, in devoting time to ascertaining that the

[16] (1828) 8 B&C 456- a valid seizure has taken place when the bailiff announces his intention, walks around the premises and makes a list of goods.

furniture removers never entered the café, assumed that had they done so they would though innocent have been guilty of pound-breach. It is also true that section 3 of the Act of 1689 seems to subject an innocent owner of goods to treble damages: for if there be pound-breach by anyone, treble damages may be claimed against the owner of goods distrained if afterwards found to have come to his possession: so that it would seem that if the claim in this case had alleged pound-breach by the tenant - of which he was undoubtedly guilty by procuring the defendant to remove the impounded article - and that the defendant was the owner of the article which had come to his possession, the defendant might have had no answer.

But these matters do not deter me from asserting, and no binding authority forbids me to assert, that pound-breach is not committed by a wholly innocent person, ignorant of the impounding. I would on that ground allow the appeal."

Commentary

This judgment is included not so much because of its decisions on the nature of the offence of poundbreach, but because of the consideration given to the nature of the pound. The judgment is useful as a reasonably contemporary statement of the law on poundbreach, especially considering the rather unusual nature of *Lavell* as discussed in the judgment. The liability of third parties for pound breach was rather uncertain before *Abingdon RDC.*[17]

In addition, it is interesting to note that, during the debate over the scope and impact of walking possession, the judges observed that an impounding ought to be visible so that a third party owner may be alerted to the situation and thereby is able to make a claim under the first section of the Law of Distress Amendment Act 1908. Similar arguments might be made in respect of goods seized in execution, so as to enable an owner to initiate interpleader proceedings.

The development of the law on pounds is reviewed and discussed in some detail. Naturally, there cannot be an offence of breaching a pound unless a pound exists, and the Court of Appeal thoroughly examined the law on this. It must be confessed, nonetheless, that the court was not unanimous in its conclusions. This exposes the unsatisfactory status of walking possession, which is widely used and accepted but is of uncertain effect, extent and legality. The majority of the Court agreed that walking possession would not

---

[17] *Gosling v Bridgman & Chiesman Bros* (1911) 104 Property Owner's Journal 6 (a bill of sale holder) and *The Times* January 7th 1909 6c, a hirer.

prevent innocent third parties without notice of the agreement recovering goods that belong to them, it only bound those who agreed to it.

Walking possession is an arrangement for the benefit and convenience of the parties making it. As the Court says, it benefits the debtor by avoiding the cost and disruption of removal. Nevertheless, the agreement is primarily for the bailiff's benefit: it saves the expense of leaving an employee is close possession; it saves the expense of removal and storage which might not be recovered on sale.

This much is obvious and rather well known. There were, however, other reasons for devising walking possession agreements. Landlords levying distress for rent *had* to wait five days before proceeding to sale under section 1 of the Distress for Rent Act 1689.[18] This five day period came to be seen as the norm so that to retain possession beyond that was regarded as not just unusual but unlawful.[19] A reasonable time to appraise and to arrange the sale might be allowed (eight days in the case of *Pitt v Shew* in 1821),[20] but retaining possession any longer than that amounted to trespass.[21] To get around this, so as to give more time to pay, the consent of the person occupying the premises was required- although the courts were prepared to accept quite minimal evidence of an agreement.[22] That said, legal writers tended to stress that it would be prudent to obtain assent in writing, that the acquiescence of *all* persons (including sub-tenants and lodgers) should be secured so as to avoid a trespass and, finally, that "the necessary consent has relation to the possession or right of possession of the *place*, and not to the right of ownership of the *goods*."[23] These early possession agreements, then, had three functions. They granted the debtor time to clear the debt and, in default, they acted as:

- a licence for the bailiff to resume possession and to deal with the goods as if they had just been distrained for the first time;[24] and/ or,
- a licence for the bailiff to re-enter the premises.[25]

---

[18] See chapter 1 earlier. Note that this is five *full* days, rather than five *clear* days excluding the days of seizure and sale- *Wallace v King* (1788) 1 H. Bl. 13.
[19] *Dod v Monger* (1704) 6 MR 215; *Griffin v Scott* (1726) 2 Ld Raym 1426.
[20] (1821) 4 B&A 206.
[21] *Winterbourne v Morgan* (1809) 11 East 395.
[22] *Washborn v Black* 11 East 405 fn, in which Mrs Washborn said 'what a gentleman' the bailiff had been.
[23] Bullen, p.155- for other forms of words see Bradby, *The law of distresses,* 1808, p.224, Gilbert, *The law & practice of distress & replevin,* 1823, p.231 or C. J. Jones, *On the collection and recovery of rent charge,* 1849, p.100. On the position of lodgers see *Fisher v Algar* (1846) 2 C&P 374.
[24] *Fishwick v Milnes* (1850) 4 Exch 825.

Modern prescribed forms of walking possession still stipulate a minimum duration. It is notable from the older case law that the initial, reasonable time for retaining possession is quite short (five to eight days). Further, given the concern with licencing the bailiff's return, the signature of the householder/ tenant/ owner ought, ideally, to be obtained. Although other 'responsible persons' may sign, it is clearly preferable to have the occupier's agreement so as to overcome any risk of trespass being alleged. Unsigned walking possession agreements are never satisfactory, but the risk of a claim for damages for trespass is yet another reason to avoid them. Without a signature, the duration of any consent will be very limited and the risk of allegations of trespass much increased.

Quinlan v Mayor & Burgesses of London Borough of Hammersmith & Fulham [1989] Court of Appeal [26]

Facts In February 1985 the local authority's records showed that there were rates arrears of £1,597.68 due from the plaintiff. Its bailiffs were therefore instructed to levy distress. On February 5th they purported to levy distress upon equipment in a launderette. The washing machines remained on site and no walking possession agreement was signed. On February 8th the plaintiff appealed against this purported execution of distress to the Crown Court. Despite this, the auctioneers left a note at the premises on 12th February 1985 to the effect that they had "lotted" his machines for auction. The next day the plaintiff went to the town hall and complained that the council had "levied twice" whilst there was an appeal pending. He asked them to refrain from completing the levy on the washing machines and this they did.

However, one week later on February 20th 1985, the council's bailiffs levied distress on the plaintiff's Toyota motor car in the street outside Baron's Court Underground station. On the instructions of the bailiffs he got out of the car and removed his belongings. The car was then taken by the bailiffs to an auctioneers in Wandsworth. On the following day the plaintiff paid the sums claimed to be due as rates arrears, a total of £1,631.16, including bailiffs and auctioneer's fees and thereby obtained release of the car.

The appeal to the Knightsbridge Crown Court was heard in early March 1985 and was dismissed. Then on March 12th the plaintiff issued proceedings against the council in the county court claiming "aggravated general and special damages and costs for the illegal levy of distress carried out by the

[25] *Hill, Clerk v Ramm* (1843) 5 M&G 789.
[26] (1989) 19 WL 649926.

defendants" against his car. The claim was dismissed by the assistant recorder and Mr Quinlan appealed to the Court of Appeal.

Judgment of Slade LJ: [Mr Quinlan sought to disprove the arrears claimed from him by the council. A considerable part of the time of both the county court and the Court of Appeal was taken with examining the parties' figures, but it was concluded that there was no basis for his dispute. The judges then turned to Mr Quinlan's other arguments.]

"The assistant recorder's conclusion that at very least an outstanding balance of £1,526.77 was due from the plaintiff in respect of rates on 5th February 1985 was thus a finding of fact with which there are no sufficient grounds for this court to interfere. However, on this appeal, as in the court below, the plaintiff has raised a number of other points on which he has sought to rely for the purpose of establishing that the distress on his car was illegal. We will deal with them in the same order as that in which they were dealt with in the judgment of the assistant recorder.

1) The rate demand ... the demand was lawfully served in the manner permitted under the 1967 Act...

2) Payment by instalments ... there was no instalment facility such as to disentitle the authority from levying distress ...

3) Excessive distress The thread running through the whole of the plaintiff's argument is that the distress levied on 20th February 1985 was excessive because, as he would say, he was not in arrears with his rates at that date, or indeed on 5th February 1985 when the earlier attempted distress took place. On the contrary, he says that he was in substantial credit. The assistant recorder explained her approach to this submission in these words:

> "Whether or not this court is bound by the magistrates which led them to issue the warrant, it cannot be lawful to levy distress if by the time that the levy takes place the rates due have all been paid. On the other hand, if at all time there were arrears of at least as much as the approximate value at auction of the goods distrained upon then the levy cannot be excessive. Indeed, a complete exactitude cannot be expected of those levying distress, so that a margin one way or the other must be permissible. Therefore, the only question for this court is whether the plaintiff has satisfied me on the balance of probabilities that the distress levied on his car was excessive in relation to the rates which were then due".

We have already mentioned and upheld her conclusion that as at February 5th 1985 a balance of £1,526.77 was owed by the plaintiff in respect of rates.

The assistant recorder took into account the fact that on February 5th 1985 the bailiffs had purported to distrain for arrears of £1,597.68 together with a levy fee of £33.48, making a total of £1,631.16. She also took into account the fact that three sums of £50 were paid by the plaintiff to the authority in February 1985 and a further sum of £3.54 in March 1985. She concluded that it was none the less clear that as at February 20th 1985 the arrears were still so substantial that the plaintiff could not sustain an argument that it was excessive to levy distress upon his motor car. We agree.

4) The second levy The plaintiff submitted that the authority cannot levy twice for the same cause, and therefore that the levy on February 20th was unlawful since distress had already been levied on his washing machines on February 5th. The general principle precluding the levying of a second distress was stated thus by Lord Mansfield in *Hutchins v Chambers*:[27]

> "Now a man who has an entire duty shall not split the entire sum; and distrain for part of it at one time, and for the other part of it at another time; and so *toties quoties* [28] for several times; for that is great oppression; and that is the case of *Wallis v Savill*:[29] where the second distress was holden unjustifiable because both distresses were taken for one and the same rent; and it was the lessor's folly, that he had not taken a sufficient distress at first".

Lord Mansfield, however, went on to state a second principle:

> "But if a man seizes for the whole sum that is due to him, and only mistakes the value of the goods seized (which may be of very uncertain, or even imaginary value, as pictures, jewels, racehorses, etc.) there is no reason why he should not afterwards complete his execution by making a further seizure. And how can the officer who seizes, judge of the real or perhaps imaginary value of the horses or goods seized? The value of them may be quite unknown to him; or may even depend upon whim and fancy".

In relation to his second principle Lord Mansfield pointed out that it is to the advantage of the owner of the goods that this should be so, for otherwise the creditor might be tempted to take too much in the first instance for fear that, if it was not sufficient to satisfy the debt he could not try again.

---

[27] (1758) 1 Burr 579.
[28] "as often as occasion shall require."
[29] (1701) 2 Lutw 1532.

It appears to have been assumed by the court in *Hutchins v Chambers* and also in the subsequent decision of the Court of Exchequer Chamber in *Lee v Cooke*,[30] that the common law rule against levying twice for the same cause applied equally to a statutory distress for rates. The assistant recorder expressed herself content to assume that it does so apply, provided that it is properly understood. We proceed on the same assumption, which seems to us a correct one. Nevertheless, the decision in *Lee v Cooke* shows that there is at least one important qualification to the common law rule against levying twice for the same cause. The rule does not apply where completion of the first distress has been frustrated by the conduct of the person distrained on. In such circumstances such a person cannot complain of the second distress; this is treated as lawful.

As their opening submission under this head, the council attempted to argue that the purported distress on the washing machines did not amount to a distress in law, on the grounds that they were not goods and chattels, but fixtures. Fixtures, he submitted, cannot be the subject of a distress. We did not allow him to pursue this line of argument, since it had not been pursued in the court below, and, if it had been, might have called for further relevant evidence. We express no view as to whether fixtures are capable of being the subject of a distress.

The council was disposed to accept that if (as we assume for present purposes) the washing machines were capable in law of being distrained, the bailiffs had on 5th February done as much as they could to distrain them. Nevertheless, he submitted, the subsequent distress on the motor car was not unlawful because the distraining authority was entitled to treat the goods distrained as being of uncertain value within the second of Lord Mansfield's principles. Alternatively, in his submission, the first distress had been rendered abortive by the plaintiff's conduct, who had untruly represented that they belonged to or were charged in favour of a third party.

As to the latter point, it is necessary to refer again to the facts. On 12th February 1985 the auctioneers had left a note at the plaintiff's premises to the effect that they had lotted his machines for auction. The plaintiff told the assistant recorder that on the next day, 13th February, he went to the magistrates' court in order to obtain a stay of execution. The justices' clerk, he said, telephoned the local authority and was apparently told that the authority would hold off the bailiffs. There was, however, an acute conflict of evidence on this point. Mr Salmon said that the plaintiff came to the town

[30] (1857) 27 LJ Exch 337- a second levy was justified where the debtor's violent obstruction prevented completion of the first.

hall and asked why they had 'levied twice' when there was an appeal. He produced at the trial what purported to be a contemporary memorandum bearing his initials, dated February 13th 1985 and giving the time 11.38. The note read as follows:

> "Mr Quinlan at counter. Q. Why have we levied twice when appeal lodged. Are we going ahead despite appeal. A. Yes. Mr Q. stated goods not his, but had bank loan etc. Told Mr Q. to produce documents within next couple of days. If Mr Q's goods then would be removed by bailiff. Mr Q. to come back".

Mr Quinlan vigorously submitted to us, as he submitted to the assistant recorder, that this note was completely fictitious. The thrust of his submissions appears from the following passage in her judgment:

> "The plaintiff alleges that that is a false document, because he could not be in two places at once and would not have referred to levying twice when the levy on his car had not yet taken place. However, although there is obviously no love lost between the plaintiff and Mr Salmon, I see no reason to disbelieve Mr Salmon or the note. Indeed, it is more than likely that the plaintiff, on receiving a second communication about his washing machines, would go straight to the Town Hall and ask as recorded in the note 'Why have we levied twice when appeal lodged?' It is by no means impossible that there was some kind of misunderstanding between the plaintiff and Mr Salmon because it would appear that relations between them are very bad and that each may perhaps be prepared to believe the worst of the other".

The assistant recorder had the great advantage, which we have not, of seeing and hearing both of them give evidence in the witness box. Having done so, she preferred and accepted the evidence of Mr Salmon in regard to this incident. No sufficient grounds have been shown for us to reject her finding. Though the plaintiff hotly denies that he ever said any such thing, and tells us that the machines were not in fact subject to any charge, we must therefore proceed on the footing that he made a representation to this effect to the authority. In these circumstances, the council is, in our judgment, justified in submitting that in accordance with the principles of *Lee v Cooke* the second distress on the car was lawful because the completion of the first distress had been frustrated by the conduct of the plaintiff. Further or alternatively, after the authority had first attempted to levy distress for the whole sum due to them on the washing machines, they had mistakenly regarded the goods in question as being of no value because of the plaintiff's representation that they were not his. In such circumstances, as appears from the second principle stated in Lord Mansfield's judgment in *Hutchins v*

Chambers which we have cited above, there is no reason why the authority should not subsequently levy second distress on other goods.

5) Distress on the highway Chapter 15 of the Statute of Marlborough, which is still in force, provides:

> "It shall be lawful for no man from henceforth, for any manner of cause, to take distress out of his fee, nor in the King's highway, nor in the common street, but only for the King or his Officers [having special authority to do the same]".

The plaintiff has submitted that this provision rendered it unlawful for the authority to levy distress on his motor car in the public street. There is, however, a conclusive answer to this particular complaint. Section 99(3) of the 1967 Act provides:

> "A warrant of distress under this Part of this Act [Part VI] may be executed anywhere in England or Wales by any person to whom it as directed ..."

Accordingly, whether or not distress under Part VI of the 1967 Act is otherwise subject to the Statute of Marlborough (a question to which we will return below) Parliament, in enacting the 1967 Act, has made quite plain its intention that a warrant of distress under Part VI, such as the warrant in the present case, may be executed in any place in England or Wales. We agree with the assistant recorder that it is impossible to hold that Parliament, having enacted section 99(3), intended that a levy of distress under Part VI of that Act should be unlawful merely because it was effected in the public highway.

6) Delayed execution The plaintiff submitted that the authority had no right to delay the levy of distress and that, having so delayed, it had lost its right. He relied partly on para.18 of Sch.3 to the Supreme Court Act 1981, which inserted section 133A into the County Courts Act 1959. However, we agree with the assistant recorder, for reasons stated by her, that this sub-section has no relevance at all in the present case. No authority has been cited to us for the proposition that a local authority must execute a distress warrant promptly, and we agree with her that the point is misconceived.

7) Notice of distress and inventory Article 8 of the Distress for Rates Order 1979, made under section 101 of the 1967 Act, requires a person levying distress for rates to hand to the ratepayer or to leave at the premises where the distress is levied a copy of the order or of Articles 3-8 of it, and a memorandum setting out the sum due. The plaintiff asserted at the trial that, when his motor car was taken on February 20th 1985, he was not given the usual blue form headed "Notice of distress and Inventory". Although this assertion was denied by the authority, the assistant recorder accepted it. However, as she said, this did not take the plaintiff's case much further. In her words: "There is nothing in the Act or in the Order to suggest that failure to comply with article 8 makes the whole distress illegal. The object of the notice is clearly to tell the ratepayer what it will all cost him, but not to tell him all his rights: there is, for example, no mention of his right of appeal against the distress to the Crown Court. No sanction is provided for failure to comply, and it would be, to say the least, surprising if such a failure were to render the whole distress unlawful so as to justify an award of substantial damages for trespass".

We agree with this analysis. The failure to give the plaintiff a blue form was, in our judgment, an irregularity in the execution of the warrant of distress. Section 99(7) of the 1967 Act states the effect of such an irregularity as follows:

> "No person making a distress under this Part of this Act shall be deemed to be a trespasser from the beginning on account of any subsequent irregularity in the execution of the warrant of distress, but a person who has sustained special damage by reason of the irregularity may recover full satisfaction for the special damage (and no more) by proceedings in trespass or otherwise".

The wording of the sub-section shows that a plaintiff can only recover damages thereunder if he can show that he has sustained special damage " by reason of the irregularity"- that is to say by reason of the failure to serve him with the blue form. We agree with the assistant recorder that he showed no special damage falling within this category.

The plaintiff referred us to the decision of Hilbery J in *Interoven Stove Co Ltd v F. W.H. Hibbard & another* (1936) which demonstrates that in an action for illegal distress substantial damages can be awarded even without proof of any actual damage.[31] However, to recover such damages under this head the distress must be shown to have been illegal. As we have indicated, the failure to serve the blue notice in the present case did not in our judgment render the distress on the motor car illegal; it merely amounted to an irregularity.

8) Replevin The plaintiff addressed no separate argument to us under this head, and we do no more than respectfully endorse the relevant passage in the assistant recorder's judgment:

---

[31] 1 All ER 263.

> "The plaintiff argues that he was not given five days to replevy his goods. Replevin is, of course, the right to seek to recover goods which have been illegally distrained. These goods had not been illegally distrained. In any event, the plaintiff has misconstrued what happened after they were taken. He alleges that he brought the car back from the auctioneers when in fact he obtained its release by paying the sum required of his from the Local Authority. He was given full credit for that sum in their accounts. It follows that the plaintiff cannot succeed on this point".

9) Driving distress out of the county The plaintiff's last point stemmed from Chapter 4 of the Statute of Marlborough, which provided:

> "None from henceforth shall cause any distress that he has taken, to be driven out of the county where it was [taken] ..."

His argument in this context was a simple one. He claimed that a breach of the statute had occurred because his car had been driven to the premises of the auctioneers, and those premises are south of the river in Surrey. The learned judge found for the authority on the basis that these premises were still in the County of Greater London.

Counsel for the authority, to whom we express our thanks for his clear, fair and patient argument, did not adopt this point with great enthusiasm. He told us that he had not argued it before the assistant recorder, but had argued another point, to which we will refer below. According to the information which he had been able to obtain, the position was briefly as follows. An administrative County of London was brought into being by London Government Act 1888 s.40. From that time onwards until 1st April 1965, Wandsworth, where the auctioneer's premises are situated, formed part of the administrative County of London. However, on 1st April 1965 the London Government Act 1963 came into force, and on that date the administrative County of London was abolished. For the next 21 years there existed Greater London and 32 London Boroughs. However, the Greater London Council was abolished on 1st April 1986 by virtue of the Local Government Act 1985. In these circumstances, the highest at which counsel felt he could put this particular point was that at the material time there was in existence the Greater London Council, which was the successor to some of the functions of the former administrative County of London. If, therefore, the Statute of Marlborough had any application at all, he submitted, the auctioneer's premises could be regarded for the purpose of the statute as being within the same county as the road outside Barons Court Underground station where the distress was levied.

In our judgment, however, his better point was the principal point on which he relied in this context, namely that the scheme for the payment and enforcement of rates embodied in the 1967 Act is not subject to the Statute of Marlborough. That was, he submitted, a statute passed with the intention of governing the enforcement and collection of fees and dues owed by a tenant to his lord under the old system of feudal tenure. Chapter IV has subsequently been held to apply to a relationship of landlord and tenant at common law.[32] However, the right of distress dealt with by the Statute of Marlborough did not carry with it a right of sale. Lord Mansfield in *Hutchins v. Chambers* himself drew a distinction between the old common law distresses, which were in the nature of a penalty to compel payment, and a statutory right of distress which enabled the thing distrained to be immediately sold by way of satisfaction. This, he said, though called distress, "yet really is in this respect an execution".

Lord Wright made much the same point in *Potts v Hickman* saying:

> "It is no doubt clear that a distress for rates is much more akin to an execution under a writ issued by the Court than to a distress for rent or the similar distress for cattle damage feasant. Both these latter distraints are acts of self help, though the former at least is now closely regulated by statutes starting from the Statute of Marlborough 1267."[33]

In the context of a statutory scheme of distress empowering the sale of the goods taken, a provision that the goods in question were not to be "driven out of the county where they were taken" would make little or no sense. The situation is a quite different one from that in which a landlord is permitted at common law, as an act of self help, to retain goods by way of a sort of pledge without a power of sale. The difficulty of reconciling Chapter IV of the Statute of Marlborough with the scheme for the payment and enforcement of rates embodied in the 1967 Act is one indication that that scheme was not intended to be subject to the earlier statute. Another indication is section 99(3) of the 1967 Act which runs quite counter to the provisions of Chapter IV of the old Act, containing restrictions on the places in which distresses shall be taken. It was open to Parliament, in enacting the 1967 Act, to provide for a form of statutory distress which should not be subject to the Statute of Marlborough. We are of the clear opinion that the council is right in submitting that it did so. It must follow that the plaintiff's point based on Chapter IV of the old statute is not well founded.

---

[32] See *Lynne v Moody* (1729) 2 Stra 851.
[33] [1941] AC 212.

Conclusion The assistant recorder expressed considerable sympathy for the plaintiff in the events which took place on 20th February 1985. She considered it understandable that he should feel aggrieved at the treatment which he had received. His motor car was taken from him while he was driving along the public highway. He was on his way to hospital for treatment. He also felt aggrieved at the timing of the incident in view of his pending appeal against the levy of distress on his washing machines. She also recognised that there had been some impatience with the plaintiff on the part of some of the authority's officials, and that relations between him and Mr Salmon, at least, were not good. However, she totally rejected the serious allegations of conspiracy which he had made against the authority's officers. The question for her, as it is for us, is whether the distress on the plaintiff's motor car was illegal. After a most painstaking and thorough review of all the main points of law and fact which he had raised, her conclusion was that he had failed to substantiate any illegality and accordingly that his action must fail. Our conclusion is the same for much the same reasons as those given by the assistant recorder. We accordingly dismiss this appeal."

Commentary

This extended judgment provides helpful clarification of a number of points:

- *Excessive distress* Mr Quinlan tried unsuccessfully to show that he owed little or nothing to the council and that, accordingly, any seizure was unreasonable. His rates arrears were in fact appreciable and the Court therefore dismissed the suggestion of excessive distress by comparing the sums due to what the sale of a four year old car was likely to raise and by allowing the bailiff a reasonable margin of error;
- *Second levies* The analysis of the case law on second levies is also useful. The circumstances in which a second levy may be made are limited (see chapter 4) but the court was satisfied that, by persuading the council that the goods seized were in fact subject to a third party claim, he established to their satisfaction that the first levy had been of no legal effect, entitling them to try again;
- *Washing machines* In passing we may remark that the first levy of the laundrette's washing machines was challenged as a seizure of fixtures.[34] The test of whether or not an item is a fixture is the purpose and degree of permanence of installation.[35] Items fixed solely by their own weight (such as commercial washers and tumble driers) are not fixtures;[36]

[34] See generally *Law of Seizure of Goods* 9.5.

[35] *Botham & Others v TSB plc* (1996) EGCS 149/ 73 R&CR D1 CA.

[36] *Hulme v Brigham* [1943] KB 152; *Re: Richards ex p Astbury* [1869] 4 Ch App 630.

domestic appliances are certainly not fixtures.[37] The questions in the Quinlan case would have been- how were they secured? Were they built in? Were they removable? Would Mr Quinlan have removed them if he had moved to other premises? It seems that it was most likely that he would and that, accordingly, the items would not have been protected for this reason. It they had been fixtures, their removal by the bailiffs would have been trespass and the levy would have been illegal.[38] However, as we have seen, their seizure was abandoned by the council.

- *Irregularity* The failure to provide a notice of distress is merely an irregularity for which only special damages can be recovered. No such damages were proved and, as a result, the claim failed.
- *Statute of Marlborough* The plaintiff challenged the levy under both chapters 4 and 15 of the Statute. For the reasons already sketched out in chapter 1, these claims inevitably failed. Chapter 4 does not apply to levies of statutory distraint and was expressly contradicted by s.99(3) of the General Rates Act; that part of chapter 4 relating to excessive levies is of general application but no excess was proved whilst chapter 15 also was inapplicable to statutory rather than common law distress. The judgment clearly distinguished between distress for rent and distraint under statute, such as for business rates or council tax. This differentiation is important, as it has major consequences for the powers of bailiffs levying distress under statute. The rights and duties applicable in distress for rent cannot simply be carried over because of the identity of name. Comparison to a county court execution would be far more apt.

Steel Linings Limited, Mark Harvey v Bibby & Co (1993) Court of Appeal[39]

Facts The first plaintiffs were manufacturers of raised steel floors; the second plaintiff was a director of the company. Tendring Borough Council obtained from the magistrates a liability order against the first plaintiffs in respect of unpaid non-domestic rates totaling £9869 and instructed the first defendants to levy distraint. On three occasions thereafter a certificated bailiff employed by the defendant firm called at the first plaintiffs' premises with a view to securing payment of the sum due. These visits were respectively on October 15th 1992 when the second defendant left a distress notice, November 10th when a cheque was promised and 27th January 1993 when one of the first plaintiffs' employees said she would chase their accountant. In fact, only one

---

[37] *Allan v Lane* [1942] 1 DLR 731.
[38] *Moore v Drinkwater* (1858) 1 F&F 134.
[39] 1993 WL 964281.

payment was made. That was on about December 11th and was for £2484, reducing the outstanding liability to £7385.

Because the debt was still outstanding, the defendants returned to the company's premises on February 5th 1993. This visit involved at least six bailiffs and took some 12 hours, which resulted in a more than usually large bill of charges from the defendant company. In part this seems to have been the result of the bad relations between the parties during the removal. The bailiffs seized and removed a good deal of industrial equipment, which included three vehicles, a forklift truck, three large boxes of tools, and a lathe. The company placed a minimum value of £46,340 on these goods. As a result a county court claim was issued by Steel Linings claiming damages for an excessive levy and for damage to property. This was combined with an application for injunction, which was granted by Colchester county court on February 19th. The defendant bailiffs appealed the injunction.

Judgment of Simon Brown LJ: "The appeal raises questions of some importance both as to the proper construction and application of the Non-Domestic Rating (Collection & Enforcement)(Local Lists) Regulations 1989 ('the Regulations') and as to the powers of the county court in relation to the manner and extent of the levying of distress for unpaid rates. In a sentence, the appellants' contention upon this appeal is that the county court judge had no power to grant an injunction restraining the sale of the goods seized or to order the return of those goods. Subject only to limited rights in the county court to order replevin - not here applicable - as well as to award damages for "special damage", the statutory scheme is, the appellants argue, such that the magistrates' court alone has the jurisdiction to receive appeals in connection with distress for rates and alone has the power to require bailiffs to return distrained goods. In the alternative the appellants argue that upon the particular facts of this case the judge ought not in any event to have made the order he did.

Although there is a good deal of evidence before the court, much of it goes to the detailed circumstances of what happened whilst distress was being levied on 5th February, and who was to blame for the conflict which undoubtedly developed, circumstances not for present purposes relevant. The facts relevant to this appeal can, indeed, be quite shortly stated.

Regulation 14 of the Regulations provides that:

> "1. Where a liability order has been made, the authority which applied for the order may levy the appropriate amount by distress and sale of the goods of the debtor against whom the order was made.

> 2. The appropriate amount for the purposes of paragraph (1) is the aggregate of-
> (a) an amount equal to any outstanding sum which is or forms part of the amount in respect of which the liability order was made, and
> (b) a sum determined in accordance with Schedule 3 in respect of charges connected with the distress."

When distress was levied on 5th February, the outstanding sum due in respect of rates was, as stated, £7385. The bailiffs' charges for levying distress are provided by Schedule 3 to the Regulations to be their reasonable costs and fees. These charges were eventually billed in the total sum of £5910.

On 16th February, the first return date under the order of 11th February, the injunction was continued. On 18th February, the plaintiffs served their particulars of claim. On 19th February, following a full hearing between the parties, the judge made the order now under appeal. It provided that upon the first plaintiffs' cross undertaking in damages and further undertaking to issue an application for taxation of the defendants' charges pursuant to para.3 of Sch.3 of the Regulations, the first defendants be restrained from selling or otherwise disposing of the seized goods and "do within 48 hours of service upon them of (a) a notice of payment into court of the sum of £3,000 to abide the event pending taxation of the 1st defendants' charges and (b) a notice of application for taxation of the said charges pursuant to [the Regulations] make the goods available for collection by the first plaintiff." Those, then, are the essential facts.

We turn next to regulations 14(7) and 15, those most directly pertinent to the issues raised upon the present appeal:

> "Reg.14(7) A distress shall not be deemed unlawful on account of any defect or want of form in the liability order, and no person making a distress shall be deemed a trespasser on that account; and no person making a distress shall be deemed a trespasser from the beginning on account of any subsequent irregularity in making the distress, but a person sustaining special damage by reason of the subsequent irregularity may recover full satisfaction for the special damage (and no more) by proceedings in trespass or otherwise.
>
> Reg.15(1) A person aggrieved by the levy of, or an attempt to levy, a distress may appeal to a magistrates' court.
>
> (2) The appeal shall be instituted by making complaint to a justice of the peace, and requesting the issue of a summons directed to the authority

which levied or attempted to levy the distress to appear before the court to answer to the matter by which he is aggrieved.

(3) If the court is satisfied that a levy was irregular, it may order the goods distrained to be discharged if they are in the possession of the authority; and it may by order award compensation in respect of any goods distrained and sold of an amount equal to the amount which, in the opinion of the court, would be awarded by way of special damages in respect of the goods if proceedings were brought in trespass or otherwise in connection with the irregularity under regulation 14(7).

(4) If the court is satisfied that an attempted levy was irregular, it may by order require the authority to desist from levying in the manner giving rise to the irregularity."

As stated, the defendants' primary contention is that these Regulations provide a self-contained code or scheme which restricts an aggrieved ratepayer to his rights of appeal to a magistrates' court, at least in regard to securing the return of his distrained goods.

The defendant's barrister pointed first to the reference in reg.14(7) to the right of a ratepayer who, during a distress, sustains special damage, to recover "full satisfaction for the special damage (and no more)", a provision, he submits, inconsistent with a right to seek injunctive relief in the county court. Next he points to the power expressly given to the magistrates' court by reg.15(3) to "order the goods distrained to be discharged if they are in the possession of the authority". Finally, by way of putting those particular provisions into their wider context within the Regulations, he reminds us that the ratepayer is given express rights to stop the levy or redeem his goods by making payment of "the appropriate amount"- under reg.14(3) if he pays before the goods are seized, under reg.14(4) if he pays before they are sold. All that, submits the defendant, should be regarded as excluding the existence of any parallel jurisdiction in the county court to order the return of the ratepayer's goods.

The plaintiffs submit to the contrary. Their argument was that neither reg.14(7) nor reg.15(3) have any application whatever to a case like this involving a complaint of excessive distraint. Many passages in *Halsbury's Laws* (4th edition) Volume 13, they point out, draw the clearest distinctions between respectively illegal distress, irregular distress, and excessive distress. The Regulations here in question refer only to "irregularity in making the distress", not to excessive distress. The real purpose of that argument was, we suspect, to try to distance the plaintiffs' claim here from the express limitation imposed upon it by these Regulations to the recovery of special damage only. But, whatever its purpose, we entertain no doubt that the argument was misconceived and, as we conclude, unnecessary too. That, indeed, it is unnecessary, the company came to submit when drawing our attention to *Smith v Enright* (1894), a Queen's Bench Divisional Court decision holding that damages in replevin are not limited to the immediate pecuniary loss occasioned by the distress but extend to damages for annoyance and injury to credit and reputation in trade.[40]

The second limb of reg.14(7) seems to us to be directed to the following matters. First, it relates to "any subsequent irregularity", by which is meant an irregularity subsequent to the liability order dealt with in the first limb of the regulation. Second, it provides that any such irregularity is not to make the distraining authority a trespasser *ab initio*. Third, it allows a person sustaining "special damage" by reason of that irregularity to recover full satisfaction for the "special damage" but for nothing else (so that no recovery is possible for the mere trespass alone). Fourth, "special damage" does not mean special damages in contradistinction to general damages, but has a wider meaning to cover all damages caused by the irregularity, including, it may be, annoyance and injury to credit and reputation in trade. Fifth, to recover that damage, proceedings may be brought in trespass or otherwise in the ordinary way in the courts. Sixth, "irregularity" is not limited to irregular distress but includes illegal and excessive distress. This is clear from the provisions of reg.15 itself, which, by paragraph 1, creates a right of appeal in respect of any grievance arising out of the distraint process.

The mere fact, however, that by virtue of reg.15 it was open to the first plaintiffs to make complaint to the magistrates in regard to what they say was an excessive distraint is not sufficient to indicate that that was their exclusive avenue of redress to restrain the sale or to secure the return of their goods. The critical question raised on the appeal is whether they cannot also seek redress in the county court. To this question we now turn.

The starting point must be this: distress for rates being a statutory remedy, authorising what otherwise would be a trespass to land and a trespass to or interference with goods, the levying of excessive distress being not authorised by statute is plainly a wrongful act. It differs from the largely common law distress for rent in a number of respects, and as Lord Wright in *Potts v Hickman* said:

> "It is no doubt clear that a distress for rates is much more akin to an execution under a writ issued by the court than to a distress for rent or

[40] 69 LT 724.

> the similar distress for cattle damage feasant. Both these latter distraints are acts of self help, though the former at least is now closely regulated by statutes starting from the Statute of Marlborough, 1267."[41]

As this court held in *Quinlan v LB Hammersmith & Fulham*,[42] distress for rates is not subject to the Statute of Marlborough. But just as the seizure of an excessive amount under a writ of *fieri facias* amounts to an actionable wrong, so an excessive distress for rates is a wrongful act.[43] Reg.14(1) itself empowers the authority to levy only "the appropriate amount by distress and sale." That wrongful act in earlier times would have constituted the tort of trespass. Now it is the tort of wrongful interference with goods under the provisions of the Torts (Interference with Goods) Act 1977.

Section 15 of the County Courts Act 1984 gives the county court jurisdiction to hear and determine any action founded upon tort. By section 38, moreover, the county court is empowered in such proceedings to grant any final or interlocutory injunction. More specifically, s.4 of the Torts (Interference with Goods) Act 1977 confers express power "to make an order providing for the delivery up of any goods which are or may become the subject matter of subsequent proceedings in the court, or as to which any question may arise in proceedings" - a power exercisable equally by the county court as by the High Court.

There further exists in the county court - by virtue of s.144 and Schedule 1 to the 1984 Act - the power (to be exercised by district judge) to grant replevin. Not only, however, is it common ground before us that replevin is a remedy available only in cases of illegal distress - distress, that is, where there is no right to levy the rate and not, therefore, this case - but we note with approval the reference in *Clerk & Lindsell on Torts* to the Law Reform Committee's observation that the power to make interlocutory orders for delivery up of goods under section 4 of the 1977 Act may pave the way for its eventual abolition.[44]

Why then should the Regulations operate to displace what would otherwise be the county court's clear jurisdiction in the matter? There are, of course, cases where a right is given by statute that does not exist at common law and

---

[41] [1941] AC 212.
[42] See earlier.
[43] See *Gawler v Chaplin* (1848) 2 Exch 503 & *Watson v Murray & Co* [1955] 2 QB 1. In the former case the court decided that an excessive seizure was *prima facie* wrong, even though the officer was allowing for possible claims; in *Watson*, though, the judge decided that although a walking possession agreement impounding all goods was excessive, no actual loss resulted.
[44] *Clerk & Lindsell on Torts*, 16th edition, para.s 22–87.

where such right is held enforceable only in the way provided by the statute: "The right and the remedy are given in one breath and the one cannot be disassociated from the other."[45] But that clearly is not the position here: the right here is the common law right of a ratepayer to the enjoyment of his own goods- save only to the extent that these are lawfully seized by due process of distress. Nor in our judgment can it possibly be suggested here that the Regulations by clear language expressly exclude ordinary remedies. Quite the contrary: reg.14(7) contemplates in terms the recovery of damages "by proceedings in trespass or otherwise".

Given, therefore, that aggrieved ratepayers can bring a civil action in trespass or otherwise, why should they not in the ordinary way invoke where appropriate the court's injunctive powers? Merely to point to the option given to them by reg.15 provides no answer to that question. Recognising, indeed, the inevitable delay inherent in the complaint process specified by reg.15 - suggested by counsel to be of the order of two weeks - this on occasion would prove an ineffective means of redress. Unlike some forms of statutory distress which provide for a period after seizure of the goods before a sale can be made (see for example Taxes Management Act 1971 s.61), a distraining authority is free to sell immediately it seizes the goods. The county court's jurisdiction, in addition, is more flexible, accommodating, as reg.15 process does not, the possibility of returning at least some of the debtor's goods before any final determination of the dispute can properly be made. In short, it is our clear conclusion that the arguments here overwhelmingly favour the plaintiffs' case: there can be no question of these Regulations operating to oust the county court's general jurisdiction in the matter.

We turn then to the appellants' remaining grounds of appeal. First it is submitted that damages are an adequate remedy in this case so that injunctive relief should on that account have been refused. As to that it is sufficient to note, as the judge himself observed, that the goods seized here were the tools of the plaintiffs' trade urgently needed to fulfil customers' contracts on which they were already working. Finally, the appellants contend that the judge should in any event have put the plaintiffs upon altogether stricter terms as a condition of ordering the interlocutory return of their goods. The council urged in this regard: first, that the plaintiffs have already, by their failure to make due payment of outstanding rates, proved financially unreliable and exposed themselves to the process of statutory distraint; second, that there has as yet been no decision in their favour either (a) upon the taxation of the disputed distraint charges, or (b) as to whether this was in fact an excessive distraint - i.e. whether in truth the value of the

[45] *Barraclough v Brown* [1897] AC 615.

seized goods was disproportionate to the sums properly recoverable. It should be noted in this regard that to be proved excessive the value of the goods seized must be clearly disproportionate to the arrears and charges, taking into consideration the conditions under which a forced sale of the effects must take place; to avoid an excessive distress all that is required is that the distrainor should exercise a reasonable and honest discretion in estimating what the goods will realise at auction; he need not consider what value the ratepayer himself could have obtained for them or what they would be worth to a business successor.

The council pointed too to the rule applying in replevin cases: that at the first stage of this two stage process, the plaintiff seeking return of his goods must give security not merely in the amount of the alleged debt for which distress was made but also for the estimated costs of the action (which he is then required to prosecute without delay). Albeit replevin is not available here - the defendants' alleged default being less fundamental then the illegality required to found this remedy - it would be odd if on that account the plaintiffs were by different civil proceedings able to escape putting up comparably stringent security.

In our judgment there is force in these submissions. But that notwithstanding, we conclude that the judge's order here was one properly within the ambit of his discretion. He was not bound to accept the charges now claimed by the defendants as being what would be found on taxation to be their reasonable costs and fees. Further, as the judge himself observed in giving judgment, the very fact that the levying of this distress had been on any view a tense and hostile process might well be thought, irrespective who was to blame, to lend credence to the plaintiffs' contention that this was indeed a case of excessive distraint. And as to the limited extent of the security required to be put up by the plaintiffs, one must recognise that the defendants' charges as billed clearly reflect the length and hostility of the distress process and so are unlikely to be capable of proper taxation until the responsibility for these problems has first been decided as part of the determination of the action itself. Accordingly, whilst in a normal case we find it difficult to see how a judge could properly require payment into court of less than the amount alleged to be outstanding by way of rates and charges, we regard the circumstances of this case as far from normal. In the result we would not think it proper to interfere with the exercise of the discretion which the judge undoubtedly had.

That said, however, we would sound this note of warning to future debtors tempted to build upon this present decision. Only very exceptionally will it be appropriate to invoke the interlocutory jurisdiction of the county court to secure the return of distrained goods. Defaulting ratepayers (or other debtors) will need to present a powerful *prima facie* case for saying that the distraint has indeed been in some respect unlawful. Where, as here, the allegation advanced is one of excessive distraint, debtors should expect a generally sceptical reaction to their own estimation of their goods' worth. In short, the civil courts will not allow themselves to become a ready means of escaping the proper processes and consequences of statutory distraint.

That, however, is but a cautionary word to those who would seek to read too much into this decision. On the facts of the present case we have found no error of principle in the judge's approach. This appeal is accordingly dismissed."

Commentary

This case provides valuable analysis of several matters:

- *Irregular levies* the meaning of 'irregularity' in the context of appeals to magistrates' courts by those aggrieved by levies for local taxes and child support maintenance is *not* limited to irregular distress in the narrow sense of the word. The phrase comprehends also illegal and excessive distraints. Similarly, 'special damages' in the regulations is not the same as 'special' as opposed to 'general' damages.
- *Appeal* to the magistrates' court is not an exclusive remedy. The aggrieved person 'may' appeal, rather than 'shall' appeal, and resort to the county court is also possible.
- *County court remedies* there is a useful summary of the redress available through county courts - primarily replevin and damages claims coupled with injunctions. Certain preconditions apply to these and they vary in their applicability to different levies but they offer clear benefits as against magistrates' court procedures.
- *Injunctions* will be granted rarely and in most cases subject to the payment of "stringent" security into court, based upon the debt, the bailiffs' charges and the legal costs. In this case an injunction had been issued requiring return of the company's goods and the Court of Appeal was not prepared to rescind it, given that without the property the firm would have been unable to trade until the trial was finally heard.
- *Excessive distress* goods worth £46,300 were taken for rates arrears of £7400. The court agreed that an excessive levy would be one in which the relationship between the value of the goods seized and the sums due was "clearly disproportionate" given that there would be a forced sale of assets. The duty of the bailiff is to avoid an excessive levy but this is achieved by applying a "reasonable and honest discretion in estimating what the goods will realise at auction." Conversely, debtors are warned

as to the "generally sceptical reaction" of the courts to their own estimates of what their property is worth.

Andrews v Bolton Borough Council (2011) HHJ Holman, Bolton county court, June 2011

Background This case was concerned with the correct manner for the enforcement of warrants of execution issued by Traffic Enforcement Centre (TEC) at Northampton county court in respect of road traffic penalties due to local authorities. These penalties arise under the Traffic Management Act 2004, they are processed by TEC under the Civil Procedure Rules (CPR) and are collected by bailiffs exercising powers set out in the Enforcement of Road Traffic Debts Order 1993.

Mr Andrews' car was seized by a bailiff acting for Bolton Borough Council in November 2010. The sum due was £438.72 and, because it remained unpaid, in March 2011 the car was removed to a pound preparatory to sale. Mr Andrews then applied for an injunction requiring return of the car on the grounds that the levy was illegal. This application was dismissed by a district judge in April 2011 and that decision was appealed by Mr Andrews in front of circuit judge.

Judgment The claimant had been assisted by an individual who traded as a parking campaigner and legal adviser. This person was not legally qualified and was refused the right to represent Mr Andrews in court. The judgment begins with a quite lengthy critique of this representative's knowledge and practices. The judge then outlined the relevant law before turning to his analysis.

"The claimant's contentions are:

1. that no valid warrant was issued (indeed he described the document produced as a forgery);
2. that the authorisation for the warrant was issued under County Court Rules Order 48 rule 5, which has been revoked, so the warrant was not lawful;
3. that he was not provided with a copy of the warrant; and,
4. that the fees charged were improperly calculated....

I can deal very shortly with two of the claimant's contentions. As to the challenge to the bailiff's fees, rule 11 of the Distress for Rent Rules 1988 provides for detailed assessment by a district judge in the event of any dispute about fees, charges or expenses. If the district judge concludes that there has been overcharging of such magnitude as to call into question the bailiff's fitness to hold a certificate, he notifies the court which granted the certificate and that court shall treat the notification as a complaint under rule 8. The claimant has not applied for such assessment.

As to the reference to CCR O.48 r.5 on the authorisation form from the TEC, it is undoubtedly the case that this order has been revoked. It has been replaced by CPR Part 75. The procedure regarding warrants of execution is essentially exactly the same. This objection attacks a matter of pure form, not substance, and is devoid of merit. Even if it did have any merit, CPR 3.10 would come into play and there would be no rational basis on which it would be open to me to conclude that I should invalidate the steps taken.

Both of those grounds of appeal have no prospects of success and I refuse permission to appeal on those grounds. The two other grounds merit proper scrutiny. I accordingly have decided to give permission to appeal. That in itself is sufficient to dispose of the defendant's attempt to have the appeal struck out, although I am bound to say that it might in any event have faced considerable difficult in establishing the "compelling" reasons which are required by CPR 52.9(2).

Was there a valid warrant? The TEC sends out authorities to issue warrants in batches by fax. The defendant produced the fax authority dated February 12th 2010. It contained 199 authorisations, the TEC having rejected one request. It bears the seal of Northampton county court. This, they informed me, is followed by an electronic transmission of the data. Given the volumes with which the TEC is concerned, the use of computers is of obvious advantage and it is specifically permitted by CPR 75.4. The electronic data was sent to the defendant, and it is used to prepare the warrant of execution (in effect filling in the blanks in the warrant). The claimant pointed out that the warrant produced in court to me (dated February 16th 2010) appeared to have been generated not by the defendant but by Marston Group, which is a company which provides the services of certificated bailiffs ... the position appears to be (and I indicated in court that I would act on this basis) that the electronic data is forwarded immediately (again electronically) by the defendant to Marston. It then produces the warrant. The claimant contends that this renders the warrant invalid, because para.5(4) of the Enforcement of Road Traffic Debts Order 1993 provides that only the authority shall be empowered to issue the warrant and further that CPR 75.7 stipulates that the authority must prepare the warrant. He argues that these are strict requirements. I note also that the code of practice issued by TEC, to which I shall refer later, refers to the local authority producing the warrant and forwarding it to the certificated bailiff.

There is no doubt that it was the defendant which requested authority to issue the warrant and which received that authority. If the defendant on receipt of the electronic date had then generated the warrant itself on its computer, there could be no possible argument. Given that this data was simply passed on to the bailiff, so far as the CPR provision is concerned, any difficulty would be overcome simply by applying CPR 3.10, because this was an error of procedure, which would not invalidate the step unless the court so ordered. There is no rational basis to invalidate it, there being no prejudice to the claimant. CPR 3.10 cannot, however, operate in relation to the 1993 Order. In that regard a purposive approach is required. The warrant correctly states that it has been authorised by the TEC. It does no violence to the Order or its underlying principles to regard Marstons as the agent of the defendant. It is processing on behalf of the defendant precisely the same data as has been supplied to the defendant by TEC. Accordingly, I conclude that the warrant was valid.

Should the bailiff have given a copy of the warrant to the claimant? The claimant referred me to a variety of sources for the proposition that he should have, and contended that the failure to do so rendered the seizure invalid. The sources are:

i. the warrant of execution itself bears a statement in bold type "If your possessions are seized, you will be left a notice of seizure of goods and an inventory (list of items seized) together with a copy of this warrant."
ii. The TEC issued codes of practice in 2007. Para.9.22 states "the certificated bailiff must have the warrant in his personal possession when he visits a person or premises with a view to enforcing it and he must produce it on demand to anyone who has reasonable grounds to see it."
iii. The Department of Transport issued *Operational Guidance to Local Authorities: Parking Policy and Enforcement* in March 2008. Para.10.69 states that the warrant must be carried by the certificated bailiff and must be produced on demand to anyone who has reasonable grounds to see it.
iv. The observation of Jack J in *JBW Group Ltd v Westminster City Council* [2009]: "it is to be borne in mind that it is only the holder of a warrant who can execute it. That is because, *inter alia*, the bailiff must be able to produce it to the debtor."[46]

[46] EWHC 2697 (QB)- and see chapter 6 *Introduction*.

The codes of practice issued by the TEC have no statutory authority. That does not mean that they can be ignored. They provide very helpful and comprehensive guidance to users of the system. The same applies to the Department of Transport *Operational Guidance.* It is of note that s.87 of the Traffic Management Act 2004 enables the "appropriate national authority" to publish guidance to local authorities. The appropriate national authority is defined at section 92 as the Secretary of State, so far as England is concerned. Whether the Secretary of State has actually exercised this power is unclear, but there is no evidence to indicate that he has. The *Operational Guidance* does not state that it is issued by the Secretary of State pursuant to s.87 and I infer therefore that it is not. In both instances, guidance means precisely that. It does not have force of law. The observation of Jack J in *JBW* is *obiter.* The case actually concerned a claim brought by a company of bailiffs against a local authority for fees alleged to be due to it.

I can find no statutory or legal authority which actually requires the bailiff to produce the warrant. Nevertheless, as a matter of common sense and in the interest of justice and fairness, a debtor must be entitled to ask to see the warrant, just as he or she is entitled to ask a certificated bailiff to produce his certificate. The statement on the warrant that a copy of the warrant will be left with the notice of seizure is an obvious demonstration of good practice. It was not followed in this case.

I can, however, see no valid justification for holding that this invalidates a warrant lawfully issued upon the authority of the TEC. Were it Parliament's intention that such a consequence should follow, I would have expected this to be clearly spelled out either in primary or, more probably, subordinate legislation. Although not directly on the point, the defendant referred to a statute and a case which they suggested by analogy undermined the proposition that a bailiff must have the warrant with him. The statutory provision is section 126 of the County Courts Act 1984. This concerns actions against county court bailiffs, where a demand for inspection and provision of a copy and a failure to comply are pre-requisites to the action. I do not find this of any assistance. The case is an old one: *Percival v Stamp.*[47] In that case, the bailiff unlawfully forced entry into a house to execute a warrant. It was held that this did not invalidate the seizure of goods under a lawful warrant; it merely gave the debtor a potential claim in damages for trespass. This is of assistance, and provides some support for my conclusion. There is a difference in this case that it is difficult to see that the failure to provide the warrant to the claimant could create any cause of action. It might give rise to a complaint about the bailiff, but that is not the issue

[47] (1853) 9 Exch 167.

before the court. Also, complaints about bailiffs fall to be dealt with under the procedure contained in the Distress for Rent Rules.

Accordingly, the district judge was right to dismiss the injunction application and the appeal must be dismissed."

Commentary

Although not shown the considerable case law on this area, the judge arrived at the correct conclusion on equitable grounds- the warrant has to be available in case the debtor asks to see it, which s/he is entitled to do. If no warrant can be produced, the levy may be rendered illegal. In the present case, though, Mr Andrews did not ask to see the warrant and we do not know whether the bailiff had a copy on him or in his vehicle that he could have produced forthwith. The Judge found no grounds to invalidate the levy and the appeal was dismissed.

The basic common law position on warrants of distress was established long ago. In *Buller's Case* (1587) the court decided that "when a bailiff distrains he ought, if he be required, to show the cause of his distraint, but if he be not required, he is not tied to do it."[48] In other words, if the debtor asks to see the warrant, the bailiff should produce it; if no request is made, it doesn't have to be shown voluntarily. Nonetheless, it clearly should be available to be shown if need be. For most forms of distress and execution, this situation has not changed materially since the late sixteenth century.

Almost all the succeeding case authority has actually been concerned with constables executing warrants of arrest. This does not detract from the relevance of these cases: the execution of an arrest warrant for a fine is a civil matter, just like the execution of a distress warrant. This is why the law developed on constable's rights of entry is also directly applicable to bailiffs' law.

The fundamental principle applicable to a warrant is that it should be in the actual, ongoing possession of the person executing it. This has not altered since *Buller's Case* - it has simply been elaborated upon. A warrant that is in the hands of the bailiff company, held at the firm's office, rather than in the hands of the individual bailiff, is *not* in the bailiff's possession.[49] A warrant kept in an office is too remote a possession- nevertheless, possession does not have to be immediate,

[48] (1587) 1 Leonard 50.

[49] *Galliard v Laxton* (1862) 2 B&S 363; *R v Chapman* (1870) 12 Cox CC 4; *Codd v Cabe* (1876) 1 Ex D 352; *Horsfield v Brown* [1932] 1 KB 355; *De Costa Small v Kirkpatrick* (1979) 68 Cr App R 186. See too *Rhodes v Hull* (1857) 26 LJ Ex 265.

physical possession: a warrant left by the bailiff nearby in his van or car but still readily accessible to show to the debtor will do.[50]

It does not matter in these cases that the person arrested never asked to see the warrant. The principle was the key thing- if such a request had been made, it could not have been complied with in the cases where the warrant was at the police station. The reasons underlying this principle are that the person is entitled to know why enforcement action is being taken against him/her and to see the authority for that. Secondly, as Roskill LJ explained in *R v Purdy* (1974) "it is essential he should be able to know for what he is being arrested and whether he is being arrested for a matter of non-payment of a fine, arrears of maintenance...; he can, if I may be forgiven the phrase, "buy" his freedom from arrest by instant payment of the sum stated on the warrant."[51] In distress cases the debtor would be paying to release their goods from imminent seizure.

If goods are distrained in a situation where the warrant is *not* in the possession of the bailiff, what is the consequence? The courts have been clear that the distraint would be unlawful and the debtor would be entitled to resist, using reasonable force (but no more than that). A claim for damages, combined if necessary with an injunction, would be the most likely remedy, however. If excessive violence was employed, an offence could be committed to which the absence of the warrant would be no defence.[52] Of course, the fact that a levy had been invalidated by the absence of a warrant would not prevent a subsequent lawful levy being made.[53]

There is one statutory exception to the common rule, which was made as a result of recommendations by the court in *De Costa Small v Kirkpatrick* (1979). Bailiffs executing magistrates' court distress warrants are granted greater flexibility under Criminal Procedure Rules Part 52.8(2). This states that the person who executes the warrant must either show it to the defendant, if s/he has it, or arrange for the defendant to see it if a request is made to see it but the bailiff does not have it with him.

A few final observations may be made. The warrant should be in the correct prescribed form, otherwise any levy will be illegal.[54] Secondly, as the purpose of the warrant is partly to identify those executing it, it should name the bailiffs to whom it has been directed. Warrants endorsed with another

---

[50] *R v Purdy* [1974] 1 QB 288.
[51] [1974] 1 QB 297A; see too *Hall v Roche* (1799) 8 TR 187.
[52] *Codd v Cabe* (1876) 1 Ex D 352; *R v Purdy* [1974] 1 QB 288.
[53] *Plomer v Ball* (1837) 5 A&E 823.
[54] *Horsfield v Brown* [1932] 1 KB 355.

bailiff's name will be illegal.[55] The only exception to this will be where the relevant statute treats such defects in warrants as mere irregularities.[56] Lastly, these considerations only arise if an actual levy occurs or is attempted. If the bailiff simply visits the property to deliver a letter, to verify the address or to inspect the premises, with no intention of levying, argument about possession of the warrant does not arise.[57]

The Bolton case confirms that this older case law continues to be of relevance. As Roskill LJ warned in *R v Purdy* (1974) "The courts must never appear to condone an unlawful arrest, however unhampered by merit the argument may seem to be in relation to the facts of any particular case."[58] The same will apply to distraint- however unsympathetic the debtor's record, the correct procedures must be followed. That said, onerous demands are not made of the bailiff. Possession means "control coupled with some sort of physical proximity." As long as the warrant can be shown to the debtor within a reasonable time, that will do.

Conclusions

If the rules of distress and execution are strictly followed by enforcement agents, they will be protected by the courts. If the law is not adhered to, whether through deliberate malfeasance or because agents have fallen into erroneous ways, the courts will protect debtors from their wrongful acts.

This text has offered all parties the key statutes and case authorities at first hand. The vital issues and essential arguments have been canvassed and the most important materials supplied. The law has its complexities but it is nonetheless clear enough in many respects. Hopefully this book will have assisted in finding that clarity.

---

[55] *Symonds v Kurtz* (1889) 61 LT 559; *R v Whalley* (1835) 7 C&P 245; *R v Patience* (1837) 7 C&P 775; see also *Collins v Yewens* (1838) 10 A&E 570.
[56] These are s.78 Magistrates' Court Act & s.125 County Courts Act.
[57] *Robins v Hender* 3 Dowl PC 543.
[58] [1974] 1 QB 292F.

Also by John Kruse from PP Publishing

Bailiffs: The Law and Your Rights

This text will be of wide interest to individuals affected by debt collection actions that have reached the stage that bailiffs are called. This includes civil actions for debt as well as Business Rates and therefore affected hundreds of thousands of businesses. It also includes many hundreds of thousands of individuals who are being pursued for debts from civil actions, family courts, road traffic offences and many others. Abuses of the law are many – from seizure of goods illegally, to overcharging costs. *Contents:*

- Preventative measures
- General Matters - How should the bailiff behave? - Harming children and acting with an effect that is discriminatory - Using the Freedom of Information and Data Protection Acts - Financial status
- Bailiffs Visits Warning - First visits - What day and what time is allowed? - Where is the visit to take place? - Can the bailiffs enter premises to seize goods? - Identification
- The levy process the procedure bailiffs must follow when seizing goods - the implications of the bailiff failing to do this correctly - the goods which may and may not be seized - the remedies available for the wrongful seizure of goods
- Removal & sale-how to prevent it - how payment may be made and its effect - how and when the bailiff will remove - how and when the bailiff will sell - what information you will receive about this
- The bailiff's bill what charges are permitted by law - the status of the extra charges that some bailiffs make - your remedies if you feel you've been wrongly charged
- What to do if things go wrong remedies outside the courts and through the courts - how to actually apply to court etc - the arguments for and against

ISBN 1 85811 711-9 £14.99 2011

Law of Seizure of Goods: Debtors' Rights and Remedies

This is the only substantial treatment of the topic, providing litigators and enforcement agencies with a major work of reference. It has been updated to take account of the Tribunals, Courts and Enforcement Act. *Contents:*

- The legal context: history and current regime
- Pre-Levy Tactics: Preventing Seizure
- Pre-Levy Tactics: Insolvency
- Levy Procedure: Forms and Remedies
- Levy Procedure: Issue
- Levy Procedure: Procedure
- Levy Procedure: Goods
- Levy Procedure: Removal and Sale
- Levy Procedure: Charges
- Complaints

ISBN 1 85811 603 7 £49.00 2008

www.ingramcontent.com/pod-product-compliance
Ingram Content Group UK Ltd.
Pitfield, Milton Keynes, MK11 3LW, UK
UKHW020138290926
15471UKWH00003B/563

9 781858 117171